BETWEEN MANAGEMENT AND LABOR

Oral Histories of Arbitration

TWAYNE'S
ORAL HISTORY SERIES

Donald A. Ritchie, Series Editor

PREVIOUSLY PUBLISHED

Rosie the Riveter Revisited: Women, the War, and Social Change
Sherna Berger Gluck

Witnesses to the Holocaust: An Oral History
Rhoda Lewin

Hill Country Teacher: Oral Histories from the One-Room School and Beyond
Diane Manning

The Unknown Internment: An Oral History of the Relocation of Italian Americans
during World War II
Stephen Fox

Peacework: Oral Histories of Women Peace Activists
Judith Porter Adams

Grandmothers, Mothers, and Daughters: Oral Histories of Three Generations
of Ethnic American Women
Corinne Azen Krause

Homesteading Women: An Oral History of Colorado, 1890–1950
Julie Jones-Eddy

The Hispanic-American Entrepreneur: An Oral History of the American Dream
Beatrice Rodriguez Owsley

Infantry: An Oral History of a World War II American Infantry Battalion
Richard M. Stannard

Building Hoover Dam: An Oral History of the Great Depression
Andrew J. Dunar and Dennis McBride

From the Old Country: An Oral History of European Migration to America
Bruce M. Stave and John F. Sutherland with Aldo Salerno

Married to the Foreign Service: An Oral History of the American Diplomatic Spouse
Jewell Fenzi with Carl L. Nelson

Her Excellency: An Oral History of American Women Ambassadors
Ann Miller Morin

Doing Oral History
Donald A. Ritchie

CLARA H. FRIEDMAN

BETWEEN MANAGEMENT AND LABOR

Oral Histories of Arbitration

TWAYNE PUBLISHERS
An Imprint of Simon & Schuster Macmillan
New York

Prentice Hall International
London   Mexico City   New Delhi   Singapore   Sydney   Toronto

Twayne's Oral History Series No. 10

Between Management and Labor: Oral Histories of Arbitration
Clara H. Friedman

An Imprint of Simon & Schuster Macmillan
866 Third Avenue, New York, New York 10022

Library of Congress Cataloging-in-Publication Data

Friedman, Clara H.
    Between management and labor : oral histories of arbitration /
Clara H. Friedman.
        p.   cm.—(Twayne's oral history series ; no. 10)
    Includes bibliographical references and index.
    ISBN 0–8057–9101–9 (alk. paper).—ISBN 0–8057–9116–7
(pbk.)
    1. Arbitration, Industrial—United States—History. 2. Collective
bargaining—United States—History. I. Title. II. Series.
HD5504.A3F75   1995
331.89'143'0973—dc20   94–44559
                                                                                     CIP

The paper used in this publication meets the minimum requirements of American
National Standard for Information Sciences—Permanence of Paper for Printed
Library Materials. ANSI Z3948–1984.∞™

10 9 8 7 6 5 4 3 2 1 (hc)
10 9 8 7 6 5 4 3 2 1 (pb)

Printed in the United States of America

To Milton Friedman
in whom sense and sensibility were inseparable

Contents

Foreword   ix
Acknowledgments   xi
Note on the Text   xiii

1. Introduction   3

2. Early Years in Arbitration
   Emanuel Stein   9

3. Development of Arbitration
   Walter Gellhorn   17

4. The Wagner Act and More
   Ida Klaus   35

5. Becoming an Arbitrator
   Arthur Stark   53

6. An Arbitrator's Secret
   Israel Ben Scheiber   75

7. Decision Making in Arbitration
   Milton Friedman   79

8. Mediating and Arbitrating
   Benjamin H. Wolf   95

9. Dispute Resolution in the Public Sector
   Arvid Anderson   105

10. Understanding Both Sides
    Irving Halevy   115

11. Roles for Neutrals
    Eric J. Schmertz   123

12. Legal Chess in Arbitration
    Thomas G. S. Christensen   133

13. Limits in Arbitration
   Daniel G. Collins   139

14. Expanding Dispute Resolution
   George Nicolau   147

15. American Arbitration Association Procedures
   Robert Coulson   157

16. The Historical Context: A Short History of Arbitration
   Irving Bernstein   165

Appendix: Methodology   181
Notes and References   189
Index   213
Photographs follow page   114

Foreword

Both oral history and arbitration are essentially about communication. The oral history interviewer seeks to stimulate informed dialogues, prompting interviewees with thoughtful questions; providing names, dates, and other basic information that may have been forgotten or mistaken; listening attentively; and making an accurate history of past events. Similarly, labor arbitrators seek to open the lines of communication between parties at impasse, helping to define and narrow the issues for adjudication, providing a fair and full hearing on the facts and on the parties' contractual obligations, in a dispute-resolution process that ends with reasoned findings by the arbitrator.

Between Management and Labor joins these two methodologies by employing the interview process on the arbitrators. Here, in a series of lively interviews, a cross-section of arbitrators explain their means of operations, offer a record of their most memorable assignments, and demonstrate their considerable communication skills.

Oral history may well be the twentieth century's substitute for the written memoir. In exchange for the immediacy of diaries or correspondence, the retrospective interview offers a dialogue between the participant and the informed interviewer. Having prepared sufficient preliminary research, interviewers can direct the discussion into areas long since "forgotten," or no longer considered of consequence. "I haven't thought about that in years," is a common response, uttered just before an interviewee commences with a surprisingly detailed description of some past incident. The quality of the interview, its candidness and depth, generally will depend as much on the interviewer as the interviewee, and the confidence and rapport between the two adds a special dimension to the spoken memoir.

Interviewers represent a variety of disciplines and work either as part of a collective effort or individually. Regardless of their different interests or the variety of their subjects, all interviewers share a common imperative: to collect memories while they are still available. Most oral historians feel an additional responsibility to make their interviews accessible for use beyond their own research needs. Still, important collections of vital, vibrant interviews lie scattered in archives throughout every state, undiscovered or simply not used.

Twayne's Oral History Series seeks to identify those resources and to publish selections of the best materials. The series lets people speak for themselves, from their own unique perspectives on people, places, and events. But to be more than a babble of voices, each volume organizes its interviews around particular situations and events and ties them together with interpretative essays that place individuals into the larger historical context. The styles and format of individual volumes vary with the material from which they are drawn, demonstrating again the diversity of oral history and its methodology.

Whenever oral historians gather in conference, they enjoy retelling experiences about inspiring individuals they met, unexpected information they elicited, and unforgettable reminiscences that would otherwise have never been recorded. The result invariably reminds listeners of others who deserve to be interviewed, provides them with models of interviewing techniques, and inspires them to make their own contribution to the field. I trust that the oral historians in this series, as interviewers, editors, and interpreters, will have a similar effect on their readers.

DONALD A. RITCHIE
Series Editor, Senate Historical Office

Acknowledgments

This book could not have been produced without the cooperation of the 14 arbitrators whose extensive oral history interviews in 1983 and 1984 are the source. (Why and how the interviews were undertaken is set forth in the Appendix.) For sharing candidly their experiences and insights, and for taking time from demanding professional schedules to do so, I am grateful to Arvid Anderson, Thomas G. S. Christensen, Daniel G. Collins, Robert Coulson, Milton Friedman, Walter Gellhorn, Irving Halevy, Ida Klaus, George Nicolau, Israel Ben Scheiber, Eric J. Schmertz, Arthur Stark, Emanuel Stein, and Benjamin H. Wolf. (For Tom Christensen, Milton Friedman, Ben Scheiber, Manny Stein, and Ben Wolf, who died some years after the interviews, poignant memories of their lives in arbitration survive in their oral histories.)

Dan Collins and Eric Schmertz were encouraging and helpful when I first suggested undertaking an oral history. Arthur Stark has been a valuable resource throughout and a heartening friend as well when unanticipated difficulties occurred. Arthur's in-depth arbitration experience yielded many obscure details during my fact checking of names and events that figure in the oral histories but do not appear in published materials. Having additionally checked records and recollections with other colleagues and reached into my own remembrances, which go back to arbitration's beginnings at the National War Labor Board some 50 years ago, any footnote errors that might nevertheless turn up are my responsibility and are certainly unintended.

The conscientious work of 10 law students who conducted some of the interviews in 1983 and 1984 is appreciated, as are the time and interest they committed in briefings before and after the interviews. From the New York University School of Law graduate seminar in labor law taught by Professor Christensen, they were Stanley Comet, Robert L. Levin, James A. Madden, Jr., Raymond T. Mak, and Robert McConnell. From Hofstra University School of Law, there were third-year students in labor law courses: Dolores Gebhardt, Diana Munkel, Michael Noonan, Martin Rainbow, and Catherine Sagos.

I was very fortunate in 1983, at the inception of the oral history project, when I walked into Columbia University's Oral History Research Office as a novitiate in oral history and encountered Elizabeth Mason. She was then the associate director of the Oral History Research Office and a former president of the Oral History Association, and she generously shared her encyclopedic erudition in oral history and enthusiasm for the subject. So did Debra Bernhardt, the very knowledgeable archivist of New York University's Robert F. Wagner Labor Archives, whom I also met for the first time in 1983.

Special thanks go to three other individuals who advanced and enhanced publication of this book. I am grateful to Donald A. Ritchie, a leading oral historian and series editor for Twayne's Oral History Series, who thought this book would be a worthy addition to the series. I appreciate that Prof. Irving Bernstein took time in 1994, immediately after completing his book on the Lyndon B. Johnson presidency, to write the historical chapter for this book; his expertise as a historian and also as an arbitrator adds a special dimension and puts this oral history into historical context. Last but by no means least, I was fortunate in having a very capable and patient editor, Mark Zadrozny of Twayne Publishers.

Choosing for this book the portions from the lengthy interviews that would seamlessly present the pith of the arbitrators' accounts has been difficult. I have tried to make selections that convey how substantial and engaging these 14 individuals are, how valuable their work in arbitration has been, and how interesting it is to hear what they had to say.

Note on the Text

In this book 16 individuals address the reader: arbitrator Clara H. Friedman, who planned the oral history project; 14 arbitrators who were interviewed for the project; and historian and arbitrator Irving Bernstein, who wrote the chapter on the history of arbitration. Italics are used throughout the book to identify the separate voices. But to avoid recognition difficulty, please note:

- Chapter 1 is written by Clara Friedman, as are the brief biographical introductions to chapters 2 through 16. Chapters 2 through 15 are the respective arbitrators' words as uttered during the interviews. Everything the arbitrators recounted during interviews that lasted hours or days could not be included in the book; editing was necessary for chapters of reasonable length. Friedman, who did the editing, selected portions of the transcripts to comprise the chapters; arbitrators had no role in the selections and did not preview or review the chapters. For the book, Friedman deleted interviewers' questions. But in the book's chapters, she did not alter the arbitrators' words, either substantively or grammatically.
- All notes and references for chapters 1 through 15 were determined and written by Friedman; content, style, and responsibility are hers. The need for notes became apparent in preparing for book publication; the 14 arbitrators had no input in the notes and references.
- Chapter 16, as well as chapter 16 notes and references, are by Bernstein.
- The appendix on methodology is written by Friedman.

BETWEEN MANAGEMENT AND LABOR

Oral Histories of Arbitration

I

INTRODUCTION

The Arbitrators' Role

Labor arbitrators speak for themselves in these oral histories. They do not, of course, speak with one voice on all issues; their views differ on some matters and concur on others. Whether arbitrators see three sides of a question, as has been said of some triers of fact, their stock-in-trade is weighing evidence and interpreting contracts. That process does not make for unanimity, anymore than it does among judges or other decision makers.

Certain subjects recur throughout these interviews. They include starting a career and inadvertencies in becoming an arbitrator, differences between mediation and arbitration,[1] misgivings or enthusiasm about interest arbitration (where terms of the collective-bargaining agreement are established by arbitration, unlike grievance arbitration, where the parties establish their collective-bargaining agreement and submit disputed contract interpretations to arbitration), differences or similarities between arbitration in the public and private sectors, contrasts between ad hoc arbitration and permanent impartial chairmanships, the decision-making process and how arbitrators live with their decisions, differences and similarities between arbitration and the judicial system, the limits and/or potential of the process, special qualities of arbitration as a dispute-resolution system, and facts of life such as arbitrator expendability.

The arbitrators' comments on these and other topics provide substantial insights into matters that, however, continue to generate more questions than answers. All recognize that the process belongs to the parties. Still the arbitrators have different conceptions of their role. Some see it as expansive and flexible, others are strict constructionists. Still others adhere to views of the arbitrator as "reader" of the parties' contract and "listener"[2] to the parties' evidence and argument.

The parties' joint responsibility for selecting their adjudicators is distinctive and crucial in arbitration. This does not occur among adversaries in other settings. Attorneys in court cannot choose their judge. Contestants in sports cannot pick their umpires or referees. But unlike these other adjudicators, an arbitrator—whose decision is final and binding upon the parties—is subject to the parties' case-by-case selection.

How vulnerable are arbitrators to the harsh financial consequences to them that may result from their awards? No "Black Sox" scandal has ever tarnished arbitrators' reputations, although enormous sums of money and momentous principles have frequently hung in the balance. Fortunately, arbitration is a profession in which integrity is not only the rule but also the basis for success. It has been demonstrated over the years that the best way to remain acceptable is to render decisions without regard to where the chips may fall. Were that not the case, individuals for whom ethical conduct is the norm would not continue to function.

What qualities do parties look for in entrusting their vital and important concerns to a neutral whose decision is final and binding? Desirable qualities, these histories reveal, include impartiality, evenhandedness, knowledgeability, maturity, experience, and civility, along with ability to comprehend evidence and analyze the record, to conduct a fair and orderly hearing, and to write a reasoned award that makes clear the basis for the decision.

Such qualities do not spring solely from intellectual stature, valuable though that is. Nor are such qualities enhanced just by years of experience. Subtly and intangibly, decision makers bring to bear in their work a range of life experience as well as professional experience.

Biographical material collected in these oral histories indicates that individuals' life experiences have made them better arbitrators and steadfast impartials. To different degrees they have been tempered by the Great Depression, the New Deal, the rise of trade unionism and the modern labor movement, the development of a corpus of labor law, World War II, the Truman administration, the Kennedy years, the war on poverty, Johnson's Great Society, the struggles against racial discrimination, the far-reaching changes in race relations, antidiscrimination laws for minorities and women, collective bargaining in the public sector and in service industries and in major league sports, extensive changes in public attitudes and behavior in the family and the workplace, and other traumas and triumphs of the twentieth century.

The arbitrators' interviews interweave with the history of our times. Their stories are recorded with fidelity in the oral histories from which this book is mined. Historic events they witnessed and even participated in, illustrious individuals they knew as mentors or colleagues, pathbreaking legislation they helped to implement, pioneering agencies they helped establish, complex issues in arbitration presented to them—all come to life vividly in the spoken recollections of these veteran arbitrators.[3]

The Need for Oral History

Included here are arbitrators whose experience goes back to the beginnings of modern arbitration in the 1940s and encompassed the dramatic developments in the decades following. Their experiences, together with those who became arbitrators in the 1950s and 1960s, constitute a major resource in the history and practice of arbitration, as well as a prime source in labor history and law. Yet for the most part direct recollections had not been previously elicited from arbitrators. Few had given oral histories, and as for memoirs, there are none, perhaps because arbitrators are too busy or very discreet.

Arbitrators' written output has a different purpose and style than oral history. All arbitrators produce awards. Some deliver papers at professional meetings or write articles for professional journals and books on particular aspects of arbitration. These may incorporate insights gained in their work, but ordinarily deal with substantive aspects of the process. These oral histories focus on what brought arbitrators to the profession and what their distinctive experiences were.

As arbitration's growth continues and expands and veterans leave the scene, many of the current advocates, as well as new arbitrators, have no firsthand familiarity with the field's landmarks and leading lights. If present-day practitioners look through the window of oral history, they will see aspects of arbitration not found even in the compendious literature. They will also find insights useful in newly emerging dispute-resolution milieus in other fields.

The Arbitrators

The 14 persons interviewed for this project are all highly regarded arbitrators. Among them are three generations of arbitrators. The first consists of the few who began arbitrating in the 1940s and even earlier, and who were at the National War Labor Board, which became the birthplace of modern arbitration. The second generation includes the larger number who became arbitrators in the 1950s and 1960s, many of whom matriculated in federal or state labor-relations agencies. The third generation started arbitrating in the 1970s and soon reached the top ranks of the profession. All three generations were associated with major developments since the 1960s, such as the widespread grievance and interest arbitration for government employees that paralleled the growth of unions in the public sector.

The interviewees were selected because each had something important to contribute in the history of arbitration. They are not necessarily a representative sample of arbitrators in the United States. The mix here has characteristics found generally among arbitrators, but the distribution in these oral histories is skewed to high-level experience and distinction.

Most of the arbitrators here have law degrees and practiced in law firms or government agencies in their prearbitration careers. Among the nonlawyers, economics was the major academic interest. About one-half had their academic studies delayed by financial exigencies during the Great Depression or by time out for military service in World War II or the Korean War.

The arbitrators are almost evenly divided between full-time and part-time practitioners. The latter are law professors, except for one economics and one industrial-relations professor.

The 14 arbitrators include one who served only occasionally as a labor arbitrator but was a major figure in the world of arbitration.[4] The time-honored tradition of turning to public figures as arbitrators, to help resolve disputes, continues still.

Arbitration was not the initial career for any of these individuals. It was a second career, or even a third or fourth career, after they had achieved experience and eminence elsewhere. Most of them came to arbitration accidentally or fortuitously. But in almost every case they came with solid, related experience at such agencies as the National War Labor Board, National Labor Relations Board, or state boards of mediation and labor relations. About one-half the arbitrators had previously been advocates for labor or management for rather limited periods. Partisan associations were succeeded by positions as neutrals in capacities of greater import and longer duration. One individual, formerly a lawyer representing unions and later a neutral in government agencies, was designated as arbitrator under each of the contracts he had serviced as a union advocate years before. Both sides accepted him as a fair-minded and neutral person.

At the time these interviews were conducted, the arbitrators' ages ranged from 54 to 93; most were at least 60. Some have since died, retired, or cut back on arbitration work.

Many honors are clustered in this group of arbitrators. Three were honored by their universities as outstanding professors. A number were awarded honorary degrees; one has 10 honorary doctorates from major universities in the United States and Europe. Two served as president of the National Academy of Arbitrators (the prestigious professional organization of labor arbitrators), and a third will become president in 1996; more than one-half were vice presidents or on the board of governors. One was president of the Society for Professionals in Dispute Resolution. Three received the American Arbitration Association's annual award for "most distinguished arbitrator."

Umpireships and impartial chairmanships in major industries were held by many of these arbitrators. Most also served on rotating permanent panels in major contracts, including those in airlines and railroads, baseball, basketball, and football, electrical products, motion pictures and television, schools and universities, steel, telephone, and trucking.

One was appointed to the Federal Services Impasse Panel by three successive U.S. presidents, then appointed by U.S. secretaries of state in two successive presidential cabinets to chair the Foreign Service Grievance Board. Two served as chairman and vice chairman of the National War Labor Board in the New York region. One served for 20 years, by successive presidential appointments, as councillor of the Administrative Conference of the United States. At least half of the arbitrators were appointed to presidential emergency boards, by successive presidents, for airlines and railroads under the Railway Labor Act.

Arbitrators with this kind of experience, at work during decades of great change in labor relations and law, have things worth saying, worth being heard. Their oral histories make evident, without pretension or preachment, some major truths about the very small yet influential labor arbitration profession.[5]

One truth is that the success of the labor arbitration process rests in large part on the character and capability of the arbitrators who are selected to implement the process. Another is that arbitration's continued effectiveness and undiminished neutrality have been accompanied by the flexibility inherent in labor arbitration as it has developed in the United States during the past half century.

Labor arbitration may be the best exemplar for the alternative dispute resolution that is very actively advocated now and attempted for a wide range of nonlabor disputes: community disputes, discrimination grievances from various groups (racial, sexual, ethnic, disabled, and other so-called minorities), divorce and family disputes, environmental disputes, investors' claims against brokerage houses and other investment officers, medical malpractice claims, and employment-related grievances of management staff and other employees not covered by collective-bargaining agreements. The far-reaching disputes rife in present-day society, the increase in litigiousness, bitterness, incivility, polarization, and violence—these are among the factors that strain the legal system's ability to adjudicate disputes without undue delay. What has worked outside the legal system in settling labor disputes expeditiously and inexpensively, and how it has worked, cannot be cloned for nonlabor disputes, which have their own distinct characteristics and considerations. But undoubtedly the experience and insights of labor arbitration can be drawn upon in devising settlement mechanisms in nonlabor matters.

2

EARLY YEARS IN ARBITRATION
Emanuel Stein

Emanuel Stein taught economics, labor relations, and labor law at New York University from 1930 until 1982. In 1973 he became professor emeritus, continuing to teach for another decade. From 1955 to 1967 he was also chairman of the university's economics department; earlier he had chaired the economics department in the undergraduate division. A superb teacher, and exceptionally popular with the thousands of students who filled his classes in the course of more than half a century, he received the Great Teachers Award in 1964 from the Alumni Federation. Founder of the New York University Institute of Labor Relations in 1948, he was its executive director until 1963.

His contemporaneous career in arbitration was, like his professorial life, long, distinguished and very active. It extended from the early 1930s (when arbitrators were what he termed "amateur men of good will") until his death in 1985. Stein was a public member of the National War Labor Board in the New York region during World War II and of the Wage Stabilization Board during the Korean War. Over the years he arbitrated major disputes, frequently by presidential or gubernatorial appointment, in transit, airlines, public utilities, hospitals, electrical equipment, telecommunications, and other industries. For decades he was sole umpire or rotating permanent arbitrator under collective-bargaining contracts between the City University of New York and Professional Staff Congress, United Parcel Service and Teamsters, New York City and Policemen's Benevolent Association, General Electric and International Union of Electrical Workers, American Airlines and Transport Workers Union, and others.

What is it we mean by the term "arbitration"? It has meant remarkably different things from the time when one can say "there are cases which have been settled by arbitration." If we think in terms of the contemporary definition, there isn't such an awful lot of difference between the concept of arbitration and the concept of a trial in a court of law. Both of them may involve labor matters. As a matter of fact, they may involve the same statutes and the same people defining them. And a lawyer would feel, probably, about as completely at home in an arbitration hearing as in court.

What really occurs amounts to a trial, with the usual array of things involved in a trial. And we call this arbitration. In effect, it is a settlement of a dispute between persons or between parties: a settlement which involves having some outside person come along and act as the umpire in the ball game. Which is to say, that he has as much status as the people want to give him.

Do the parties boo that outsider the way the fans boo the umpire? Well, they might, they might. They might use a different forum to do their booing; they might decide that "this guy is not for us, we made a mistake when we picked him as the umpire." But functionally the person called in by the parties to adjudicate the matter is making a decision with which they have to live, whether they like it or not.

If you look at the overall picture, arbitration (in other words, this kind of dispute resolution) is a settlement of an argument between people who are disagreeing with each other. But it also has been many different things. It is interesting to note that the ancient Greeks in the period of Thucydides were familiar with the practice of calling in an outsider to settle an argument. And that concept of settling an argument, which we know as arbitration, involved the same kind of thing. That is to say, people got together and had a discussion of the issue, decided in effect what standards they would apply. "How do we determine the truth or the falsity of the claims which are made? And in either event, how do we decide the case?"

In ancient Greece, did threshold questions of arbitrability arise, as they do in present-day arbitrations? They sure did. The question as to whether you would be willing to appear before a neutral would include (on some occasions anyway) a determination as to whether you want to appear on a particular issue. Thucydides remarks in one case actually that one of the city-states, which was being urged to go to arbitration, refused to go. Until the troops of one of the opponents were removed from the area, said the Greeks of that city-state, there was nothing to take to the arbitrator. The issue, in other words, was what we would today call "arbitrability."

If we were to move on about 700 to 800 years, from Thucydides to the Talmud, we would find a society which was quite familiar with the concept of arbitration, with the concept of committing to neutrals. The interesting footnote is that the Talmud is really not so much interested in the justice of a cause as in the compromise aspects. Which is to say, they viewed arbitration as an opportunity to settle a dispute. And the crucial thing was the settlement of the dispute, without altogether too much regard for the abstract rights and wrongs. The Commentaries, on that bit of learning, would have it that "it was better to have a compromise than it was to have justice." Better to have people agree and accept a suggestion, a resolution of a problem, than to have some abstract finding.

Louis Brandeis[1] (a lot of centuries later!) remarked once that "it was better for the law to be certain, than for it to be just," again indicating that perhaps abstract allegiance to a theoretical concept was not altogether desirable—or at least not desirable in all cases.

Would this be a tradition that would justify present-day arbitrators disregarding rights and obligations in collective-bargaining agreements in order to award a compromise? Oh, no! All that I meant was that if you can have two satisfied people walk out of the hearing room, you may—in this tradition—feel that you have accomplished greatly.

If you were to pick up a volume of proceedings of the National Academy of Arbitrators,[2] you would find that one of the tests or standards which is urged most often (by this or that speaker) is that the arbitrator made a powerful mistake in the application to a new set of facts of what he should have considered. This presumes that the arbitrator approaches the fact of arbitration with a view not unlike that of the judge in court. And that the arbitrator might be judged in the same way as a judge would be judged: on the basis of the decisions written. Yet what I am trying to say is that there are many different kinds of things in arbitration.

When the United States and Canada went into an arbitration in the case of the Alaska fishery, one of the reasons they went in was that there were really no well-defined benchmarks for the law of international relations in this area. The people very often in those cases had to make the law first. And then, making the law, decide what the law should be. As a matter of fact, I suppose one of the nearest analogies were the Nuremberg cases after World War II.

Usually we say, "In order to have arbitration, it is important to have well-defined benchmarks so we know what law or standard applies, so we know what the arbitrator is supposed to be capable of doing."

Why do we go to the arbitrator? The answer is that there are advantages which we see in arbitration. It's interesting to observe, in a historical sense, that in the early days the advantages which were being urged upon people were frequently not labor advantages. Today if you talk about arbitration, you really are talking for the most part to people who are familiar with the litigation of disputes in labor cases. But the United States Arbitration Act was not passed for labor disputes.

And the American Arbitration Association was not formed primarily to deal with labor matters. As time went on and people were more familiar with labor matters (and there were more labor matters to be familiar with), a larger and larger proportion of the cases coming to the American Arbitration Association, or involving resolution of disputes under the United States Arbitration Act, began to have overtones of labor matters.

I think I was roughly contemporaneous with the AAA [American Arbitration Association]. My impression is that it was formed in the latter [19]20s. Its work was largely confined to business disputes, as in the textile industry. The movie industry is another which made use of arbitration at an early date. Also the New York Stock Exchange. I have done a fair amount, in the early years of arbitration, in commercial matters. (And I never was paid for services as arbitrator. Arbitrators never got paid in commercial arbitrations.)

I've even had a divorce case, many years ago, in commercial arbitration. It was very funny. The case involved a claim by a lady for child-support money from her former husband. (If I were to mention the name, which I'm not going to, you would recognize it.) These were very intelligent and kind of sophisticated persons. When their divorce was impending, they agreed that their child needed to be supported. The father agreed to pay $500 a month, which in those days was a lot of money, plus tuition for a private school.

The parties recognized that the money which was appropriate at age 8 would not be appropriate at age 12, and agreed (in this agreement) that when the child was 12 years of age, the mother had the right to come in and demand more money, on the ground that the old sum was no longer enough. And if they couldn't agree how much was appropriate, they would go to arbitration. So she asked for more money when the child was 12 years old. I was the arbitrator.

The mother did what was unusual in those days, even in a labor case. She brought in an employee of the U.S. Bureau of Labor Statistics to testify on the cost of living and what had happened to the consumer price index from the time the child was 8 until she was 12. The claim was that $500 a month was nowhere near enough for the child's support.

Evidence was produced that in the one year when the girl was 12, her clothing alone cost $6,105. The child went to a private school, where the children were obliged to wear uniforms. The mother said she bought 35 sweaters for the child. Comparable numbers of evening gowns also had been bought for this 12-year-old, costing about $150 each, along with other articles worn with evening gowns. There was a sheared beaver coat for $950; I asked, "Surely you can't charge that all to one year?" She said, "Oh no, you're right. That was a mistake. She might, if she was careful, get another year's wear out of it."

The hearing continued, and the mother said she could not afford to give the child piano lessons for $5 apiece, because the husband was stingy. Then the father said, "Mr. Arbitrator, believe me, it isn't the money. I don't really care about the money. Because when the child is 21, she will receive $3 million as the first installment on her grandparents' estate. But what kind of a life would this child have, owning 35 sweaters at age 12?"

12

The arbitrator awarded an additional $5 per week to pay for the piano lessons.

In the early years, arbitration was very informal. And one thing has to be kept in mind about the development of labor arbitration: arbitration was not enforceable, for the most part. As late as the 1920s, the only state in which an agreement to arbitrate a future dispute could be maintained was New York. Some three or four years later, there were two other states (Ohio, as I recall it, and Wisconsin) which had adopted arbitration laws.

In this whole country you could not enforce an agreement to arbitrate. The collective-bargaining agreement was an "agreement" only in quotation marks. It could not be literally enforced. It was not until the [Steel] Trilogy[3] that we began to get some real teeth in the enforcement of arbitration awards. Until then what you had was a "gentlemen's agreement." Now if they were not gentlemen, which happened fairly often, you had nothing to enforce. You could whistle for it.

I can't go into the long history, but the law in England, which we had adopted here for many years, was that until the arbitrator's award was practically put into the employer's hands, he could renege if he didn't want it enforced. In those circumstances the only way arbitration could be enforced was by, in a sense, the power of the trade unions.

There were a fair number of interest arbitration cases in which the good offices of respected people would be called on to bring to bear upon a recalcitrant party whatever weight could be found. The weight was more likely to be manifested in the collective bargaining which preceded arbitration. Thomas Dewey, for example, sometimes got involved in labor disputes when he was governor of New York. But most of us thought that one of the conditions that Mr. Dewey exacted for his services was a preagreement to settle. The parties went through the motions of negotiating in the governor's office, but by that time they had already reached agreement to settle.

Years later I myself was involved in that kind of situation with another governor. This was a Long Island Railroad strike dispute. (Were they striking that far back? Oh, my goodness, yes!) I think we were locked up for weeks at the Hilton Inn near Kennedy Airport, while we were settling a dispute involving 13 separate unions. And they had an agreement on unanimity; nobody would settle unless they were all satisfied. So it took weeks; I'd get home at two or three o'clock in the morning.

Finally came the big day, and our three-man board procured what looked like it was going to be an agreement. While we were going through preliminaries of getting the agreement in writing, Governor Nelson Rockefeller was hiding out in the kitchen of the Hilton Inn until he got the word that the parties had actually signed. And when he finally learned that their signatures were on the paper, he emerged and "settled" the dispute.

There were cases in which (in the more active days of Catholic workers' groups) it was not uncommon to have an arbitrator appointed by the suggestions of the men of the cloth. Some of my early designations came from the cardinal. But I don't want to give a false impression; there were also designations from some of the rabbis in New York.

Were arbitrators in those years serving chiefly pro bono and coming from other fields? My recollection is that until about 1936 or 1940 (my recollection of the dates is not exact) I never was paid in a labor dispute and certainly not in a commercial dispute. To be an arbitrator was, for a college professor, like being invited to give the commencement address at the Weehawken High School. It was a kind of function which you were expected to perform as part of your academic duties.

Here's one illustration from some 35 years back. New Jersey was one of the states which, after the shooting stopped in World War II, enacted a compulsory arbitration statute in public-utility labor disputes. This involved the seizure of the property by the governor. When a telephone strike loomed, Governor Charles Edison[4] acted under his authority as general of the New Jersey militia. He ordered continued operation of the company with no interruption in service to telephone users.

The governor ordered arbitration of the dispute before a five-man board which had three public members: Dave Cole,[5] Paul Hays,[6] myself. The telephone workers' union was represented by Henry Mayer.[7] And the company was represented by a very talented lawyer who ultimately became a justice of the Supreme Court: William Brennan. So they were high-powered guys.

This was a case in which Mr. Brennan (who was a very articulate lawyer) remarked that these "carpetbaggers" (meaning Cole, Hays, and Stein) come over here and they are going to raise the telephone charges for the people in the state of New Jersey, if you give them the opportunity to do so.

My recollection is that the governor said (I'm not sure about this in every detail) he didn't think it was right for the public members to work for nothing, and so he was going to see to it that we were paid. And if he had to raise a private slush fund for this purpose, in simple justice he would do so. And so he did and we were paid the scale which the governor adopted. It was $10 per man per day, with a maximum of $25 for the whole case.

Arbitrators generally didn't really get paid for their services until almost the [19]50s when arbitration became much more widespread. Let me put it this way. Arbitrators would say to each other, perhaps just in casual conversation, "Gee, I have two arbitrations booked for the next month." And that we would regard as indicating that the parties were pretty satisfied with our role as arbitrators. If we could get two arbitrations back-to-back that would be great.

But then came the time when you could go out every day and be an arbitrator. You could build up a sizable backlog of respect in Syracuse, Rochester, and Buffalo. People from all different places were pressing you to come arbitrate their disputes. And then it seemed appropriate for arbitrators to be paid for their time and services. In the beginning we'd be paid $25 or $30 for a case. Later it escalated. Arbitration began to be a way of making a living.

That the service was valuable, I have no doubt whatever. It was valuable, and in some cases priceless almost. So it was reflected in the charges. And reflected also in the fact that many people began to turn to arbitration as a full-time career, as a way to make a living.

3

DEVELOPMENT OF ARBITRATION
Walter Gellhorn

Walter Gellhorn's long and notable service as an arbitrator began in 1936, when arbitration of labor disputes was a rarity. During the 1940s he was public member and chairman in the New York region of the National War Labor Board, at the center of the establishment of modern-day arbitration. In the years since he has arbitrated many controversies, some of small dimensions but large emotional content, many of more sweeping nature. He has served by presidential appointment on presidential emergency boards under the Railway Labor Act. His assistance has been invoked at state and local government levels by the New York State Public Employment Relations Board and the New York City Office of Collective Bargaining.

This substantial record in labor arbitration is nevertheless a footnote in Gellhorn's remarkable career as professor of law and expert in administrative law. In 1931 he was law clerk to U.S. Supreme Court Chief Justice Harlan F. Stone. Since 1933 Gellhorn has been on the law faculty of Columbia University and since 1937 on the political science faculty. On a number of occasions he left the classroom to serve in a variety of federal posts at the Social Security Board, Attorney General's Committee on Administrative Procedure, Office of Price Administration, Department of the Interior, and National War Labor Board. In 1974 he became University Professor Emeritus at Columbia University. He has continued to teach and study throughout the world; from 1984 to 1986 he directed the China Center for American Law Study.

The subject of administrative law, as studied and practiced, was shaped from the beginning by Gellhorn. His seminal text Administrative Law—Cases and Comments *is used in more than 80 institutions. In the mid-1960s he was a leader in the research and development that produced the Administrative Procedure Act and created the Administrative Conference of the United States (ACUS). Five successive U.S. presidents, beginning in 1967, designated him a councillor of ACUS.*

The word "ombudsman" was introduced in the United States, along with ideas that have taken hold widely, by his 1966 book Ombudsman and Others *and the companion* When Americans Complain.

Honors include the Columbia Law Alumni Medal for Excellence, Learned Hand medal, Oliver Wendell Holmes Lecturer at Harvard University, president of the Association of American Law Schools, and fellow of the American Academy of Arts and Sciences. In February 1988 he received the American Bar Foundation Fellows Research Award; presenting the award, now Supreme Court Justice Ruth Bader Ginsburg saluted Gellhorn as "a prodigious scholar of surpassing intelligence." In 1991 the Walter Gellhorn Chair was established at Columbia University School of Law. Not limited to administrative law, the chair, like Gellhorn's achievements, is all-embracing.

I have to talk somewhat indirectly about how I became involved in labor arbitration, because one's activities don't proceed in a straight line from one point to another by precise design.

In 1933 I joined the Columbia [University] law faculty as an assistant professor. One of my interests then was in public law; it still is. In my early days I served as an assistant to Joseph P. Chamberlain, who was a professor of public law and the head of the Legislative Drafting Research Fund here at Columbia. That fund was created (I think in 1912) in recognition of the fact that though statutory activity in the United States mounted steadily, the quality of legislative drafting and the thoroughness of research—that should underlie the preparation of a statute which might affect other statutes on the books or might have some impact on existing case law—should be undertaken more thoroughly than had been the case usually in the past.

Professor Chamberlain was a highly respected scholar, a very public-spirited person, a reformer in the best sense, not at all a stuffy type of reformer but a person who examined social problems and, instead of wringing his hands, undertook to do something about it. I served as a junior to him in connection with a number of projects which had to do with the elaboration explicitly of "labor law," as we referred to it in those days. Labor law then had not to do with "labor-relations law" (as I think the current usage of labor law connotes), but rather the body of statutes or decisions that bore on the status and well-being of working persons. One of the things on which I worked with Professor Chamberlain was the drafting of New York State's Unemployment Insurance Law. I remember, also, having worked on the preparation of statutes to restrict opportunities for industrial homework; it was a very complex sort of legislation to draft.

In those days I served not only as a toiler in the library (I almost said "the vineyard" but that would suggest too much jollity about it), but also as a member of, or an aide to various committees and commissions that were created by an act of one or another branch of government.

I recall, for example, having worked with a commission appointed by Governor Lehman to consider creating a system of unemployment insurance. And I recall very well George Meany, whom I met for the first time in that setting. He was then the president of the New York State Federation of Labor, and only later became president of the American Federation of Labor. George Meany was among those who at first strenuously opposed the idea of unemployment insurance, likening it to the detested "dole" of Britain, which had been thought by some to have taken the starch out of the British workingman and made him dependent on government handouts instead of on union organization. In short, Mr. Meany at that time required fully as much education as did employer groups before he was able to perceive the beauties of some sort of insurance against the irregularities of employment which were experienced by many persons, especially in the blue-collar and service industries.

I was appointed by the state of New York to be a public member of various boards that were created in connection with the administration of some of the recently enacted labor legislation. For example, the New York State Minimum Wage Law provided that, though the minimum wage was to be set by action of the industrial commissioner (as the head of the New York State Department of Labor was called), the commissioner was to act on the basis of a report and recommendation by a body that represented the public, the employer group, and the affected union organizations, or at least workers' organizations in general.

One of the episodes that comes back to me (because it suggests how much change has occurred and how rapidly indeed it has occurred) is that in setting the minimum wage for the restaurants of New York in those days, I believe we fixed upon 17½¢ as the permissible hourly minimum wage for waiters and waitresses. By hypothesis, of course, that wage would be supplemented by tips. But I will testify from recollection that in the early 1930s tipping was not one of the most heavily engaged-in social activities.

Work of that sort did extend my acquaintanceship with people in the management-labor area. One of those with whom I worked then was a man called George LeSauvage, who was one of the high officials in the Schrafft's chain of restaurants and tearooms. His company maintained a decent rate schedule. Because his company felt the competition of others who did not maintain as high a wage structure (25¢ an hour, I think, was the Schrafft's rate), he was supportive of the effort to set minimum wages. And that incidentally perhaps leads to the irrelevant observation (but nevertheless it does bear, in a way, on almost everything that has to do with labor relations): there isn't a single pattern of employer sentiment and of union sentiment.

As we read the newspapers, they tend to speak of "labor's point of view" and "management's point of view." But the truth of the matter is that, within either of those two groups, there are all sorts of subdivisions. And so I've discovered early in my career, through activities of the sort that I've just been outlining.

Earlier today you asked if I could recall when I had first undertaken to serve specifically as an arbitrator, rather than in some other relationship to problems of management or labor. And I do remember. That's another instance perhaps of how serendipity, rather than design, may affect one's later career. In 1936 I became the regional attorney of the newly created Social Security Board. One of the persons employed there was a man named Jules Freund. He was (I'm pretty sure) the executive assistant to the regional director who was a very well-known woman in the management-advisory field (and business consultant and counselor field) named Anna M. Rosenberg,[1] who among other things was a close associate of Senator Wagner's.[2]

Jules Freund left the Social Security Board to become the executive secretary of the New York State Board of Mediation. I think the board was newly created, and he left the federal service to undertake that activity in the state administration.

In some instances the state mediation board, having entered a controversy involving management and union, was able to persuade the contestants to submit their disagreement to the decision of an outsider, an arbitrator. This was not a widely practiced thing at the time.

Freund asked me on several occasions to serve as arbitrator in one of these situations in which the mediation board had persuaded the parties that instead of continuing warfare they should submit their disagreement to a tribunal, as it were. A one-man tribunal usually, but I do recall even then that on some occasions it was a three-person board of a tripartite nature: two chosen by the respective parties (one each by each of the contestants), and the third to be appointed by the mediation board.

I have never represented parties in a labor controversy. My role has always been that of the middleman so to speak, rather than that of a partisan. In any event, my first experience as an arbitrator was in response to these requests by the New York State Board of Mediation to step into some of their situations.

I should stress that the work at that time was regarded as a contribution to public well-being. It did not produce fees. It was not a service to the state, it was not a service to the parties, it was just a public service that was being performed upon somebody's request. I stress that in a way to emphasize how infrequently arbitration existed as an ongoing enterprise, as a regularly established and expected activity prior to the National War Labor Board days in World War II.

I stress in that connection that despite the infrequency of arbitration some persons were already strongly identified as persons of influence, whose judgment about how matters should be handled was so respected that they were called upon. One of them was Arthur S. Meyer who was chairman of the New York State Board of Mediation, a highly respected businessman in terms of his prior activity.[3] David Cole, a lawyer in Paterson, New Jersey (who subsequently was a public member of the National War Labor Board, region two, New York–New Jersey), is another person who comes to my mind as having been very actively involved in arbitration even before it became commonplace.

But the real emphasis upon arbitration, as a means of avoiding the continuation of warfare about matters in contest, came about with the National War Labor Board itself: in furtherance of its efforts to maintain continuity of production during the war years, when any interruption of productive activity (as by strike or a slowdown) was regarded as a setback for the national war effort. And I am sure that was the motivation, rather than some philosophical conviction, for the National War Labor Board insisting that when management and labor entered into a contractual relationship they should include in their contract some sort of machinery for dealing with grievances and should have as the terminal step (if agreement was not reached) the submission for final and binding arbitration to somebody who was chosen by the parties or by some means that the contract set forth.

I became vice chairman of the National War Labor Board, region two, in 1944, and in 1945 I became chairman. The [National] War Labor Board had two main functions. One had to do with the stabilization of wages, so that some coordination with the work of the Office of Price Administration could exist. OPA, as it was known, was responsible for maintaining some sort of bridle upon the galloping of prices and residential rents during the war years. As for price control, that seemed to be unlikely of achievement unless some harness could be put on wages. So the War Labor Board undertook to stabilize wages. No agreement could be reached between management and labor, and no unilateral decisions could be made by management, to raise wages without first receiving the approval of the National War Labor Board. Criteria were at hand for determining whether an adjustment would or would not be destabilizing. And so each application, even if there were complete agreement between the affected parties, required governmental approval.

In addition, in order to maintain the continuity of production, the War Labor Board required that if disagreement existed concerning the terms and conditions of employment in a new contract, every unresolved labor dispute came to the National War Labor Board. It was considered by a tripartite panel of the board with employer representatives, representatives of unions, and at least two (and usually three) representatives of the public.

We dealt with what is nowadays called "interest arbitration," fixing the terms of the continuing relationship between the parties. In order to do that, in each instance, an investigation (something in the nature of a hearing, the reception of the parties' evidence, and so on) had to be organized, so that the board would know what the circumstances of the particular matter were. The board named persons drawn from the public at large, persons who were thought to be qualified by experience or training or community stature, and to be effective in receiving and analyzing the evidence. Those persons of course sought to bring the parties to agreement. But agreement failing, the controversy had to be referred to the board, which then issued what it confidently called an "Order" to incorporate in the new contract certain provisions and not other provisions which might have been sought by one or another of the parties. The Orders were not enforceable directly by the Regional War Labor Board. In the first place, they were appealable to the National War Labor Board sitting in Washington.

When I say that our regional [National War Labor] Board's Orders were subject to appeal, I think most of them were not appealed; the parties by and large accepted them. The national board was in a position to affirm or modify what was done on the regional level, and generally supported the regional board's Orders and decisions.

Now suppose the national board, having affirmed the position taken regionally, was ignored. Was there some enforcement device there? No enforcement device in the sense of a direct remedial method that was set forth by statute. But the president had the power, as an ultimate sanction, to seize the company that was recalcitrant and ignored Orders of the board. And that happened in two or three dramatic instances during the war. Montgomery Ward was seized, and the mines were seized at one point, and so on. This was all in furtherance of the war effort, not in furtherance of the National War Labor Board or of the union or indeed of the management, but in order to ensure continuity of production. Because in those days (differently from now, I think) the notion was still accepted that "you can not strike against the government!" So if the government was nominally operating the company, that pretty much ended the likelihood of strike activity, and so production went on.

By and large the decisions of the National War Labor Board were prudent. And one thing that I say reflectively about them, is that they themselves were confined by the stabilization program. That is to say: a radical member of the board could not incorporate in Orders what might ever have been his or her personal preferences or idiosyncrasies.

If the labor union, for example, demanded a pay increase of 10¢ an hour and one were terribly, terribly sympathetic with the poor workingman and wanted to increase his income, one couldn't order a wage increase of 10¢ an hour, because that might be destabilizing. One had to confine the Order to whatever the level of wages that was regarded permissible in that industry and for that line of work and at that particular time.

So also with innovative things that one might abstractly have thought to be highly desirable. I well recall that one of the demands many people deemed virtually revolutionary during those years (now only 40 years ago!) was that workers should have some paid sick leave: if they got sick, they shouldn't lose a day's pay or a week's pay but at least for some number of days in the year some illness might be anticipated, and they should be protected against being made virtually destitute by loss of their current earnings. Most contracts nowadays do have something of that sort in them. But 40 years ago that was a rarity. So if one were to order that type of provision into a contract, it would obviously make wage costs increase even though it didn't go directly into the workers' pockets in the form of an increase in the hourly wage. It would increase the total wage growth, for the year, of the employer.

So we had to think about that in terms of whether it was or was not destabilizing. It would be destabilizing if it were innovative. It really comes down to that. If what was set was simply to bring some laggard company into line with the bulk of the companies in the industry, that would not be destabilizing; that would simply be forcing the rear guard to catch up with the main procession.

That happened in a number of instances where people wanted paid holidays. We didn't have a formula that everybody is entitled to 6 paid holidays or 8 paid holidays or 10 paid holidays a year. But we made studies of the prevailing practice, industry by industry. And if in some industry 6 days was the normality, then one could order 6 days in the new contract for a company that at that time wasn't getting as many as 6 days. But my best recollection is that we didn't undertake innovation, even on an industry basis. We didn't say, "Six paid holidays are the norm, taking the country as a whole for most employments." But we said, "What is the norm for this particular industry?" And then we maintained that pattern. I'm sure that many people in the staff, and the board itself, felt in various industries that their levels of compensation or their levels of fringe benefits might be too low; but this wasn't an occasion to be raising them.

After the war ended, a history of the National War Labor Board was written. One of the questions that was put to the board members in that connection was what would be our recommendation about continuing in the future the process of disputes resolution that had functioned so well during the war. I responded that in my estimation we should not continue by having a labor court, as it were, to which disputants might take their disputes because, unless we were to forestall innovation for all time, we could not over the long term halt the sorts of demands which were being made and routinely rejected by the War Labor Board.

Health insurance is a perfectly good example of that. Someone would say, "We want a system of (what we now colloquially refer to as 'Blue Cross–Blue Shield') insurance." Now medical insurance is just routine in labor contracts. We would have disallowed any such claim during the war years because it was innovative.

One could think of many other changes in the content of the worker-employer relationship which abstractly can't be argued for or against. You argue for it if you think the workers' lot should be a happier one, and you argue against it if you think the employer's circumstances make it difficult to honor that demand. But it was very easy for a member of the War Labor Board to say, "I sympathize with you, my dear Mr. Union, but nevertheless I deny your request because. . . ." And that was the end of the matter. But to do that year after year would have made us a very stagnant nation.

Any change, from one level to another, I don't think is dictated by some abstract principle of justice that emanates directly from heaven, but by perceptions of competing considerations. During the war we limited the number of competing considerations because we had only one consideration: to win the war. And we were sure we had the formula for doing it. But I don't think that could be continued over the long term.

I have been struck (in the instances when I have been asked to serve as an arbitrator in the interest-arbitration type of situation) by the difficulty of deciding abstractly whether demands should or should not be granted. Plainly I do not take the view in my life that every innovation is to be resisted. I remember actually in a Supreme Court decision in 1912 the constitutionality of workmen's compensation (as it was then called) was being challenged. The Supreme Court upheld the challenge but wasn't able to give very good reasons for doing so. Mr. Justice McKenna wrote in his Opinion: "Resist first steps. Who can know to what they may conduce?"

That isn't my philosophy. I believe in taking some first steps, or we'd just be marking time and society would mark time. So I am not generically against first steps. But as a determiner of the fate of a management or a union organization, I have some difficulty in knowing whether the step which seems to me to be in the right direction is one which should be commanded that others take. Or whether it is simply one that I would take if I were taking it for me.

So I'm troubled by the interest-arbitration cases, unless the parties themselves have given some criteria that can be applied by the arbitrator. (I said in connection with the War Labor Board work that we did have the criteria of maintaining stabilization as well as continuity of production.) I recall one instance in which the *Washington Post* and the Newspaper Guild were at loggerheads. The Guild had been seeking a large increase in pay; the *Washington Post* agreed that some increase was warranted, but disagreed as to how much it should be. If I had simply been called upon to say how much I thought a newspaper reporter should get, or a subeditor should get, I think I would have been stumped.

But they had also gotten to the point where they had agreed that *Washington Post* reporters ought to get paid as much as reporters on comparable papers. I think that was the agreement they had reached. What they could not agree upon was which newspapers were comparable. The *Washington Post* reporters wanted to be compared with the *New York Times,* which had very good rates compared with the then *Washington Post* rate. The *Washington Post* wanted to be compared with the *Washington Star* and other newspapers in Washington, not with some New York paper. And (according to the *Washington Post*) if the *Washington Star,* which was an afternoon paper and not as widely circulated perhaps as the *Washington Post,* was not comparable, then let's look at morning newspapers in cities other than New York; let's see what is the pay rate for reporters on morning newspapers in Detroit or St. Louis or whatnot.

But at least I had the notion of comparability. And I could receive testimony as to why one side or the other thought its choices of comparable newspapers should be sustained as correct. That seemed to me to be putting me in the position of making a decision, rather than simply formulating a policy of what I thought was sound. And I had less discomfort in that than in some other situations in which a union was pressing for a change because it was seeking in effect to break new ground through the collective-bargaining process.

I can give an example of that in a case in which I sat with Prof. Emanuel Stein of New York University and Robert Coulson, president of the American Arbitration Association. The three of us were asked several years ago by the New York City Office of Collective Bargaining to serve as adjudicators of a dispute between the Policemen's Benevolent Association on the one hand and the New York City Police Department on the other, in connection with formation of a new contract to govern their relationships. To state the issue fairly simply: the police wanted to break out of an historical mold that limited how much they were likely to accomplish. Historically in this city (and I believe it to be true still today) the policemen and the firemen have the same wage rates. At the time that this controversy arose, the entry salaries were the same and the length-of-service increments were the same.

That arrangement seems to have been advantageous to both groups—or I can't imagine that it would have been entered into in the first place. In this particular controversy the police (having been dissatisfied with an agreement made by the firemen's representatives for a new contract) wanted to break the mold and say, "We shouldn't be bound by what was done by the collective-bargaining representatives of the firefighters. They're another group. We have our own collective-bargaining representative and want to bargain for our wage rate without reference to what their wage rate is."

I can't say that this is an implausible position if you once accept the notion that each bargaining unit is to have its own agent. Then it seems to me, abstractly, that an agreement made by unit X should not automatically foreclose a demand by unit Y for something quite different. But the whole course of history for years and years had been to the contrary; the two scales were on a parity. And the consequences of changing that pattern were unforeseeable; they weren't even foretellable.

In those circumstances, Stein, Coulson, and I were in agreement that not a strong enough showing had been made for innovation. And we stuck with the past, not because we were forced to (as in the War Labor Board examples I was giving earlier), but just because it seemed imprudent for us to command that the city depart from what had been an historical practice. And, I must say, an historical practice which had raised the rates for both categories of employees at a fairly satisfactory pace over the years. The pattern was not established at the city's behest, but had been demanded in the past by the unions. So we in effect said, "Let's stick with the status quo until some real compelling argument is given for change."

That's the trouble with interest arbitration, as I see it. The union that is no longer satisfied with the past (and very frequently indeed a new union or new union leadership has come into power because of dissatisfaction with the past) may be at the mercy of the past, in a sense. An arbitrator will rarely (or, at least in my estimation, should be reluctant to) disregard history and say, "By my command, let the parties move off in a new direction." If one party can persuade the other, well and good. But I, the arbitrator, am not Jove. And I'm not in a position to say, "You must start up a new pact."

So, having that in mind, I've not been an enthusiast for interest arbitration where the parties have not themselves created some criteria that can be applied. The criterion that I mentioned, in the one example I gave, was comparability with some other newspaper. Very frequently, quite a different formula will be designed: "We think that the workers in this plant are entitled to an increase because their pay raises are lagging behind that of the industry as a whole, and that requires an economic study of the industry as a whole, and so on." At least there they have given the arbitrator some guidance as to what it is they are disagreeing about. It isn't just a disagreement between the new and the old, but a disagreement about some fact which, once resolved, would lead to a conclusion. That type of thing does not bother me, but the other continues to bother me.

I was recently exposed to some of these difficulties in a fairly acute form, about two or three years ago. The public transport facilities in New York City were involved in a citywide bargaining situation. And I was a member of a three-man board which was trying to bring the parties to an agreement. It was not an arbitration board; I suppose "mediation board" would be the right way to describe it because we didn't have power. We were called simply "the Board"; we were named by the parties. Each of the parties, management and labor, had chosen a representative; then they chose me as the middleman.

It was a highly complex problem; the whole subway system is marked by history unrelated to practicality. Work rules that were prudent when adopted, and designed to overcome some managerial abuse, had become themselves abusive to management. When the union in that situation (or unions, because there were more than one) would put forward a demand, management would say in effect, "Yes, but where is the money going to come from? Will you change this or that in response to our request? Then we would have something to give you." "Oh, no, we're never going to give up our hard-won gains," would come the bellowing answer from the union.

I'll show you how irrational that can be. One of the hard-won gains that they would "never give up" had to do with the grinding of the wheels of the subway trains, which wear from contact with the rails, obviously, so that periodically, just as a tire needs to be changed, the wheel has to be taken off and reground so that it will ride smoothly over the rails. I think that sometime in the distant past there must have been unusually burdensome demands made on the workers in that particular branch of maintenance; their output was held at too high a rate. And finally the then union and then management agreed that grinding two wheels would constitute a day's work. I think the grinding equipment must have been very limited at the time that agreement was made; I'm prepared to assume that that was a fair measurement of a day's work at the time that agreement was reached.

But today's machinery does most of the grinding. And I was satisfied, from what I heard in the course of this controversy, that the day's work of grinding two wheels was now completed in about two hours. Then the wheel grinders remained on the premises for the rest of the day, in order to earn eight hours of pay. They did no additional work; they played cards or read a book or something to fill in the time. But when the suggestion was made, "Why don't we change work rules like that so we'll have money to put someplace else?" then would come that bellowing response, "You can't expect us to give up our hard-won gains."

Another aspect of interest arbitration that has to be taken into account, and that troubles me a lot, is that many unions are not nearly so unified (or perhaps I should say "authoritative") as they have been in the past. This was a product of the democratization of the unions. But one consequence of making the rank and file the real owners of the unions, instead of the entrenched union executives, is that even a prudent settlement by an existing leadership may be challenged often by demagogues—not by genuine rival leaders, but seekers of power within the union. "Those fellows have sold us out to the management," say the dissident element. So getting an agreement that will stick is very difficult.

And that is, incidentally, exactly what happened in that transit situation.

If it had just been left to our board of three and the union spokesman (who unfortunately had two very powerful rivals at that time) and the head of the Metropolitan Transit Authority [MTA], we would have been able to reach an agreement. But just as the union fellow had to worry about outsiders, so did the MTA have to worry about the mayor and the governor—neither of whom ever spoke to the members of the board, or had any part discernibly in the negotiations, but both of whom outside the meeting room were saying, "Don't give this, don't give that."

It was a very difficult situation to deal with. A strike did occur. The strike was ultimately settled on precisely the basis that the board had recommended before the strike began. So it was just a waste, from everybody's point of view.

I'll tell you perfectly truthfully that to me arbitration has been professionally rewarding. I have done too little of it to have been rewarded in a major economic way. But it's been professionally rewarding for me in two senses that bear on my academic work.

In the first place, the nature of arbitration hearings has many points of resemblance to administrative hearings. My field of special professional expertise is asserted to be administrative, as in the War Labor Board and the Social Security Board and in other public posts at various times. But this labor arbitration has been a very valuable addition to my exposure to the problems of investigation, reception of evidence, determination on the record that has been brought before the arbitrator, rather than something the arbitrator might conceive outside.

I don't think there is a single pattern of administrative procedure in government agencies, and certainly there is not a single pattern in the arbitrations in which I've engaged. In some arbitrations the lawyers seemed to want to conduct the proceeding as though it were the trial of a tort suit or of criminal action, with stenographic record and with attention to all of the rules of evidence that most trial lawyers magnify beyond their real worth. Others are conducted informally and more—how shall I put it?—through colloquy, through exchange rather than through the strict effort to re-create a past event by the presentation of testimony.

It depends a little bit on the nature of the grievance, of course. If you have a wrongful discharge case and the question is, "Is it true that this worker hit the foreman in the nose with his fist on the night of June the sixth?" then as to that you're re-creating a past event and one has to receive testimony about it.

If the grievance is about whether some activity done by a person within a wage classification is or is not within the dimensions of that wage classification, it seems to me there it would be silly to proceed as though one were conducting an ordinary trial. So I think that the variety of procedures is very large, and that in itself has been illuminating for me, just to have a sense of how one can proceed informally and yet with a good deal of confidence that one was learning what one had to know.

I think the other aspect of arbitration that's been personally most illuminating for me—though it's something that would be absolutely impossible to quantify—is simply the accruing confidence that comes from lengthy contact with a variety of persons and personalities. I don't suggest that that has made me a highly adaptable or easy-to-get-along-with person in different settings. But it has at least enhanced my acceptance of the settings, if not the settings' acceptance of me.

I have been in some arbitration proceedings where one or the other representative was unable to speak words that had more than four letters in them, and he used those words repetitively for everything, and usually shouting at the top of his lungs. But if one can get over one's wish that the proceedings were being carried on in a different manner and just deal with the situation as it comes, it must have some contribution to make to one's social agility. (Shall I put it so?) So I've felt that I've been the beneficiary in a lot of the arbitration I've done.

In a number of situations I've been the sole contract arbitrator. And I must say that on the whole I've found that to be a more constructive relationship than the ad hoc where one comes in and disposes of a particular dispute but leaves no deposit behind on which the parties can base their own decision in the next instance—the next instance, by hypothesis, not being precisely like the one that went before. Whereas where you have a more continuing relationship, the line of decisions that comes out begins to take a shape that elaborates the contractual language, and the parties come to apply the body of decisional law, just as the courts apply precedents themselves.

And I have felt in the instances where I have had that sort of relationship, that over a period of time the volume of controversy is diminished. The good relationship between the parties has been strengthened because I've tried very hard in rendering a decision to do more than simply decide "you are right" and "you are wrong," but rather to suggest how matters of that kind might be dealt with more effectively in the future. When it works, it works very well. I know that was George Taylor's philosophy: proceed not to ignore a contract, not to expand a contract, but to suggest in advance of controversy how a contract might be utilized advantageously to both parties.

But I have had one experience where I feel confident that that has occurred. Some 22 years ago the state mediation board asked me to go to a city in western New York where a six-month strike had been in progress, because the parties had finally agreed to submit to an arbitrator the issues that remained in dispute between them. At that time there were 32 issues in dispute. I heard three, rendered my decision there on the ground; I didn't leave. I think most arbitrators don't like to render bench decisions; I wrote it out, right then and there, and gave it to them. But then I suggested that they go back; in the light of these decisions they saw how my mind was running—and perhaps with that they might be able to make some progress on the remaining 29 issues. They did indeed go back, and they disposed of the other 29 without needing me further. Maybe they thought they'd make their own mistakes, instead of my making them for them.

But then they asked me to be their grievance arbitrator. And I have now, as I say, for 20-odd years. In the last two years I think I have had to go there only once; I used to go surely once a month. It's a difficult place to get to and from, so I'm just as happy not to go. They give me an annual retainer, just so I'll come when they want me to come. But then they don't want me to come. But they're happy, they say they're happy, and I believe that it's so. And they seem to think that I helped them become happy in this way. So of course that gives me tremendous satisfaction. I feel that I've accomplished something more than simply ending a dispute, that I suggested a fruitful relationship for the future.

In those days I had the feeling that the union in this particular plant was too unsure of its constituency, as it were, to be as demanding of itself as it should be. If someone came storming in to the union office and said, "Let's fight this case to the Supreme Court if necessary!" the union would then fight it to the Supreme Court, namely me, without really exercising as much censorial judgment as I thought would be desirable. But instead of leaving it to the union to explain to a disgruntled member why the member had not prevailed, I undertook to talk to him before the day was out.

At any rate, that was for me not merely a personal satisfaction triumph but seemed to me to be an exemplification of what the arbitration process can do in a situation. I agree that it's not because the arbitrator does it; the parties must want to have it done. But one "can do." I would be insincere if I disclaimed belief that I had made some contribution to this, and that it wasn't simply the process producing the result. People are what make processes work. So obviously you have to have people (not only the arbitrator, but the representatives of the parties) who want to make things work out.

I don't know that I have anything more to say about "permanent" umpires versus ad hoc arbitrators, but that doesn't mean I won't say it. When Arthur Goldberg (who had been the general counsel with the steelworkers) was secretary of labor, the maritime industry, which had a nationwide contract with the International Organization of Masters, Mates and Pilots, wanted to have a permanent arbitrator, and asked the secretary to name somebody. He asked me whether I would be willing to be permanent arbitrator in that industry. I served for some years until after a change in union leadership I was no longer persona grata with the new union president—who was certainly not one of the people who were most grata with me either. So that was all right.

In the very first cases that I heard under that agreement, there were five cases: I rendered all of them in favor of the employers. (I don't say "the employer" because this was a nationwide contract and one dispute might be with steamship company A and the next one with steamship company B, and so on.) But the union was involved in all five, and I held in five consecutive cases for the employer's side. I was pretty sure that my tenure in that instance would be very brief.

The then president of the union, however, a man named Captain Charles Crooks, was so impressed by the fact that I decided five cases in a row for the management, that he was convinced that I was a man who would exercise my judgment honestly. Far from having been turned off, he seemed to have an enhanced confidence in me. Over the years I had a very pleasant relationship with him and with the industry. I really enjoyed that one a lot. ("Crooks" was an unfortunate name, but I want to tell you that he did a wonderful job of cleaning up a corrupt union. He was a reform leader, and he did actually achieve reforms during his administration.)

You asked me not to engage in "war stories" and I won't. But since you said to share really good ones, I'll tell one that really was damn near a war story. At one point our nation built an atomic-powered freight-carrying ship called the *Savannah*. So far as I know it's the only nuclear-powered ship, other than submarines, that we've had. It was not a gigantic ship—15,000 tons, something of that sort.

Everyone agreed that the wage rates for the deck officers (that is to say, the master and the mates) and for the engineer officers (chief engineer and the assistant engineers, and so on) would have to be increased, considering the novelty of the vessel. You couldn't just put an old sea dog on one of those ships with all of its special attributes. But neither the [International Organization of] Masters, Mates and Pilots on the one hand, nor the Marine Engineers Beneficial Association on the other, wanted to start the negotiations. Each of them was fearful that whichever one first made a contract would then be outstripped by the second one, which would insist on getting more than was given the first bargainer. The consequence was that the vessel was in effect immobilized because no one could agree on what were to be dominant wage rates aboard.

Finally the Masters, Mates and Pilots did get up enough courage for me to decide their case first, before the [Marine] Engineers came aboard, and I did set the rates. But I put in my award something that infuriated the [Marine] Engineers: that the captain of the vessel, who is responsible for everything, should in any event receive more than the chief engineer. I ordered that he should get X thousands of dollars a year, but in no event less than $100 more than the chief engineer (or some such formula).

The pay differences between those two classifications had been variable but it was well known in the industry that the unions were professional rivals, as it were. "We engineers are skilled people. You people, you deck officers up there, you just turn a wheel every now and again." So everyone thought that the engineers were going to demand a very large pay for working nuclear machinery.

In point of fact, the operation of the machinery was not very complex. The consequences of not operating were very complex, but the operation itself was pretty well routinized. But it did seem to me that was the critical issue: who was going to be the top man on the ship? The chief engineer or the captain?

The Marine Engineers were furious that I had designed a formula which put a "cap" on them. I said that the chief engineer could get as much as he can bargain for; there is no limitation on collective bargaining. Go ahead and bargain for whatever you want; but when your bargaining is over, the master is still going to get $100 more. They didn't like that very much.

One other "war story," then I really will subside. At one point I was the permanent arbitrator of grievances involving all of the newspapers in New York [City]—of which there were more then than there are now—and the union that represented the news deliverers. That was a very tough union; I don't know what it is now. In any event, the union was thought to have a very large corrupt element in it; whether it is so now, or not, I don't know.

But in one of the early cases I decided there, I held that a newspaper had properly disciplined the driver of one of the trucks. Afterwards one of the union representatives came up to me and said, "Jeez, you sure got a lot of guts." And I said, "What do you mean?" He said, "Why, you upheld the paper in that case." And I said, "Yes, why not? I felt that the fellow was properly disciplined." "That's Socks Lanza's brudder, you dummy!" Socks Lanza being one of the more notorious gangsters of that period in New York, that led the people in that industry to believe that I was a fair-minded person. Then I rendered some decisions that the *New York Daily News* didn't like. And so, when the contract terminated, I was terminated. I don't want you to think it's only unions that fire me. I could be fired by managements as well. My rear's even-cushioned to receive kicks from both sides.

Today I do a certain amount of grievance arbitration in small public units, school systems, police departments, things of that sort. The Public Employment Relations Board frequently asks me to step into some situation, not always of great dramatic content though of local heat. And I have felt in a number of instances that my function is not so much to resolve a controversy as to take responsibility for having resolved a controversy. Sometimes public officials, just as is true of officials in companies, are unwilling to take the responsibility of giving something that they think probably ought to be given. And sometimes union leaders are unwilling to take the responsibility of saying that the claim lacks merit, but are willing to have someone else say it lacks merit—if not willing, not surprised.

In that respect one function of the arbitrator may be to preserve face for the contestants, rather than to resolve a genuine disagreement between them.

It's not an acknowledged agreement; it's a declared disagreement. But I think that on the inside, sometimes, there's an acknowledgment. I think that's a perfectly desirable function: for someone to take the heat. And at the end of it, the union leader can say to his disgruntled constituent, "Well, it's that stupid son of a bitch, the arbitrator. We'll never have him here again." And the member goes off happily, knowing that the good fight has been fought, even though it was not won. And similarly the city official who doesn't want to be identified as being soft on unionism or something of that sort, can say, "I did my best, folks. Vote for me again." But he knows that the right thing was done.

So if we think of arbitration as a way of furthering peace, I don't believe that it's too demeaning for an arbitrator every now and again to receive the brickbats that would otherwise be thrown at persons who need to have a continuing relationship with one another. So we can make continuity possible in that way; it does make for discontinuity of the arbitrator.

The final point that I have to make is that labor arbitration has itself been, I think, educational for people who are not involved in direct management-labor matters. It serves as a demonstration, that becomes widely known and recognized, of a simple means of resolving disagreements. In short, labor arbitration in my view has stimulated the use of arbitration in other nonlabor areas, or at least nonlabor-contract areas. One labor-related but nonlabor-contract area in which I personally had experience involved a trust fund which was created to provide pensions for retired employees of one of the Washington newspapers.

The contract had indeed provided that the trust fund should be created, and that the company was required to make contributions to the trust fund to assure that retired employees would receive some sort of pension. But after a period of time, when all of the pensions that had been contemplated had been provided, the trustees of the fund discovered that they had almost $1.5 million left in their possession. What to do with the $1.5 million? Whose $1.5 million was it? No contract gave an answer to that. No precise precedent, that anyone knew of, gave a precise answer to that. Nobody had ever expected that there would be a penny left over, let alone $1.5 million.

In this instance the trustees of the pension fund (not the company and the union as such) utilized arbitration, and specifically used me as arbitrator to resolve the impasse. The contributor of the money, that is to say the newspaper which had set up the trust fund in the first place, said, "Give it back to us." The union on the other hand said the purpose of the employer's contribution was to provide pensions. "So why don't you give the pensioners the benefit of the extra money, by increasing pensions? After all, they must have given up wage increases, or given up something, in order to get those pensions. The fact that the pensions cost a little bit less than was expected shouldn't mean that the extra money should go back."

As I recall the formal aspects of the matter, the trustees didn't say, "Let's submit the matter to Gellhorn, as trustees." There were three trustees who had been nominated originally by the publisher, and three trustees who had been nominated originally by the Newspaper Guild. They functioned independently of their respective appointers; they would be personally liable if they didn't function as trustees. In effect the six trustees elected me to be a seventh trustee for the purpose of deciding this particular issue: what to do with $1.5 million? I sat with them and, at the end of two or three days of very hotly contested proceedings, the six usual trustees were still deadlocked, three to three. Then I, as the seventh trustee, cast my vote and that was the end of the matter.[4] It was in essence an arbitrator's decision, though in form it was the trustees' decision.

I use that simply as an illustration of what I believe to have been one of the benign and spreading influences of labor arbitration. I feel confident that it would not have occurred to those trustees to forestall long drawn-out litigation had they not in one capacity or another observed the use of arbitration in a different setting.

4

THE WAGNER ACT AND MORE
Ida Klaus

Before Ida Klaus became an arbitrator in 1976, she had already "pointed the way"[1] in two of the areas that made widespread arbitration of labor disputes possible and necessary: the development of labor law (particularly the National Labor Relations Act), and of labor relations in the public sector. In 1948 she became solicitor at the National Labor Relations Board,[2] serving for six years as the board's principal legal adviser, including conduct of litigation at circuit courts of appeal and the U.S. Supreme Court. Later, from 1954 until 1962, she was counsel to New York City's newly established Department of Labor, serving as principal labor relations adviser to Mayor Robert F. Wagner; the program she designed for the city as employer culminated in the landmark law known as the Little Wagner Act.[3]

In 1961 and 1962 Klaus was consultant to the Cabinet-level task force established by President Kennedy to devise a program for employee-management relations in the federal government.[4] The result was President Kennedy's Executive Order No. 10988, "Employee-Management Cooperation in the Federal Service," the first system of labor relations for federal employees.

In 1962 the New York City Board of Education asked Klaus to complete its first efforts at collective bargaining with teachers. She negotiated the first agreement ever entered into by the board for its teachers, an agreement that became a model for school districts throughout the country. In 1962 she became executive director of the Board of Education's Office of Labor Relations and Collective Bargaining, serving until her retirement in 1975; she directed labor relations and negotiated contracts covering more than 100,000 pedagogical and administrative employees. In 1976 she began a decade-long service as one of the three neutrals constituting the New York State Public Employment Relations Board. The Public Employment Relations Board (PERB) governs labor relations under the Taylor Law for state employees.

Klaus began arbitrating in 1976 as an arbitrator under the national collective-bargaining contract between U.S. Steel and the United Steelworkers of

America. She also served on the grievance arbitration panel for the U.S. Postal Service and the various unions of postal employees, and on the panel in Railroad Adjustment Board cases involving contract disputes between railroads throughout the country and the unions representing railroad employees. On three occasions she was appointed to presidential emergency boards under the Railway Labor Act.

I started my arbitration career very late in my professional life. It was, I believe, my fourth career. However, it was a logical, I thought, outcome of the prior experiences in my previous "incarnations." I started in the labor field when I was very young, in the early days of the New Deal—which starts with 1933 when Franklin Roosevelt was trying to bring this country out of the worst depression since the nineteenth century. He intended to do it by various kinds of legislation which would remove the causes of cyclical depression in a structural way.

By 1937 one of the pillars of the New Deal program was the National Labor Relations Act. It was passed in 1935 and was known as the Wagner Act. Its purpose was to remove the burdens on interstate commerce caused by long strikes (which seriously affected the growth and continued growth of commerce between the states) labor strife, and unrest.

The general philosophy of the Wagner Act was to prevent (or at least to minimize) the frequency of strikes by attempting to remove or minimize the causes of employee dissatisfaction which led to strikes. Fundamentally it granted the right of collective bargaining to employees to form organizations of their choice in order to equalize the economic power of those who performed labor. By 1937 the statute had been declared constitutional. That was a great surprise to many people because it followed a whole series of Supreme Court decisions which had found that one or another of the New Deal statutes was unconstitutional for one reason or another. The National Labor Relations Act was saved because of its very clear statement of policy, which centered its functions on the protection of commerce as the objective of the Congress.

In 1937 the National Labor Relations Board came to life, and I came to work there. I spent many years there, years of great excitement, years of dedication to the true mission of enforcing the policy of free and unhampered collective bargaining.

It was an experience in industrial democracy of which I had a full part, along with many of my young colleagues, all very eager to achieve the same kind of work ideals. We had a role in helping the board to forge a fund of principles with administrative force and administrative philosophy that filled in bit by bit the structural outline of the Wagner Act and its policies. Primarily,

I think, the greater contribution of the board was the development of the foundation for the practical and theoretical concept of "the duty to bargain" and its antecedent aspects.

We thought little in those days about arbitration because it was not particularly evident in industrial relationships. Workers were struggling to join unions and achieve full collective bargaining and improvements in their terms and conditions of employment. There were not many written agreements at that time. Many were oral, and few provided for any kind of grievance procedure. It was believed that the agreements would be observed; as a matter of fact, under state law some of them were not recognized. They weren't regarded as contracts, and so it was difficult to apply any kind of legal guidance to these documents, or these oral arrangements. It was all, in a sense, a voluntary system of collective bargaining enforced by the prescriptions of the Wagner Act.

As we went on we developed the practice, among others, of requiring that agreements reached in collective bargaining must be reduced to writing in order to protect the fruits of the negotiations of the parties and to prevent either side (but particularly employers who were still quite hostile to this new law) from backing down on what they had promised. This became a very important aspect of the components of the duty to bargain as it evolved.

There were various other principles which were developed, whose purpose it was to effectuate the collective-bargaining system as a basic requirement of employer-employee relationships. Collective bargaining was to be looked upon (and still is) as a legislative process in which the parties themselves are the legislators. They come together and they legislate for themselves, pursuant to the broad principles of the law and of the doctrine laid down under the law. It is a system of government by which they govern themselves. The executive function under that system of government is performed later, again by the parties themselves who administer the document which has been agreed upon, or at least the basic legislative mandate for the instrument. The judicial function under that system is the process of arbitration.

Arbitration is the recourse of one of those sides (usually the union) to a third party unrelated to the parties themselves. It is a system of determining and declaring claimed rights under the legislated document, the agreement. That was about as much as we needed to think about in those days with respect to arbitration. Arbitration did not become a real recourse until World War II when the unions gave up voluntarily the right to strike in return for binding arbitration of disputes under agreements. Many of the strikes were caused by one type of grievance or another. There were also bargaining disputes, and those too were a matter of voluntary agreement by both sides, called a "compact," a "social compact," or a "social contract." These did not have binding aspects, just "honor" at the highest levels.

I won't go into the [National] War Labor Board, which in 1941–45 really brought arbitration into the entire system of conducting labor relations on a stable, mature basis. It was, I might say, the War Labor Board that was the fount of talent from which the present arbitration roster drew its strength. Names come to mind, all very important: Ralph Seward,[5] Sylvester Garrett,[6] Saul Wallen,[7] just to name a few that are very important. Those people made tremendous contributions to the development of arbitration and of its function as a very important aspect of the collective-bargaining system and industrial government in this country.

I will go back to the beginning of my [National Labor Relations Board] NLRB service, before I go on. I started as a review attorney. That was where most of the thinking was taking place, that was where most of the development of the doctrines occurred. I read huge records, transcripts of hearings that were held in cases of extreme antiunion conduct on the part of the employers. It was not uncommon to have the ordinary transcript run to 3,000 pages. Some cases went on for a year, some for more. We had very serious struggles with employers who refused to recognize the authority of the statute, even after the Supreme Court decision. It was there that we lawyers, many of us, worked unceasingly. We worked day and night, we worked Saturdays and Sundays, we came back after dinner and worked some more. The board members, all very dedicated people, sat day and night hearing cases.

I gradually worked up to be supervisor in the litigation section. There again I had great pleasure in supervising a number of cases which led to very important National Labor Relations Board doctrines. I remember one case which built litigation doctrine when the case went to the Second Circuit. That was the Western Union Company, which had a "company union" they themselves had founded—and which they did not want to give up. I felt very proud that we disestablished that company union. The day the board's order came down, Western Union stock dropped five points or something like that; it affected the whole economy. It went to the [Circuit] Court of Appeals and was sustained. It resulted in very good law on company unions.

There were other major cases. I had one of a series of cases involving Ford Motor Company. In those days Henry Ford was so opposed to unions that he set up what was known as the "strong-arm squad," headed by a man named Harry Bennett. Bennett was a very well-known man whose job it was to keep unions out of Ford plants, through any means. Violence was very much one of the instrumentalities of that objective.

There were a whole series of Ford cases. I had one (I think there were four of us chosen to do Ford cases), the Dallas case. That involved the worst kind of terror I have ever encountered in labor relations. Ford's strong-arm squad got down to Dallas and beat up, cruelly and brutally, anyone coming into the city who was an organizer of some kind or another, not necessarily in the Ford plant. One man (named Baer, I believe; he worked, I think, for the Millinery Workers) came into Dallas. He was waylaid by the strong-arm squad in a field, beaten unconscious, and had his eye gouged out. There were other such acts. Through the fine efforts of the field examiners and the trial attorneys (Nat Wells was one; he is now a very well-known practitioner in Dallas), that case broke the strong-arm squad. It broke the identity of the squad and its purpose, and traced it all the way back to Detroit into Harry Bennett's office and the offices of high Ford officials.

Another Ford case was handled by Ted Kheel.[8] He had a whole series of discharges in Kansas City. He had the longest transcript and did it faster than anybody else.

I went on to become the associate solicitor and then the solicitor; this was a new job created in 1947 under the Taft-Hartley Act, which was to give the board its own lawyers. As the solicitor, I was the top lawyer of the National Labor Relations Board, giving legal advice to the board members and to the board staff, and reviewing the work of the litigation section, particularly in the Supreme Court.

That very exciting and wonderful experience gave me a chance to develop a system of legal thinking under the new statute, to accommodate the new law to the established body of labor law already developed under the Wagner Act, and vice versa to accommodate the Wagner Act to the new provisions (some of them very extensive) of the Taft-Hartley Act.

The NLRB experience was the foundation for the rest of my career. It was the philosophical foundation, the psychological foundation. It was certainly the legal frame of reference and background against which I made my professional life. Without it, I don't think I could have continued with the zeal that seemed to be inherent in my personality as I pursued one career after another. Because I felt that I was taking with me this precious "treasure chest" and using it to big advantage in other work. Indeed, I don't think I would have done the other work but for that background.

I left the NLRB in 1954, having served as solicitor from 1946 to 1954, to join the Wagner administration. This was the then New York City Mayor Robert Wagner, son of the famous Senator Wagner who was father of the Wagner Act. I came to New York City as counsel to the new labor department, the only municipal department of its kind in the country, and labor counsel to the mayor. I was given carte blanche; I could look around to see what I wanted to do. It soon became my responsibility to analyze and make recommendations as to all proposed legislation bearing upon labor and generally affecting New York City. Other problems involving legal aspects of labor relations in the city (and there were many, many such problems) also came to me.

What impressed me most was the totally chaotic atmosphere in the public sector of the city of New York. It had as many mayoral-agency employees as there were hourly paid employees of the Ford [Motor] Company, who were then very well organized and had established bargaining relationships in those plants. In the city of New York there was no such arrangement. Every little group was fending for itself: the police, the firemen, the sanitation workers, the supervisors, the clerical workers. Teachers were off by themselves, trying to be organized, although they had had for a long time a pretty well-established organization which functioned more as a professional group than a labor organization, but a very dedicated one (unlike some of the other groups who were primarily interested in promoting only their own terms and conditions of employment).

When I came to New York there seemed to be a concerted action every time a fireman was injured or died on duty. There weren't that many deaths but there were some, surely more than the number of deaths of policemen on duty (that was still before the violence that broke out against the whole police system of control). Every time a fireman died there was a demonstration around City Hall, with placards about how firemen were underpaid for their dangerous work and had to work too hard. All their grievances came out when a fireman was killed. It was very sad.

And it was a very bothersome kind of problem for a mayor, particularly a new one. Mayor Wagner was not happy with being followed, wherever he went, by a caravan of firemen carrying picket signs saying "you killed so-and-so, you killed so-and-so."

In any case, I wanted to look at what kind of labor relations New York City employees had. They wanted a system of labor relations, a union, but they didn't know quite what they wanted. Whatever the union leaders got in those days, they got through political pressure. Mike Quill was "getting it" for the transit workers by sheer political pressure, with a lot of name-calling and vituperation in public. In private Mike Quill was a very sweet little man whom you could deal with, because he knew that by simply meeting with the mayor he would get a lot of publicity. There was also the Teamsters, and there were others. AFSCME (the American Federation of State, County and Municipal Employees) was just beginning to organize; it was growing out of another organization and it already had a rival.

City employees didn't want much, but they wanted a little bit. They wanted some kind of grievance procedure, and they wanted (of all things) the check-off,[9] and they wanted some uniformity in their working conditions.

All of this seemed to me no way to conduct business as an employer. After all, the city was an employer. It should have a more rational, better-organized system of dealing with its employees. My thought was to establish a thorough-going system of labor relations in New York City, under the direction of the mayor. We were not ready for legislation; it seemed to me much too early. But there had to be, in my view, some fundamental system which would take these employees and this manifold number of organizations out of the political arena and bring them into a rational area, where they could use the powers of persuasion which are brought out in some system of collective exchange of views on working conditions.

I will not go through the whole history of how we came to have Executive Order No. 49 of the mayor of New York City. But by 1957 (after my having done a tremendous amount of research and having written a series of monographs on every aspect of the components of a labor relations program for New York City employees) the mayor signed that executive order and it became the law for those agencies under the mayor's immediate supervision. They were called executive agencies; these were all the commissioners and their employees. Other agencies having some contact with the mayor could, if they wished, come in on the program.

The executive order, also known as the Little Wagner Act, was based on the real Wagner Act. There was no other model. There was no real system of collective bargaining anywhere in the public sector at that time. It was really plowing thoroughly new ground in an effort to bring to these employees an orderly system of labor relations accommodated to the various aspects and unique characteristics of the governmental employing enterprise. Government as an employer is somewhat like a private employer, yet very much not like a private employer. And those were the characteristics which challenged and engaged me in drafting of that executive order. Along with the executive order came a report which explained the entire background of the [executive] order. There again there was not much talk about arbitration, except that at least one of the monographs covered mutual recourse under the collective-bargaining system. There were different kinds of techniques for resolving unresolved disputes in the public sector.

There was a time when our thinking, and I think the general thinking, was that of course public-sector employees could not strike. Obviously that was a given. It was prohibited by law; it was prohibited by public policy as it came to be accepted. And there simply could not be strikes. That was at the base of the frame of reference in which I worked. City employees were not going to strike. They could picket, they could use all kinds of embarrassing techniques, but they did not generally engage in any kinds of organized work-stoppage in order to gain their demands. Maybe 5 or 10 minutes, a "quickie," which very quickly got settled. But generally speaking, no strikes. Just as you simply don't steal, you don't rob, you don't set fires. It was that well ingrained, we thought, in the moral basis of the public employees' relationship to the public employer.

We were wrong. We really didn't understand. And I think we were quite unrealistic about believing that that kind of self-restraint could continue, unmoved by what was going on in the outside world. Public employees were looking around to see what was going on in the private sector, and they wanted "into" that mainstream. They didn't want to stay out.

And from that came my experience at the Board of Education. The board was excluded from the application of the Little Wagner Act, because the board was primarily a state agency (despite a number of city connections) not subject to the direction or control of the mayor. (Footnote: that is probably less and less true with a strong mayor who does want to control but yet give the appearance of the board being independent.) Control is exercised by the budget. Control is exercised in other ways by which a so-called independent agency, subject only to the state in most respects, can be regulated.

In 1961 the Board of Education was reconstructed and reconstituted by state legislation, with some very good appointments, some outstanding people. There was Lloyd Garrison who was a well-known lawyer at Paul Weiss Rifkind and Garrison; he had been a dean of the [University of] Wisconsin Law School, and had had a good career in Washington. There was Clarence Senior who had been a very active Socialist, taught at Brooklyn College, and was very much interested in labor relations and labor and the labor cause. There was Anna Rosenberg who had distinguished herself in various phases of government, starting (I believe) with the NRA (which is the National Recovery Administration) and culminating in her post as assistant secretary of defense for the U.S. Army, in charge largely of personnel problems. There was also a representative from the CIO [Congress of Industrial Organizations], named Morris Iushewitz. And there was Max Rubin, a well-known lawyer who was a dedicated educator (layman educator I should say). And several other distinguished people.

They were ready to give the employees some form of collective bargaining, after earlier boards had dragged their feet and done nothing. Those Boards of Education had really resisted, in one way or another, the efforts by employees to achieve a sound thoroughgoing formula for maintaining relations with the board. This new board brought me in as a consultant and asked me to take over the whole problem of dealing with its employees.

The first aspect of it was to be the conduct of an election, because there were many competing factions, all of whom wanted some part of this agency, and every one of which claimed some "turf." The American Federation of Teachers won that election, was certified, and became the bargaining representative for all teachers in the Board of Education early in 1962. It started with teachers, first. That was a great victory. It was a great day for them and for the Board of Education. And I departed, having handed them this certification.

But that was not enough. The teachers wanted to bargain, and they brought in something like 120 demands the very first day after the certification. The board then tried to negotiate by itself (a great mistake), the board members participating in the negotiations. They were not accustomed to spending the time that this required. They were confronted by a very persistent committee of employees, some being negotiators who were sent in to the Board of

Education to help teachers negotiate their first contract. (Several of them were sent in by the United Automobile Workers, I believe.)

The Board of Education had its first big strike in the spring (it was April 12 of 1962), which was the outcome of the beginning of a system of labor relations for New York City between the Board of Education and the teachers. That strike was over money, and it ended with Governor Rockefeller stepping in and "finding" money. This finding of money got to be a game throughout the negotiations with the Board of Education and with other public employees in New York City.

At this point the Board of Education farmed out the negotiations to inside people, the head of each department. So you had the head of a high school division negotiate for the high schools, and the head of the junior high school division (all of these are educators) negotiate for the junior high schools, the head of the elementary schools negotiate for the elementary schools. They wrote on pieces of paper. They signed so very many papers which dealt in large part with matters of educational policy.

The board realized that it could not come to terms with these unions, after the strike, negotiating by itself. They asked me to come in and negotiate to agreement: write the agreement, and present the full document. This I did. It was a very exciting experience because here again there was no guide for this new agreement. It was clear that the "little pieces of paper" had gone way beyond what was considered the permissible or the mandatory scope of collective bargaining in the public sector. That was a real problem: to bring together what had already been negotiated, into the form, style, and content of a collective-bargaining agreement for teachers in the largest school system.

The hard part was to separate terms and conditions of employment from the terms which had been negotiated, and the way in which these terms were to be effectuated. The *way* they would be effectuated was primarily a managerial question. *What* the employees were to get was clearly a negotiable matter. Somehow or other we worked around this. And we got our first agreement after working on it all summer long with some very good negotiators for the teachers. In the end, we had the first agreement for teachers anywhere in the nation.

The big stumbling block at the very close of negotiations was a "no-strike" pledge in return for a grievance procedure which would end in binding arbitration. They got such a procedure with great misgivings on the part of many that this would not stand up in court, and it would not stand up before the state commissioner of education. To prepare for that, we separated the kinds of grievances that could not go to arbitration from those that could go to arbitration. The first category was primarily those items we called "educational policy"; those would not go to arbitration. All other matters, involving terms and conditions of employment, would. But in return for that revolutionary provision, they had to give a no-strike pledge. And this was a bitter pill for the union to swallow, very bitter. But they did finally agree. The union then ratified the agreement and by October it was signed. The board had approved it at a board meeting. And they had their first agreement.

When we went into the second agreement there was not only a new face but a new voice. Charles Cogen for many years had been the moving spirit in the established teacher organization. A man with a very fine background in economics and labor and labor history, he was a high school teacher and a very good one. The "new face" which then turned into a "voice" was that of a young man: very, very tall, ungainly, gawky, wearing a beret all of the time, very "boulevardier" looking, whose voice began to be heard. He was somebody I had not known the first year; his name was Albert Shanker.

He boomed away the very last day, shouting his head off on a point about which he was absolutely right. It had to do with eliminating a certain kind of organization from the individual schools, which really was a benevolent kind of "company union" established by the board many years earlier. Gradually we did get those little "company union" type organizations out of the whole school system, but it took a while. His maiden speech (and I should say his maiden "shouting") in this context was on this point.

After that I got to know Albert Shanker, and to know him very well. I sat opposite him through many negotiations for 13 years, as we developed more and more the breadth of our bargaining, the scope of our bargaining, the concepts of our bargaining, into a really very mature bargaining relationship—before there was any Taylor Law and before there was any other guide. We really had our own personalities and our own ideas of a system of educational justice, and also a personal understanding, on both sides, of a common objective which we both pursued conscientiously.

We began the arbitration process in the first agreement. And to everybody's surprise, we actually had a case with a grievance which went to arbitration. It startled some of us because we did not think there would be such a thing as grievances going to arbitration. But there surely were, and this opened the door to many grievances going to arbitration.

Many of the early questions had to do with the use of teachers for nonteaching chores. They were very much dissatisfied with the way in which they were assigned certain tasks which they believed were not a part of the educational process: floor patrol, lunchroom patrol, stair patrol, a lot of patrols. They wanted to use the grievance procedure to free them of those duties; this freedom they had already expressed in the first agreement, but they wanted it specifically applied.

I think the very first case we had went before a fine arbitrator, Aaron Horvitz, the father of Wayne Horvitz.[10] Confronted with this first case, I decided that I'd better get someone to do our arbitration presentations because I could see that we were going to have a whole series. I had known Tom Christensen (now a well-known labor law professor and a well-known arbitrator) at the NLRB; Tom was a young man when I was already solicitor. Years later I met him again in New York City and found out that he had done arbitration work for Cravath Swaine & Moore but was now teaching at New York University School of Law. I asked him whether he would like to take over the board's arbitration advocacy, and he was delighted.

Christensen served for one year as the board's arbitration counsel and recommended Dan Collins who succeeded him. This was Dan's introduction to public employee labor relations. He was an excellent litigator, very dramatically oriented in his presentation of evidence. Dan was with us quite a while, and we were very sorry to see him go. He was becoming an arbitrator while continuing as professor at New York University School of Law. "Let those other guys do the hard work of litigating," Dan said to me, "I am going to arbitrate." And he did. He was very good and was soon chosen as an arbitrator in board cases.

We began with some good and well-known arbitrators: Aaron Horvitz I just mentioned, Arthur Stark too, Eric Schmertz on one or two ad hoc cases, Peter Seitz.[11] We also had one arbitrator, a very good man (sort of starting out at arbitration) who rendered a decision sustaining a grievance. The school principal was president of the Junior High School Principals Association. He was so infuriated (1) at the decision, namely, that he had been overruled; and (2) that any kind of unflattering reference was made to the way he ran the school (I did not see that in the arbitrator's opinion), that he wanted the arbitrator removed from all rosters. He did not get that.

When we decided it was time to get a panel of arbitrators (that came about in 1965), we brought together an excellent panel of three that would work through the American Arbitration Association and get cases in rotation. We had Abe Stockman,[12] an outstanding arbitrator and one of the best I have ever encountered. We chose Stockman because we thought that he would bring to this particular assignment a good understanding of the nature of public employment, and a very good understanding of the legal implications of what was being asked in arbitration, and a thoughtful analysis of the agreement provisions. It turned out we were right. We lost a number of cases but in each case Stockman wrote such a good award that I circulated it among our staff all over the city. These were cases which we had lost, but which were very instructive and extremely useful to people who had to run a school within the frame of reference of a collective-bargaining agreement.

Equally good were the other two people, in other ways. Jim Hill[13] was very good at individual grievances; he understood the gripes of individual people. He was a man who was very quiet, said nothing, allowed the hearing to go on as long as they wanted. He didn't limit these people at all (and there were times that I was very annoyed at him). But he really gave them a sense of being heard, and a feeling that even if they lost their case, they had had a fair chance.

Then there was Eli Rock. (Both Hill and Rock became presidents of the National Academy of Arbitrators, Hill in 1969 and Rock in 1973.) He had very good background in public employee relations in Philadelphia. Stockman, Hill, and Rock were a fine, upstanding panel. They really put arbitration on its feet at the Board of Education.

Then new groups of employees began to be organized, not the least of which were the hourly paid school-lunch employees. We agreed on a permanent arbitrator for them, and that was Lou Yagoda[14] for a number of years. He made a real contribution in this area of nonprofessional employees; it was a very informal procedure.

Then the paraprofessionals were organized. They were the people who were going to help the teachers. The Teachers Union, in a very bitter representation election, won the classroom paraprofessionals, and AFSCME won those outside the classroom. There, too, we set up a system of arbitration with one arbitrator, Milton Friedman. Both sides were pleased with the way he functioned. He is now also on the teachers panel. Today, of course, he has become a very well-known arbitrator.

By the time I was ready to retire from the Board of Education, we had had several strikes (in 1967 and 1968) and had come under the jurisdiction of the Taylor Law. But we had very little to do with PERB (the Public Employment Relations Board, a state agency created to administer the Taylor Law), practically nothing at all except toward the end of my incumbency when the union began to file improper practice charges against the board with PERB, much to my consternation. Every employer feels perfect—and to have an improper practice charge filed against it, is an eyebrow-raising experience.

I left the Board of Education in 1975, having decided it was time for me to retire. And what did I think I was going to do in retirement? Naturally I wasn't going to stay home and twiddle my thumbs! There were a number of things I could have done, but I decided that the thing I really wanted to do was be an arbitrator—because I thought it was going to be very easy. This is the real reason I became an arbitrator. I felt I had worked so hard all those years it was time for me to relax. (When I say "hard," I mean "very hard." It was not easy to negotiate for the Board of Education with all these groups pounding at our door, particularly in the early days. And it became in some respects increasingly difficult as time went on, because I stopped being "the great expert" to whom they all looked. They were becoming experts by now, as they should have been.)

I became an arbitrator, as I say, because I thought it was going to be easy. And as Dan Collins had said, "Let them do the hard work. I'm going to be an arbitrator." Well, I think he also came to realize that arbitration is not so simple as it appeared. I must say that I had a rude awakening, because I never intended to work this hard when I became an arbitrator.

My first assignment was a very fortunate one. Sylvester Garrett had been with me at the National Labor Relations Board, and had gone on to make a name for himself at the War Labor Board, and then to become the head of arbitration for U.S. Steel and the United Steelworkers of America. He asked me to arbitrate under him as what was called a "special arbitrator" under the Steel Agreement. And that was, I think, the luckiest break I had in arbitration. The Board of Arbitration was a well-established system of self-government, established by both sides after World War II. Some very interesting questions were left to be determined by arbitration because both sides wanted the issues resolved in this particular way. It was a voluntary recourse which they utilized with very good will.

The questions were difficult; they were very tough for me. I had a series of seniority cases which I had never encountered before. In all my experience I hadn't had any true seniority questions; we had some at the Board of Education but they were not of this kind. I worked day and night on my first steel cases. There were times when I went to bed at three o'clock in the morning because I already had the big momentum going and I was going to work on them very carefully and complete them. I mean *carefully*; these were not cases that one could rush through. One had to do them deliberatively, and there were times when I wondered whether what I did was right.

The first group of cases I submitted to Garrett were really submitted in fear and trembling because they were my first awards in what I considered to be a complicated situation. To my great surprise I got a very laudatory note from Syl, telling me he was extremely pleased with what I had done. I was such a perfectionist in the arbitration work (and still am—much to my discomfort, I must say) that any little imperfection upset me. In any case, the Steel Board [of Arbitration] was a very happy place for me to land. Good hard work, and very good environment, and fine colleagues, and a great "oversight" man in Garrett. This really got me started in a good way.

By the end of 1982 I decided that I was not going to do any more steel cases. My back began bothering me very much, and I was mildly disabled from sitting too long a period of time. My last steel awards were handed in by December 1982. I still miss the steel cases; for me they were certainly the most fascinating.

At the same time as I started arbitrating in steel, I became a member of the expedited panel for the U.S. Postal Service collective-bargaining contracts. Postal employees were the most numerous category of federal employees, in this now quasi-independent agency. (At the time I worked on the federal executive order, under President Kennedy in 1961, the post office was the largest single public employer in the country.) The expedited cases dealt only with discipline and required a full-fledged hearing, a very quick decision, with an award to be rendered within 24 hours after the close of the hearing. It was good experience, excellent. Employee relations were of the most chaotic, paternalistic, uncontrolled, often irrational kind. This was an absolute "mine" for any arbitration system. The challenge was to draw the essence of the grievance out of a hodgepodge of so-called testimony given under oath and to resolve the underlying dispute.

All this had to be done on one page, typewritten. It was good practice for me. It taught me to reduce, to the bare essentials, the facts and the arguments and the decision. That challenge is still present in most discipline cases and probably in other arbitration situations.

I am pleased to see how much maturity has come into the employer-employee relationship in the [U.S.] Postal Service. The employer has made great efforts to accommodate to collective bargaining in good faith. And the unions have also attempted to rationalize to some extent their recourse to the arbitration process. Much still remains to be done in some of these postal cases. It is still very difficult to know what the issue is, even though it is framed as "just cause." It is very difficult to know precisely what the employee is grieving, what he complains about. There is a highly informal and not very articulate presentation, even by an employee in his own language. This is partly due to the fact that a number of employees are not very well versed in self-expression, have minimal education, and no clear understanding of what is owed them by their employer. What also comes through in these cases is that there are still too many instances of high-handed actions by petty supervisors who are running their particular jobs in a quasi-militaristic fashion. I believe that the principles enunciated in the arbitration awards have had an educational effect on supervision generally, certainly at higher levels. And this is likely to improve more in the future because of the apparent efforts of both sides to bring about a good relationship on the work floor.

I have not accepted arbitration cases at the local government level, in New York or in any other state or municipality, since I was appointed a member of the Public Employment Relations Board in 1976. I have served at PERB as one of three board members on a per diem basis; about one-half of my working time is on PERB matters during the seven years I've been a board member. PERB is, I think, the single most important labor agency in this state, as would be its counterpart in other states. For the public employees of New York, it combines quasi-judicial functions like those of the NLRB, and quasi-administrative functions like those of the Federal Mediation and Conciliation Service. PERB has developed a body of labor law in the public sector which is a fundamental legal way of life in this now not-so-new field of labor relations. It has done over the years what the NLRB did, when I was there, and continues to do in private labor relations; PERB has done that for public-sector employees very effectively. It has become the agency of recourse wherever labor disputes arise. In the case of stalled negotiations, PERB does have a real role of intervention to bring about a peaceful settlement through mediation. It is also the arbiter, in its judicial role, of the basic legal relationships established by the parties. PERB has developed basic principles with the guidance, of course, of the principles enunciated in the statute. PERB's real function is not only to abide by the very words of the statute, but to find the deeper meaning in the policy of the statute, so as to achieve a developing broad frame of reference for the conduct of labor relations in the public sector.

PERB has no role in the arbitration process apart from its limited one in the police and firemen interest arbitration. It does maintain a roster of arbitrators; the parties choose the arbitrators. PERB believes itself to be a very important instrumentality for promoting the arbitration process, not only in interest disputes and impasse situations in bargaining, but in the implementation of collective-bargaining agreements. They maintain a very lively interest in all manner of arbitration which does find its way into this particular area of labor relations.

While at PERB I was appointed by President Jimmy Carter to three successive emergency boards under the Railway Labor Act. Each was an impasse, just before the parties are permitted to go out on strike, and all other devices for settlement have been exhausted. The first board dealt with a nationwide strike of dispatchers. This was their first strike. We were able to resolve this dispute before our report was written, working under a deadline set by the statute. Our report to the president was really a document memorializing a settlement which had already been reached through our efforts.

The second was a very complicated dispute involving the Rock Island Railroad, which was already in a state of bankruptcy. The bankruptcy aspects were themselves very complex and almost insoluble. And the third was the Long Island Railroad [LIRR], which has a perennial crisis every time its contract is about to expire. There we dealt with a whole series of operating unions. (The nonoperating unions, such as the clerks and other categories not directly engaged in the running of the railroad, had already settled.) This was a protracted and bitter negotiation between the MTA [Metropolitan Transportation Authority] and some nine craft unions. (After private ownership of LIRR was relinquished several years ago, management went to the Metropolitan Transportation Authority, the parent agency which oversees the New York City bus and subway system.) There was a very short strike following the deadline for accepting or rejecting the emergency board's report. That strike was settled, in large part based upon the fundamental conditions the board had proposed in the mediation which is part of the emergency board procedure.

These three were all mediation experiences, which I had not had before and which do not normally come to an arbitrator as an arbitrator. This was a good experience for me; in each case again I brought to bear all the facets of my background. I learned a lot about railroads, not enough, but a lot. I certainly was interested in how they settled their disputes which were called "minor disputes." Those are grievances, rather than disputes in contract negotiations, which are "major disputes."

That experience led to my being appointed to National Railroad Adjustment Board work, which is grievance arbitration on the railroads. This appointment was a "first" for this very long-established operation. It was the first in that they dared come into the year 1982 by adding to their panel their first female. I don't know what they thought I was going to be like, and I don't know what they thought I was going to do. But it was a very big step for them. The heavens have not fallen. I was accepted hospitably by both sides and enjoyed very much the work with the [National] Railroad Adjustment Board.

I suppose I ought to make a few comments (as they say, "a few brief comments") about expectations of the parties, as I observe them, vis-à-vis the arbitration process. In my experience as an arbitrator (which really isn't very long compared with some of the other arbitrators interviewed), I've observed that parties (particularly employers) have come to accept arbitration much more congenially over the years than was indicated in the early days of arbitration. It is a procedure which has great appeal to both sides. It is accessible early in the dispute, once the parties themselves have let go of it. It permits the parties to decide for themselves whom they will have as their arbitrator to resolve this issue for them. I think it gives them confidence in the outcome.

The ideal situation would be for collective bargaining to resolve all the disputes with respect to the terms of the agreement and for the parties themselves to resolve at least most of their disputes with respect to the implementation of the agreement at the various levels of the grievance procedure—knowing, of course, that the ultimate recourse would be to a third-party outsider, but not finding it necessary to use that recourse.

I don't know why in this country we have more arbitration, a more lively arbitration system, than in any other country. It's difficult to know why there is such a flood of cases into arbitration in the United States. I hesitate to venture any guesses. I think that the wartime experience was very important and probably that has remained with us. I am not critical of arbitration; I think it has performed a very useful function. But I stop to think of why there are still so large a number of cases coming to arbitration. (There also are a large number of cases that go to the NLRB, which is so bogged down with scheduling that there is some question as to whether it will extricate itself from cases *ever*, with the difficulties that it is having with the changing of philosophies and of principles.)

I think there is a danger of rushing into the arbitration system, which ought to be used more thoughtfully. Quite possibly the parties have become accustomed to third-party recourse. And that's surely very useful in mediation, there is no question about that. But there too my view is that mediation should not force the parties, or induce or encourage them, to leave the bargaining table prematurely.

5

BECOMING AN ARBITRATOR
Arthur Stark

Arthur Stark, as a very young man, wanted to be an arbitrator. This was at a time when virtually no one arbitrated on a full-time basis. Even in 1957, when (still a young man) he resigned from the New York State Board of Mediation after a decade (preceded by five years at the National Labor Relations Board) to devote himself entirely to the practice of arbitration, there were few full-time arbitrators. But this somewhat risky career choice turned out to be the right one for him. He became one of the most respected arbitrators in the country, and his interest in the arbitration process never waned.

He has been called upon to adjudicate grievances in practically every major industry throughout the country, frequently on particularly complex issues (such as merging seniority lists when airlines combine), and often in matters of especial interest (such as salary entitlement for major league football players who sustain disabling injuries on the job).

Stark serves as permanent umpire in numerous contracts, including ALCOA [Aluminum Corporation of America] and the Aluminum, Brick, Glass Workers Union; and the Maritime Associations and the International Organization of Masters, Mates and Pilots. He serves on permanent rotating panels in many industries and areas, including the National Football League (NFL) and NFL Players Association (for on-the-job injuries), General Motors and IUE (International Union of Electrical, Radio, and Machine Workers), New Jersey Bell and IBEW (International Brotherhood of Electrical Workers), New York Telephone and Communication Workers, New York City Board of Education and United Federation of Teachers, and television networks and Directors Guild of America.

Since 1955 five presidents have appointed him to presidential emergency boards in railroad and airline impasses. He was on the Federal Service Impasses Panel from 1970 to 1981. He served on the Foreign Service Grievance Board from 1982 to 1991, the last eight years as chairman.

He was president of the National Academy of Arbitrators from 1977 to 1978; from 1984 to 1990 he chaired the National Academy of Arbitrators Committee on Professional Responsibility and Grievances, which focuses on ethics. In 1990 the American Arbitration Association awarded Stark its Distinguished Service Award for arbitration of labor-management disputes.

What were the influences in my becoming an arbitrator? I would suppose that the greatest influence on me and my future development was that of my parents. My dad, whose name was Louis Stark, was a journalist. Early on in his career he started to work for the *New York Times,* and as the years went on the subject of labor and industrial relations became a prime interest to him. The *Times* itself became the first paper, I think, to have someone specializing in that subject.[1]

I was exposed at home to discussions of unionization, the early days of collective bargaining, and the whole gamut of problems which related to that. Some of my early recollections are of discussions in our home with figures who were writing and studying in this field, such as Louis Hacker, who became a prominent historian; Sterling Spero, who went on to be a professor at New York University in this field; Ben Stolberg, who wrote an authoritative work on the International Ladies' Garment Workers' Union, and others. My dad was not at home too much in those days because he had to attend conventions and meetings and cover strikes and so forth. Some of my early recollections were of going to meetings with him and being introduced to some of the major figures in the labor movement, such as John L. Lewis of the [United] Mine Workers and Bill Green who was president of the American Federation of Labor, and others.

In the early days there were very, very few persons doing arbitration. But there were a couple. One of them was a chap named William L. Leiserson, known to one and all as Billy, who later became my dad's best friend. He was a professor of economics at Antioch College [now Antioch University]. He had become interested in collective bargaining, became a mediator, and ultimately went on to hold various government jobs. He was one of the early role models for me, so to speak.

I went to school in New York and graduated in 1936 from Fieldston School. I was interested, even in my high school days, in the emerging field of labor relations. I had the feeling on graduation that I wanted to go into the labor-relations field on a full-time basis. I also had the feeling I did not want to follow in my dad's precise footsteps; they were pretty big footsteps, perhaps too big for me. I chose to go to the University of Chicago which had at that time the best program in labor relations, at least equal to that of the University of Wisconsin. When I went to college I was only 17 and in a hurry to get out and go to work; I did my B.A. in three years.

During those years I maintained my interest in not only studying labor relations but working in this field. Upon graduating from high school I took a summer job on a newspaper in Washington, D.C., where my folks were then living. The paper was *Labor,* the weekly publication of the Railroad Brotherhoods. I was a sort of glorified office boy, but they allowed me to do some rewriting, and I had a chance to learn how to write, condense, and make things clear. That certainly was good training.

While I was at college I held other summer jobs. One was working on a railroad, the Union Pacific, as a lineman, out in Wyoming. That was manual labor, which I enjoyed but knew very well I would not spend the rest of my life doing. Another was back in Washington at the Wage and Hour Division, U.S. Department of Labor, where I helped prepare statistical and economic information for minimum wage boards; the Fair Labor Standards Act had been passed just a couple of years earlier.

During college I volunteered my services in some organizing campaigns which were going forward. One was the Steelworkers Organizing Committee in South Chicago, where a young man named Merlyn Pitzele was in charge of trying to organize the Republic Steel workers. That was also the time, I recall from my first summer in Chicago in 1937, of what was called the Memorial Day Massacre, when many persons were killed and injured as a result of a strike for representation. This was before the steel industry agreed to recognize the union and really put such strikes in its past.

After graduation I decided I was young enough and that another degree would help, so I stayed on at the University of Chicago and worked for a master's degree in industrial relations. My primary professor was Paul Douglas, who already was well known at that time for his book *The Theory of Wages.* He was substantially interested in collective bargaining and industrial relations. His courses were designed to teach the preliminaries in this field including the development of labor laws, which were just beginning. He was a very fascinating and challenging teacher. Ultimately he did other things with his life, such as joining the [U.S.] Marines as a volunteer at the age of 50; he became a major, was wounded, lost the use of one of his arms. He came back, went into politics, and ended up as one of the most distinguished senators from the state of Illinois. (As a footnote, his successor was a classmate of mine at the university. He is a current [U.S.] senator: Percy.)[2]

Paul Douglas was one of the early arbitrators, and he would tell us about his experiences. He invited his students (as others of us, now, still do) to attend arbitration hearings. And that was my really first, very first, exposure to the process itself. He was umpire for the printing trades and for the needle trades in Chicago.

My other professor was Harry Millis, chairman of the economics department. He also was one of the early arbitrators and became the first umpire under the initial agreement between General Motors and the United Automobile Workers. They had just been recognized, in 1939 or 1940, and decided to set up a permanent umpireship. Dr. Millis was their choice to start this machinery. It's still in effect today. (I became the eighth umpire under that system, having been there now for about the last nine years. In 1940 I was a young kid; I certainly never dreamed that some day I would step into Dr. Millis's very large shoes.)

He was also very interested in the National Labor Relations Board and was in the process of writing the first authoritative book on the subject, with Emily Brown, a professor from Vassar College. We were given the galleys to read as part of our course. Again this was fascinating and challenging to me, and only enforced my feeling that labor relations was the field I wanted to go into. After finishing at the university, I sensed that working for the National Labor Relations Board would be the most attractive post at that time, and I applied for a job. I was told, however, that I was too young and that the board would not be hiring any field examiners who were only 21 years old.

So I looked elsewhere. I was too young to be anything! But fortuitously a job came along. Sam Levin, who was chairman of the Joint Board of the Amalgamated Clothing Workers of America in Chicago, had need of what wasn't "a gal Friday" but "a man Friday." He offered me a job as sort of a chief assistant; my fancier title was head of the Educational Department, Amalgamated Clothing Workers [of America] in Chicago. I worked for Sam and I wrote speeches, attended meetings, acted as liaison with the CIO (where a young man named Arthur J. Goldberg was general counsel; he went on to do many other things in his life, including becoming Justice of the Supreme Court). I prepared education programs for the members of the union. I did some work in New York at the union headquarters for J. B. S. Hardman who was director of the Educational Department, and who had many, many innovative ideas in the field of workers' education, such as establishing correspondence courses. I did some writing for *Advance,* which was the monthly newspaper of the union. The office I occupied had Sidney Hillman's[3] name on the door. They never did get around to taking it off while I was there. The Amalgamated was a thriving, flourishing active, imaginative kind of union. I welcomed the opportunity to be there because it put me in touch with a lot of the interesting things which were happening in the labor movement at this time, which was about 1940.

In 1942 I thought perhaps I was old enough to work for the National Labor Relations Board. By that time Billy Leiserson had become a member of the National Labor Relations Board, Harry Millis had become its chairman. "Two folks in my corner," I thought, and applied once again. The National Labor Relations Board gave me a job as a field examiner and sent me down to New Orleans for training. There were long hours. There was a lot of travel; our territory included Louisiana, Mississippi, Tennessee, Arkansas, and northern Florida. It was a fascinating period. Organization was just starting in the South. Trade unions were quite new. Hostility of employers was very high. People like me, who came from the North, were considered "damn Yankees" of the worst kind, imposing bureaucratic New Deal philosophy on the poor folks in these southern states.

The racial tensions were high. In many of the elections we held we discovered (I guess I should have known it, but I came to realize it more poignantly than I otherwise would have) that most of the black employees had never voted in any elections at all. The right to vote was something which was really staggering, and almost revolutionary from their point of view. It was equally shocking to the employers who watched while their black employees (who sometimes were the majority in the bargaining units) actually won elections because the white employees (who might have been antiunion) were in the minority.

I recall an instance where after the election all the employees had left. I was surrounded by a group of very, very hostile white management people. (Incidentally, this was a northern company that had opened a southern plant.) They accused me of running "a goddamned nigger election." While I was trembling in my boots—because people had been run out of town with guns in this area—I just reacted as a government agent probably should not have. I told them that maybe a majority of their employees voted for the union and the majority were black, but that was probably due to the fact that they paid their black employees less than their white ones, and so they can blame themselves and not me. Forty years later I don't think I would have had the courage to say that.

In another case we held an election where the employer had threatened the employees with finding out how each one voted by getting hold of the ballots afterwards and obtaining their fingerprints. This was a really far-fetched threat, but some of the workers were apparently frightened by it. The principal field examiner (a fellow named Baker McAlpin) had a genius of an idea. He called a meeting of all the employees and told them that "nobody is going to get the ballots, and your fingerprints cannot be taken from them. But if anyone is afraid, I am putting a pair of gloves in each voting booth. And any of you who care to, you can put the gloves on, and then you can mark your ballots. And don't worry."

Since I'm telling NLRB stories, one more. This was a large election in a defense plant that probably had 25,000 employees. We had erected little voting booths with a little curtain in front. At one point I noticed this young black man going around to the back and trying to climb over the top of the booth to get in. I was just amazed at what I was seeing. Then I realized that his whole life he had been told that where white folks are involved he had to go around the back, and the only way he could go around the back of this election booth was to climb over the top. And that was what he was doing.

After three months in New Orleans I moved to Cleveland. During my five years at the NLRB I served as field examiner and principal field examiner and acting regional director for a while. Part of those years was also spent in Washington on special assignment. I think probably the most useful work at the board (retrospectively at least, for my interest in arbitration) were the investigations and hearings. I would guess that this is not just my own opinion but that of many others, because the board has graduated a lot of people who ultimately became arbitrators. Our job was to investigate charges, and evaluate the truth of various allegations of unfair labor practices and the like. It required interviewing witnesses, listening to employers and union members, and trying to reach the truth. We were required to write reports about the results of our investigations; the emphasis was on clearness of thought and succinctness in presentation.

Another aspect of the work, which in retrospect was certainly of great benefit for future arbitrators, was conducting hearings in the representation cases. In those days the board's philosophy, as represented by Millis and Leiserson, was to minimize the legal approach to labor relations. I was not a lawyer and in any event concurred wholeheartedly in that philosophy. The consequence was that we nonlawyers were allowed to be trial examiners and conduct hearings. This was my first exposure to sitting at the head of the table (or in some cases in the judge's seat in the courtroom, because we used courtrooms on occasion) and presiding at a more or less formal judicial-type hearing.

My years at the board went very quickly, and after five years there I started to explore the possibility of work as an arbitrator. By that time, 1947, the National War Labor Board had developed a great expertise and acceptability for grievance arbitration since they had insisted that a grievance arbitration clause be inserted in all contracts. (I had crossed paths in Cleveland with chaps like Fred Bullen[4] and Lew Gill,[5] who were heading the National War Labor Board there, and we were to meet later.) The idea of arbitration was becoming acceptable to the general public and among employers and unions.

I arranged to meet George Taylor in New York to talk about the possibility of becoming a labor arbitrator. He was a distinguished arbitrator, a professor at the Wharton School [University of Pennsylvania], and had been chairman of the National War Labor Board. "This is what I'd like to do," I said. "What do you think?" He said, "Don't do it. Don't try to be a full-time arbitrator." (I might say parenthetically that there were very, very few full-time arbitrators in those days. Most people who did this kind of work were either lawyers or professors or had some other occupation and did arbitration in addition to what else they were doing.) Dr. Taylor said to me, "If this is what you are interested in, get yourself a job at a university. Become a teacher or professor, and then go on out and do some arbitration." Well, I thanked him very much and returned to Cleveland.

A few months later I learned of an opening at the New York State Board of Mediation. That information came from Mel Pitzele whom I had known many years earlier in Chicago. He had since moved to New York, became the labor editor of *Business Week* magazine, was the advisor to Governor Tom Dewey in New York on labor matters, and was a member of the New York State Board of Mediation.

Historically the board was the oldest state mediation service in the United States; its origins went way back into the early part of the century. But it had undergone several transformations; in its most recent one, for about 10 years or so it consisted of seven per diem members appointed by the governor. There was a small administrative staff: an executive secretary, an assistant, and the counsel. There was a full-time staff of mediators in New York City and in several upstate centers.

The job which was open was as assistant executive secretary. Fred Bullen, whom I had previously met at the Regional War Labor Board in Cleveland, had held that job before becoming executive secretary. I came east and was interviewed by him and by Arthur Meyer. Meyer was the chairman at that point: a wonderful man, a superb mediator and a top-notch arbitrator who had been appointed in many highly volatile situations. And at the board he led probably the best group of mediators in the country at that time. The upshot was that I gladly accepted the offer and came to New York in May of 1947. I had several functions, one was to be the administrative head of the agency; Fred was that at the beginning, and then left a few years later. I ultimately stayed for 10 years.

The Board of Mediation was also deeply involved in arbitration. From the very outset the people who drafted the law felt that this little agency could perform two functions. It could provide mediators to help employers and unions resolve their bargaining disputes, to help prevent strikes, or settle them as quickly as possible if they occurred. And it could perform an arbitration function. It was decided early on that arbitration could be performed in several ways. One was with the members of the board, the distinguished persons appointed by the governor, who included in those days Harry Carman (the dean of Columbia College), Arthur Meyer, Mabel Leslie (a prominent figure in workers education and social work), Bill Herlands (who later became a judge), Burt Turkus (who had been in the district attorney's office),[6] Ralph Kharas (dean of the law school at Syracuse University). Later on, Jean McKelvey[7] from the Cornell University School of Industrial and Labor Relations became a board member.

While board members were called upon in some cases to perform as arbitrators, other cases were handled by the members of the staff. Incidentally, there was no charge for these services; the parties got them for free. The caseload was high, no doubt about it. I don't think that "no charge" was the only reason we were so popular, but I'm sure that was one reason many people did come to us. There was a third echelon and that consisted of the panel, a roster of experienced and capable persons. Most of them had had training during the National War Labor Board days and were accepted as individuals whom unions and employers could trust. Panel members charged the parties $50 to $75 a day for their arbitration services, as I recollect.

As a member of the agency in 1947, for the first time I actually conducted an arbitration hearing and wrote an arbitration decision. That was the beginning, so to speak, of a career which ultimately landed me in arbitration full-time. Looking back, I think that the state mediation board was probably the best training ground (if we leave aside the National War Labor Board) for arbitrators. Almost every member of the staff in those days, at least in New York City, went on to become highly successful arbitrators. I'm referring to people like Ben Roberts, Louis Yagoda, Ben Wolf, Julie Manson, Irving Shapiro, Milton Friedman, Eva Robins, and many others. The board members themselves went on to become full-time and very successful arbitrators. The panel members were already working in the field, and most of them were also on the roster of the American Arbitration Association and they too operated very successfully.

(Early on I became a member of the American Arbitration Association panel and got some assignments. Parenthetically, one of the tribunal clerks that gave me such work in the beginning was a chap named Eric Schmertz, who ultimately went on to become executive director of the state mediation board some years after I had left it. He became a successful arbitrator, and in his most recent transformation is the dean of the Hofstra University School of Law.)

There was a relatively new law in New York in 1949 which gave the industrial commissioner (he's like a secretary of labor to the governor) the power to invoke a Board of Inquiry when a serious strike either was threatened or had occurred and defied all efforts to settle it by mediation or any other means. It was about 1959 when the industrial commissioner, whose name was Edward Corsi, set up the first Board of Inquiry under the provisions of the law. A strike had occurred up in Buffalo at the Bell Aircraft plant; the union was the United Automobile Workers. Commissioner Corsi appointed a five-member board, chaired by the provost of Cornell University; among its members were Ralph Kharas, the dean of Syracuse University College of Law, and Elinore Herrick, who had been the NLRB regional director in New York. (Later she was industrial relations director for various large corporations.) I was named secretary to the board. That extracurricular assignment was eminently successful, I'm glad to say. After several hearings we persuaded both sides to submit the open items to arbitration.

The second Board of Inquiry appointed under the state law was in a wildcat strike on the waterfront in New York City, which became rather famous at the time. The Waterfront Commission, chaired by Judge Proskauer, had been appointed earlier to look into crime on the waterfront. All that ultimately ended up in a movie (*On the Waterfront* with Marlon Brando) and books. The Board of Inquiry was chaired by Martin Catherwood, who was the dean of Cornell University School of Industrial and Labor Relations; I was secretary to that board. We managed to get the strike settled by agreeing, if the strikers went back to work, to make an investigation into collective-bargaining procedures between the International Longshoremen's Association and the waterfront employers, and to recommend to the parties how those procedures could be improved. Several months afterwards we came out with a rather long report. One of the issues was hiring-hall practices; more important at that point were internal union procedures for voting democratically on such matters as acceptance or rejection of contracts.

Other special assignments in those days were on the federal level. The Taft-Hartley Act of 1947 allowed the president to establish Boards of Inquiry which were quite different than the New York State Boards of Inquiry where we were actually trying to settle strikes. Under the Taft-Hartley procedure the board's function was to determine whether a strike would substantially affect interstate commerce, and to report what the issues were to the president. In 1956 I was appointed to a board involving the longshore industry, and subsequently to some others.

Under the Railway Labor Act there was a procedure under which the president could establish what is called an emergency board to avert or resolve railroad and airline strikes. This board's function, unlike Taft-Hartley, was to actually listen to the parties present the guts of their dispute and the clauses which the union and employer were seeking, hear the evidence concerning their positions, sift out all the conflicting economic and statistical presentations, and then come up with written recommendations on how the dispute could be resolved reasonably and fairly. My first exposure to that procedure was around 1955 when I was appointed to an emergency board in a dispute between the New York Central Railroad and the Brotherhood of Railway Conductors.

In 1955 there was an interesting new development. The New York City Transit Authority was created, composed of appointees of the governor and the mayor. The Authority signed a collective-bargaining contract with the Transport Workers Union, with provision for an impartial adviser, who was in effect an arbitrator. But his decisions were to be recommendations to the Authority and not legally binding. At that time the Authority members did not feel they could legally give up their sovereignty, so to speak. The union and the Authority reached an impasse over who should be appointed impartial adviser; the union had a candidate whom the Authority would not accept. Finally the decision to appoint the adviser was put in the hands of the U.S. secretary of labor, who was James Mitchell, formerly director of labor relations for Bloomingdale's in New York City. Mitchell selected me, and I, still at the mediation board, had to obtain the approval of the attorney general of New York to take on this additional assignment. (That gentleman was Jacob Javits, later to become the distinguished senator.)

The transit assignment was my first so-called permanent arbitration experience. There were about 40,000 workers employed on the city's buses and subways. The cases covered all kinds of grievances on such matters as work schedules, differential pay, seniority, sick leave, deadheading, posting, job abolition, and so forth. The hearings were relatively informal, although both sides had attorneys. My recommendations or decisions were relatively short. From my point of view, the value of this experience was not only in the work but in the courage that it gave me to believe that I could possibly "make a go of it" in the field of arbitration. I did have a retainer from the Authority and the union, and thus out on my own I could start with at least sufficient money to pay the rent and possibly buy some groceries.

I was encouraged also at that time by Harry Uviller, who had become chairman of the state mediation board after Averell Harriman became governor and Merlyn Pitzele stepped down. Uviller was the impartial chairman for the ladies' garment industry and had long experience in the field. He thought I could also "make a go of it." In 1956 there were some impartial chairmen like Uviller and others in automobile, steel, and a few other industries. But there were very, very few full-time ad hoc arbitrators.

New York probably boasted more full-time labor arbitrators than any other area in the country. There were some very illustrious National War Labor Board alumni. Included among them were men like Abram Stockman; he was a lawyer, and I think he had "Attorney" on his office door, but for all intents and purposes he was doing full-time arbitration. Another was Joseph Rosenfarb, an alumnus of the National Labor Relations Board where he was a very distinguished attorney and author. When I ultimately went out on my own, these two gentlemen served as my mentors, helping me to get by the initial traumas of being on one's own, facing all the problems that neophyte arbitrators confront when they're beginning.

My secret weapon when I decided to become a full-time arbitrator was my wife. Dorothy[8] had a wealth of experience in collective bargaining, labor relations, writing, and related fields. What's more important is that she had a full-time job, and I didn't have to worry completely about where the next check was coming from. She also encouraged me to go out on my own. And so it was in 1956 (with the Transit Authority position in my pocket, so to speak) that I announced I was leaving the state mediation board to set up my own arbitration practice. That summer I went away on vacation, and learned how arbitration really works. In Colorado I had a call that there was a telegram for me at the mediation board from the Transport Workers Union telling me that I had been released and my contract retroactively terminated. Thus passed the umpireship in the Transit Authority.

Notwithstanding this rather rude shock, I decided to go it alone anyway and left the mediation board in 1957. At this juncture Jean McKelvey from Cornell University rode to the rescue. She was taking a sabbatical from the School of Industrial and Labor Relations and asked me to teach her graduate seminar in government and labor relations and her senior-level course in labor arbitration. Needless to say, I jumped at the chance. The arbitration workload too began almost immediately, and I was not really idle at that point or any time since.

It's really hard to know where to begin, in talking about the years since I've been a full-time arbitrator. In terms of highlights, one has been the General Motors umpireship. Rolf Valtin, who was the umpire for GM and the UAW, became so overloaded with work that the parties agreed to provide him with an associate umpire. He gave them a list of names from which to choose, and for one reason or another they selected me. I served as Rolf's associate for several years, and then as umpire when he left to become the first industrywide umpire in the coal industry. I've been GM umpire ever since, about nine years now.

It is a unique umpireship. (I might say parenthetically that every umpireship is unique because the wonders of arbitration are that the parties can adapt the arbitration process to their own needs and change it as they go along. And each industry, perhaps each employer and union in the ad hoc cases, have their own way of doing things.) In General Motors, tradition, precedent, and practice play tremendous roles. The parties have collected and printed every arbitration decision since the first one by Harry Millis back in 1940. They quote from them liberally; in almost each case presented to me I find some citation from an earlier umpire decision. The cases are carefully screened and prepared. The arbitrator (umpire) is given written submissions (they call it "the record"), which include all that has happened in previous stages of the grievance procedure. The parties have an agreement not to bring up new information or make dramatically new arguments at the arbitration hearing; they have agreed, in effect, there should be no surprises. Therefore the hearings are more controlled than you would normally find in other situations.

The parties are extremely adept at resolving disputes. In one year, when about 200,000 grievances were filed throughout the country, only about 2,000 were ultimately appealed to the umpire, and only about 30 actually presented for decision. So you can see how successful their approach to arbitration has been. This is partly due to the philosophy which George Taylor inculcated way back in the early 1940s. He persuaded them that grievance processing was part of collective bargaining and not a judicial adjudicatory procedure. Even until this day they talk about "bargaining grievances." That's what they do, and the result is that they settle virtually everything and leave only a relatively few cases for the umpire to decide. Some of those referred to the umpire are very important cases involving principle.

Others involve discharge cases where the parties just can't compromise for one reason or another, but are the most routine types involving credibility questions and things of that kind.

A special procedure in the GM/UAW arbitration system provides that, if the parties agree, they can have what they call a "memorandum decision." If that is requested, the arbitrator has 10 days after the close of the hearing to issue his award; he is requested not to write an opinion, but to merely state what the issue is and what his decision is. (I, and all other arbitrators I think, love those, but don't get too many of them.) I find it hard to recall other instances, at least in the umpireships, where the parties do not want an opinion. I think the reason is understandable: that is, that precedent does play an important role, particularly where there is an umpire who is a continuing adjudicator. The parties want to know how he thinks about a question, why he has resolved the dispute in the way he has. And they can take it from there, and probably not have to take any similar cases to him in the future. They know how he thinks, and repetition becomes unnecessary.

Another unique experience (they're all unique!) has been as "permanent arbitrator" (don't forget those quotation marks) in the last two years for the National Basketball Association and the National Basketball Players Association. Peter Seitz served as their first permanent arbitrator for six years, and George Nicolau next for three years. The players have perhaps the smallest union with the largest membership—I mean the tallest. There are about 23 teams in the league, each with 12 players, so the union consists of some 300 people. These may be the highest-priced per capita union members in the world. The issues are so different from the normal type of arbitration that basketball arbitrations are particularly fascinating.

Each player has his own player contract, which sets the terms of his employment; the overlay on top of that is the collective-bargaining contract between the league and the players association. Claims can arise from players or owners that the collective-bargaining contract is in conflict with the individual player's contract. For example, the collective-bargaining agreement will say that no club can include certain kinds of clauses in individual player contracts. Yet a club may go ahead anyway and sign proscribed clauses with a player; then there may be a dispute which puts the club and the player on the same side, opposed by the league on the other side. There are all kinds of permutations and combinations because they have all agreed in the collective-bargaining contract to have the arbitrator decide not only disputes under the collective-bargaining contract, but also disputes under the individual player contracts. (So an individual player would not go to court to interpret or enforce his individual contract.) Another interesting thing about the basketball cases is the amount of money at issue. It is not unusual for a grievance to involve $1 million or more.

Arbitration in football, where I've served since 1972, has unusual aspects.

The National Football League and the NFL Players Association have an agreement which permits players to file grievances, under certain circumstances, if they are injured during the course of practice or play and have been released from their contracts by their clubs. Trying to put it succinctly: if the player's contract is terminated following an injury, before he has been rehabilitated to the point where he can play up to par, he can grieve because termination shouldn't occur under such circumstances. These so-called injury disputes are heard by one of five or six arbitrators on a rotating panel. The issue will be whether an injury in fact occurred. If so, did it occur during the course of play or practice? Was the player rehabilitated before his contract was terminated? If not, how much money is he entitled to? In other words, how long would it have taken him to be rehabilitated?

These might be difficult questions to answer. Most of the evidence is medical. There are doctors on both sides more often than not. The arbitrators are required to sift the medical professional expertise in an effort to find the truth of the matter. Reinstatement is never an issue in these cases because by the time the case gets to the arbitrator usually two or three years have passed; the parties are only talking about how much money the player may be entitled to. The maximum is his salary for the rest of the season; it can't go beyond that.

In baseball, it's been a completely different experience. Some years ago, after baseball players were allowed to become free agents, the baseball players and their leagues agreed to what they call "salary arbitration." My little piece of the action (so to speak) about the arbitration aspect, has come to pass when a free agent and his team are unable to agree on a salary for the coming year, and the player elects to go to arbitration. What happens, simply stated, is that he puts down a salary figure which he thinks he should have. His club puts down the salary figure which it believes is appropriate. They come to the arbitrator with those two figures, having exchanged the figures far enough in advance so that they can negotiate further, if they so desire. But at some point they may not change these offers or proposals. At the arbitration hearing, each side is allowed to present in a one-hour period facts, figures, information, arguments to sustain the club's or player's point of view. They normally give the arbitrator a host of statistics. Baseball is probably more statistical minded than any other industry in the world. The figures are offered to demonstrate, mostly on a comparative basis, why the player should get what he is asking for, or why he should get what the club is offering. Statistics include attendance at games, runs batted in, earned run averages, the whole gamut, and arguments about whether older players (in terms of seniority) should get more than younger players who are not tested by time.

The arbitrator has 24 hours in which to make a decision. He is directed not to write an opinion, not to make any statements about reasons for his decision. All he does is to fill in a contract which the parties have signed at the hearing in his presence. He fills in the box which says "the salary for the next year shall be _____ dollars," and he inserts the number of dollars. The amounts are great and sometimes the difference between the parties is hundreds of thousands of dollars. It's sort of a Russian roulette kind of system, very interesting for the arbitrator and probably quite traumatic for the participants.

Entirely different than the sports arbitrations is the system in the shipping industry, headquartered in New York City, where I've been serving as impartial chairman in the last few years. The collective-bargaining agreement is between the International Organization of Masters, Mates and Pilots, which represents the deck officers on both dry cargo and wet cargo ships which sail the seas of the world, and three associations of shipowners. Their arbitration procedure is a little unusual. For each case the parties establish a Licensed Personnel Board, consisting of two representatives each from the labor organization and the association which are involved in the particular case. At the arbitration hearing the arbitrator sits at the head of the table as the presiding officer and also the note taker. The parties, represented by attorneys, present the case in full. The four members of the Licensed Personnel Board, sitting at the hearing along with the arbitrator, have first crack at the case. After the presentation they adjourn and see if they can reach an agreement. If they do, that's the end of the case, and the arbitrator writes down the decision for posterity.

But if the board members don't agree, which is what happens most of the time, then the case is turned over to the arbitrator. The parties are allowed to present some additional testimony or evidence, if they so desire; but normally they don't. And then the arbitrator goes home and does what arbitrators normally do, which is to write a decision.

One of the unique features of this arbitration system is the nature of the evidence which the parties present. There is a tremendous amount of hearsay. Most of us in arbitration are very leery, for obvious reasons, of receiving written statements or reports about what other people said. But in the shipping industry it is so difficult to assemble a group of witnesses to any incident in one room at the same time, that the parties have more or less accepted hearsay. The witnesses are scattered, serving on ships. The ships are all over the world, and you just can't get them. In the typical case I find perhaps one witness on each side. Then either party, or more likely both, present written statements to corroborate the testimony of the direct witnesses.

I'll say one more thing about arbitration in the shipping industry, and that is that it's unique. (I'm really overusing that word here, but that's what arbitration is all about.) One unusual aspect is that in almost all of the cases the opposing witnesses come from the same union. What will often happen is that a captain will discharge a chief mate or a second mate or a third mate, and it is the grievance of that mate which is being arbitrated. Theoretically the captain himself could be fired one day, in which case the union will be defending the captain because he is a member of the International Organization of Masters, Mates and Pilots. But when it's the mate's grievance that's involved, the union is representing the mate against the captain. It's a situation where the union in effect has to oppose and seek to contradict and defeat the action of the captain, one of its own members. It's a very delicate and unenviable position for a union attorney to be in. But that's the nature of the beast, so to speak, and makes the cases interesting and challenging for the parties as well as for the arbitrator.

You're asking me to go from the seas to the skies? I've done a lot of work in the airline industry and have handled disputes involving pilots, flight attendants, ground service people, mechanics, dispatchers—the whole gamut. One of the more interesting aspects of airline arbitration has been that each dispute is submitted to a tripartite board called a System Board of Adjustment. The reason is that the airlines came under the Railway Labor Act when they started their labor relations, and (like the railroads and the railroad unions) were obliged under the law to submit their grievance disputes to a so-called system board of adjustment which was bipartite in its initial stages and then tripartite with a referee, at the end. In fact, the word *referee* in airlines came from the railroad industry. The challenging (and sometimes helpful, and sometimes not so helpful) aspect of the system-board procedure is that the referee sits with either two or four other persons (an equal number from each side) who participate in the arbitration as adjudicators, not as presenters.

The consequence is that there is, in effect, an extra step in the process of deciding the matter. The referee has to not only consult his own conscience and the record, but he must also consult his colleagues. Where there is a good relationship, the members of these system boards can be enormously helpful to the referee, both in working out what an appropriate penalty might be and also in guiding the referee in terms of what he says in his opinion. Frequently an arbitrator does not know the ramifications of a statement which he or she might just offhandedly write. The parties—if they are conscientious and experienced, which they usually are—can tell the arbitrator that "Look, this is going to hurt matters more than it will help." A word or a phrase or a comment in an opinion unwittingly could lead to a substantive controversy which could even be worse than the one that you are trying to resolve.

Turning to some of the issues I've dealt with in arbitration, early on there were cases involving what are now very important contemporaneous issues. One was a "fair representation" case which became very well known because of the extended litigation in federal courts. *General Motors v. Ruzicka* started about 12 years ago with the discharge of a General Motors employee for being intoxicated on the job. It was a relatively routine case: he was fired; he had long seniority; the UAW filed a grievance that went through a couple of steps. Then the critical thing happened or, I should say, did not happen.

Under the collective-bargaining contract, the union has a certain number of days to appeal to the next step a grievance rejected at an earlier step. In this case the union failed to appeal within that time frame. The employee asked that his grievance be processed to the next step anyway. The company, acting under its privilege, said, "No, it's too late. This is a dead grievance." The chairman of the grievance committee (or the shop committee, as it's called) said it was inadvertent, he had just overlooked the deadline, and appealed to the company to reverse itself. The company refused.

As a consequence of all this, the grievant, Mr. Ruzicka, went to his local union with a grievance against the union. And they turned him down. Under the UAW constitution he had a right to go to the international union, which he did. And they turned him down. Under the UAW constitution he had a right to appeal to the Review Board, which consists of outside persons who determine whether the international union has acted properly. And they turned him down. Then he went to the NLRB, and they turned him down. Finally he went to the federal district court in Michigan; the district court turned him down. Then he appealed to the Circuit Court of Appeals. After seven years the circuit court sustained him and directed the case back to the district court, with an instruction that if the district court could not decide the merits of the case, the judge could remand it to the umpire under the GM/UAW contract.

All that happened. It was remanded to the umpire (which I was, at that time). It was the first arbitration in some 35 years of GM/UAW experience in which a dispute was being arbitrated which neither party had appealed to arbitration, but was being brought to the umpire at the direction of the federal district judge. Ruzicka was being represented by the international union, whom he had successfully sued in court. Before walking into the hearing, I thought to myself: "What's going to happen here? The union is the defendant; it lost the case and Ruzicka is suing the union for money damages, among other things. (This was under the *Vaca v. Sipes* decision of the Supreme Court.) He is suing the union for money; he is suing the corporation for money. How can the union represent Ruzicka? And what's his attorney going to say about that?"

At the hearing the corporation and the union each had its usual staff representatives. Mr. Ruzicka's attorney was sitting in the back, observing closely, and we proceeded. In the end the company decided not to call any witnesses; it just relied on the record (submitting the written submission, "the record," which is ordinarily provided for the umpire in arbitration hearings). The union, playing the same game, decided, "They have no witnesses, we'll have no witnesses." They did not even offer Mr. Ruzicka, but they offered the record too. I made a stab at trying to resolve the matter. I don't usually do that in GM cases because they've done their best already; I felt this was worth a try. I got sort of close, but did not succeed. So we all went home, and I wrote a decision.

I realized, of course, that I was not deciding a case as the umpire; I was deciding the merits of the dispute on behalf of a judge of the district court. My decision was carefully worded to tell the parties that if I had been the umpire to decide the case, and if I were the one to make the final and binding decision in this case, this is what I would do. My ruling was that I would not have sustained the discharge, but would have reduced it to a suspension without pay (I've forgotten whether a 30- or 60-day suspension was indicated). The ruling was at the behest of the district court judge; I read his decision and the circuit court's, as not telling me that I had any final powers in the Ruzicka matter, but was performing a function which was to decide the merits of the case. The case involved the duty of fair representation and who was obligated to do what.

Who was liable for back pay, if back pay were to be granted? The corporation? The international union? The local union? All this was beyond me, as the umpire from whom the district court judge had requested a ruling. The union took my award back to the district court judge who said, "Fine. That's it, and I will decide how the back pay should be paid." He decided to split it, 50–50, the union paying half and the corporation paying half. At that point Mr. Ruzicka did not return to work at General Motors; he had gone to work for the Ford Motor Company in the meantime and was doing quite well. Actually, there wasn't that much back pay coming to him, about $25,000; he had worked elsewhere. But a tremendous amount was spent in lawyers' fees.

Another General Motors case, years ago, involved genetic questions which are now a "hot issue" in many industries. Two women filed a grievance because they had been denied transfers to jobs they had applied for. Management had turned them down because of a company policy under which women of childbearing age were denied jobs which would expose them and any fetuses to lead. Scientific investigation had long since shown terrible consequences for a fetus exposed to lead. There was no dispute about that. In the past the union did not object to the company's policy. The grievance now arose in the context of the new push by the women's movement and federal agencies to protect women from discrimination of all kinds. The philosophy was that women, no less than men, should make the decisions affecting themselves. That was the claim of these two women: regardless of the future outcome for themselves or potential offspring, they should be permitted to make that choice; it was not up to a paternalistic corporation, and it certainly wasn't up to the union.

Another argument put forward in this case was that there had been some scientific indication that when men were exposed to lead there might be an effect on their offspring as well. This was obviously a fascinating issue (I will not say "unique"), a philosophical one which poses all kinds of social problems, as well as internal management-union problems. The evidence presented in arbitration was largely medical, including all kinds of research studies in this country and others. The government had not taken a stand yet. They had issued various rules and regulations which required companies to reduce exposure, but had not yet reached the issue of whether any exposure should be permitted.

I wrestled with this question and thought that what we were talking about was preservation of the human race versus preservation of job opportunities. In the end the evidence had not shown that the same kind of injury or potential injury to a fetus would result for males as for females. For a variety of other reasons, it seemed the corporation's approach was not unreasonable. My award said that if scientific studies in the future came up with more information, the parties certainly were free to reopen this kind of issue. But based on what was now known it was appropriate to protect potential children, so to speak, from the damages which might result from mothers' exposure to lead. That was a safety case extraordinaire.

In recent years, particularly in airlines, seniority-merger cases have come to the fore. Such issues go back many, many years, but in recent years there have been more, and possibly more hard fought. When two companies merge, the workforces have to be integrated. Each has its own seniority list, and the question is: "How shall the lists be merged?" In the end there can be only one seniority list. The balance may be quite different between the groups being merged. One airline may have persons who are considerably older in terms of service than the other airline's. All kinds of issues, which go to the very heart of employment, arise. In a merged list, some are going to be at the bottom, and may lose their jobs sooner or later—possibly sooner, because of the decline in business which led to the merger in the first place.

The government requires that matters of this kind be submitted to arbitration. Some organizations, like the Association of Flight Attendants, require in the union's constitution that seniority-merger disputes be arbitrated. The result is that in the end either a single arbitrator or a board of arbitration must sit to decide how to integrate seniority on two airlines. In my experience these disputes are the most bitterly fought. They are disputes essentially between union members. The employers have not too much to say. In one case, the employers didn't even participate. They just said, "We will accept whatever comes out of the case." I tried to mediate, quite unsuccessfully, between the two union groups who were in the same international union but employed by different airlines. The union groups could not have been more "poles apart," because many stood to lose positions on the seniority list and all that entails, which includes deciding the city and location where one works, the kinds of flights one can choose, et cetera. These disputes between unions are like family feuds, which everybody knows are the worst feuds of all. And the men and women in the middle get the worst clobbering of all.

A more commonplace issue is "past practice," one which most arbitrators are concerned with because it has given rise to so many disputes. The concept itself is somewhat tenuous, and different people have different notions of what it means. One high-visibility case arose in 1966 after John Lindsay became the new mayor in New York City. I think he wanted to do something dramatic at the beginning of his administration, to show how much "on the ball" he was. He announced that he was revoking a procedure which had been in existence for many years, under which city departments closed one hour early during the summer months. Prior mayors, including Robert Wagner, had actually issued executive orders on this subject in which they declared this summer-hours policy. It was not, however, written into any of the collective-bargaining agreements which covered city employees.

Mayor Lindsay announced that henceforth summer hours would not be automatic but would depend on whether particular offices in individual departments had comfortable or uncomfortable room temperatures, et cetera. All of the unions complained loudly, and the unions and the city finally agreed to arbitrate the matter. It was a very strange case (I'm not going to say "unique"). The dispute had gone on for many weeks, and by the time they came to me in mid-June, the summer hours (if they were to go in effect) were just a few days away.

Hearings were on Wednesday and Thursday; each union was represented by its own spokesperson, and the city was represented by its corporation counsel. The transcript was delivered to me on Friday, and my decision had to be made by Sunday, because Monday was the beginning of summer. (This is really a ridiculous way of arbitrating an important issue. But that's the way it was put before me.)

The parties were very emotional about summer hours. For the unions, at least as they saw it, it meant the unilateral withdrawal of a benefit long enjoyed. They just could not understand how this could occur. The city argued that there may have been some kind of a practice, it's true, but it was a practice which a mayor had put into effect and so a new mayor could withdraw it. This kind of issue arises not infrequently, but not often so dramatically. Everybody was interested; newspapers were keen on finding out what was happening. I handwrote my decision and gave it to my typist on Saturday, and my wife and little daughter helped collate it on Sunday morning. I called a press conference on Sunday afternoon, right after meeting with the parties to hand them the decision.

My decision was that this was more than just a practice, in terms of what had happened in the past. It was in effect an understanding embodied (if not in writing) at least within the parties' comprehension in their collective-

71

bargaining relationship. For example, the evidence showed that during negotiations, when the union had asked for certain monetary benefits and shown that New York City employees received lower wages than similar employees in other cities, the city representatives responded with "Yes, that's true, but you have the benefit of working one less hour during the summer months." The summer-hours benefit was taken into consideration when the parties worked out a monetary package in their collective-bargaining contracts. To make a not-so-long story a little shorter, I felt that the summer-hours practice was so embedded in the parties' relationship, that the only way it could be removed was by collective bargaining. And that was my decision. (The aftermath, for better or worse, was that I did not receive any additional cases involving city employees, except for teachers, after 1966.) Years later the city and the unions bargained the issue of summer hours. Ultimately the unions gave up this benefit in exchange for other benefits.

Still another out-of-the-ordinary arbitration system operates within the State Department. For a number of years I've been on the Foreign Service Grievance Board, which was established by statute to resolve grievances (but not issues of contract terms) for all foreign service employees, from the lowest clerks up to the ambassadors. The board has 21 members; 14 are retired foreign service officers, and 7 are arbitrators like myself. Each of the 21 has similar responsibility and authority, and a vote. A foreign service employee (including employees in the State Department, Agency for International Development, Voice of America, et cetera) may file a grievance. There are two or three unions of foreign service employees, but not everyone belongs to a union. An individual can file a grievance, the union can be involved in addition or on its own. Normally a grievance will allege that something improper has been done. The case will be assigned to a three-member panel consisting of two foreign service retired officers and one arbitrator, sitting in effect as an arbitration board.

A large majority of these matters are decided on the record. Each side presents written submissions setting forth the facts and arguments, referring to the statute or the rules and regulations, et cetera. They have a chance to rebut and to put into the record as much as they want. When the agency and the employee are satisfied that the record is complete, it will be closed, and the three-person arbitration board will sit (together with a staff member who supervises the administrative conduct of the case) and decide how the grievance should be resolved. In some cases the board can only recommend a remedy, not order it. Many of the disputes concern what the outside world might consider trivial matters, such as a critical sentence in an evaluation report. But to foreign service officers these can be extremely crucial because what goes into their personnel files may become *the* most important thing in their lives, affecting whether they are promoted or not, demoted, or taken out of service completely.

A year or so ago the statute was amended to give the board the right to decide cases involving the termination "for cause" of an employee. That means matters not connected with his or her proficiency, but such things as dishonesty or misconduct of some kind. The statute goes a long way beyond what most parties in the private sector would accept, providing that the agency may not terminate an employee (who protests termination) until the board has made its decision. Thus termination is only a proposed action, and the board will say yes or no to, "Can this employee be terminated?" This is an unusual posture for arbitrators to be in, although it is an expedited type of procedure for obvious reasons.

6

AN ARBITRATOR'S SECRET
Israel Ben Scheiber

Israel Ben Scheiber practiced law from 1913 on. In the 1920s, when the American Arbitration Association opened its doors, he occasionally served on its arbitration panel. He was very much interested in adjudicating disputes and increasingly preferred the role of neutral rather than advocate. By 1977 when he ended his long career as attorney and arbitrator, arbitration had been his major activity for well over three decades.

Industries in which he arbitrated included telephone, utilities, broadcasting, printing, airlines, and performing arts. He served on presidential emergency boards under the Railway Labor Act. President Kennedy appointed him, together with Emanuel Stein and Saul Wallen, to the presidential emergency board for the safety and manning issue on which TWA [Trans World Airline] and the Air Line Pilots Association had deadlocked: whether flight navigators were still necessary in cockpit crews or whether their presence was rendered obsolete by new technology.

A former vice president of the National Academy of Arbitrators, Scheiber delighted in meetings and conversation with arbitrator colleagues. His wit was legendary. One perhaps apocryphal story is that he would buttonhole other arbitrators and offer to listen to two of their arbitration stories if they would listen to one of his.[1]

He brought to arbitration the same unselfish values and respect for others' dignity that he expressed in community service. Improving the lives of children was a lifelong commitment for him, from the time he was a young law student doing volunteer work at Madison House, a settlement house on New York City's Lower East Side. When he came to Putnam Valley in 1920 to help Madison House establish a summer camp for boys from the slums, he also helped transform what was then a poor rural area with one-room schoolhouses into a community with a fine school system.[2] For 25 years he was president of the school board in Putnam Valley (where he maintained a country residence), and also served on the planning board there.

Scheiber died in August 1986. In 1983, when the oral history interview was conducted, he was almost 94 and quite frail; thus the interview could not be very extensive.³ But he still recalled happily his career in arbitration and his community service in Putnam Valley.

After passing the New York State bar examination in 1913, I went from door to door of lawyers' offices, seeking employment. Finally one lawyer said he could use me, but he couldn't afford me. So I offered to work for nothing. He said, "Oh, no, you couldn't do that!" I answered, "Well, if you think I'm bluffing, why don't you call my bluff?" So he told me, "All right, hang up your hat outside."

After a while my employer became ill and suggested that I take care of his clients and office in his absence. He said he didn't want to take advantage of me, so he would pay me $4 a week. I stayed there about three years, and then opened an office of my own.

Many of the people who came to me apparently felt that since I was a lawyer they could safely bring me their troubles and see if I could help dispose of them. From that point on I was quite busy with neighbors and friends and people who knew me, who brought their problems and explained them to me. And where possible, I tried to work out some settlement that was satisfactory to both sides without going to court. Sounds a little bit like mediating and arbitrating? Absolutely, though at the time I didn't know those two fancy words. But I did the best I could.

When the American Arbitration Association started, around 1920, I was designated as an arbitrator from time to time. I enjoyed arbitration tremendously and found I had up to that point done nothing in my entire life that gave me as much pleasure and satisfaction. What I enjoyed so much was, first of all, the fact that it was possible for me to be really and truly helpful, and second, that my work seemed to give satisfaction to the parties who chose me as arbitrator.

Later I became a member of the panel of the New York State Board of Mediation; Arthur Meyer was chairman then. I also was added to the panel of the Federal Mediation and Conciliation Service, when Cyrus Ching was the director.

I started as a lawyer, and then sort of began taking on arbitration work. During the time I maintained my law practice, some 40 years, I was also doing some arbitration. And in the 30 years following, almost all my work was as an arbitrator rather than as a lawyer.

Why has arbitration given me so much joy and satisfaction? It was very useful work. Any work that adds to peace on earth is important. And I found arbitrators were amongst the best people I knew. I like the fact that they are good people. They do very important work. They don't brag about it. They're content to do the very best that is possible for the parties.

You want me to tell the secret I've often told my wife?[4] Well, it's a secret that is probably worth repeating, although it would be repetitious! And that is: for me, if I was not paid for doing the work of an arbitrator, I would pay to do it.

7

DECISION MAKING IN ARBITRATION
Milton Friedman

Milton Friedman was an arbitrator and mediator with the New York State Board of Mediation for 17 years before becoming a full-time private arbitrator in 1967. He arbitrated in every major industry throughout the country and was umpire and/or permanent panel arbitrator in airlines, broadcasting, hospitals, newspapers, railroads, schools, steel, telephone, trucking, universities, and other industries and services. While the status of so-called permanent arbitrators is ordinarily not permanent, for reasons that seldom reflect upon them, Friedman had the rare experience of never being terminated from an umpireship or panel. In many contracts he served continuously from the inception of the parties' arbitration systems, as in the contract for paraprofessionals between the New York City Board of Education and the United Federation of Teachers. After he resigned from almost two decades as the neutral in the paraprofessionals' contract, the board and the union presented him with a plaque at an unprecedented private ceremony on June 16, 1989. The inscription read, "In appreciation for a man who listened with his mind, but never decided without his heart."

Friedman's mediation and arbitration expertise were called upon in the public sector from the beginning of collective bargaining in the 1960s for New York state and city employees. He served as chairman of the New York State Public Employment Relations Board's Nassau County Board from 1967 to 1969. He was a public member of the New York City Office of Collective Bargaining for five years, declining reappointment in December 1986. He and the other Office of Collective Bargaining public members, Arvid Anderson and Daniel Collins, averted a transit strike in New York City in 1982, when the state legislature designated them to arbitrate the impasse over a new collective-bargaining contract between the Metropolitan Transit Authority and the two unions representing 35,000 bus and subway workers.

Friedman was a member of the board of governors of the National Academy of Arbitrators in 1963–65 and served as vice president in 1977–78.

His awards continue to be cited frequently for their quality of judgment and clarity of expression, years after his death in October 1989.

In 1950 I started work as a staff mediator and arbitrator at the New York State Board of Mediation.[1] I sat in on a few arbitration cases and that essentially represented the training for new staff members. On-the-job observation was really the training. Apparently I had an instinct for both mediation and arbitration.

I particularly enjoyed mediation because of the great satisfaction in bringing contesting parties together. In arbitration, the decision generally leaves one party happy and the other party sad. So the neutral's satisfaction can come from mediation more readily than from arbitration.

During my early years at the board, in order to familiarize myself thoroughly with the arbitration process, I would sit down in my free time in the board's library and read *Labor Arbitration Reports,* the complete texts of arbitration awards published by the Bureau of National Affairs, a widely quoted source in arbitration. Now the *Reports* are up to about volume 80, but at that time went to volume 25, maybe less. I may have read every case in every volume.

I enjoyed the work at the mediation board. It was really gratifying, the arbitration too, and fascinating. I have a number of good friends who were colleagues I met at the board. At that time the mediation board had a very, very high reputation among lawyers, unions, and managements, with good cause, because the mediators were extremely skillful and the arbitrators were very good. In general the cases were what might be called small cases, with small companies but not necessarily small unions. The issues, however, were big. They were the same issues that I still encounter in private arbitration, including discharges, job classifications, contract interpretations.

The Korean War started a year after I was at the mediation board, and the government resumed both price and wage controls. When the Wage Stabilization Board, as the wage-control administration was called, opened a New York regional office in 1951, I went to work there, on a year's leave of absence from the mediation board. (My wife, who had been at the National War Labor Board during World War II, was asked to work for this new agency. Our first son was an infant at the time, and she said she couldn't. But when she was asked, "What about your husband?" she said I'd be great and she'd urge me to take it. And she did.) The experience at the Wage Stabilization Board, where I was in charge of metal and machinery industries and also wage incentives, gave me a good background for later work in arbitration.

Also helpful later on in private arbitration practice, was experience arbitrating in New Jersey, during my last years with the New York State Board of Mediation. Staff mediators at the New York State Board of Mediation were given permission to arbitrate on their own time, outside New York, while charging a fee as was customary with private parties. Many of us were selected by New Jersey employers and unions, who turned to the New Jersey State Mediation Board for lists of qualified arbitrators.

The great influence in my life would have to be my wife. And that was true also in connection with my leaving the New York State Board of Mediation in 1967 to go into private practice of arbitration.

There were also other contributing factors, albeit less potent. One was my work in 1966, chairing a special board established by the Nassau County government. The county had commissioned a job evaluation plan by an outside consultant and reshuffled jobs of thousands of county employees in the county's civil service structure. The result was a lot of dissatisfaction. The county set up a tripartite Nassau County Classification Appeals Board to conduct hearings and recommend changes in the consultants' job evaluation plan. I was asked to be board chairman; the labor member was a union leader and executive officer of the Nassau County Federation of Labor, and the management person was an official of the Long Island Lighting Company. (I had official permission to use annual leave for hearings during the regular workweek and to do studies and other appeals board work on my own time.) After our recommendations on revising job evaluations went into effect, the county designated another board, the Salary Appeals Board, to make revisions in the salary placement of employees. I served as chairman of the tripartite Salary Appeals Board, which completed its work during the spring of 1967.

Clara was urging me to leave the State Board of Mediation. Similar advice came from a friend who had been at the board himself before going into arbitration full-time. But I was a product of the Depression, and I had never voluntarily left any job I ever held. I was drafted from one job in World War II and lost various jobs as a result of layoffs and cutbacks, but I had never left a job on my own motion. And having a civil service job, which in those years meant lifetime security (civil service has changed since then!), I was reluctant to leave the State Board of Mediation.

Another reason that concerned me about leaving the State Board of Mediation, where I was on a salary, was that it was immaterial to me that my decision in an arbitration case might benefit some stranger I might never see again, or might adversely affect some union representative who came around the board a lot. It was just a matter of the evidence. But one of the parties might feel disaffected, and I could understand that losers don't like to lose. Thus I wondered how I would feel if I knew that making a certain decision as a private arbitrator would lose me a line of potential cases. The one thing I didn't want to do was begin an arbitration practice at the mercy of aggrieved parties. I certainly didn't want to change my own outlook. In that sense the

State Board of Mediation was an excellent milieu because there was no reason not to "call them as you see them."

But Clara felt that I would have no problem coping with arbitration in private practice; she felt I would do well. After I decided to do it, I took a year's leave so that if I couldn't make it as a full-time arbitrator, I would be able to go back to the State Board of Mediation. I did fear it might be a year without a case. I had no source of cases; I hoped the New Jersey Board of Mediation would continue to provide some cases, but I had never had any dealings with the American Arbitration Association and the Federal Mediation and Conciliation Service, which were agencies where arbitrators got cases.

Fortuitously (although I didn't realize it at that time) the Taylor Law was passed in New York. The Public Employment Relations Board, set up under the law, desperately needed mediators and fact finders. Where were they going to get them? People who had mediation experience came either from the New York State Board of Mediation or the Federal Mediation and Conciliation Service; there were very few experienced individuals PERB could call upon. The initial sources were other people (more adventuresome!) who had been leaving the state mediation board to become private arbitrators. PERB was established I think in September. I left the mediation board October 1, 1967. (By that time many parties had given up using the mediation board arbitration services. The administration changed at the board, things changed. It was much easier for me to leave the board at that time rather than earlier when I was associated with great people. It had been a real pleasure to be there.)

Soon afterwards I was asked to be chairman of the Nassau County Public Employment Relations Board, established under the Taylor Law to act in place of the state board in many respects. Entry into this kind of work promised to be very fascinating, and I was glad to accept the chairmanship, which was not a full-time position. Between this and other sources (such as the arbitration panels of the New Jersey Board of Mediation and the American Arbitration Association), I did quite well in private arbitration practice, almost from the beginning. Whatever reputation I acquired from my work at the State Board of Mediation, which apparently was quite good, generated some cases because lawyers I had encountered at the mediation board also represented clients who used the American Arbitration Association. And I began doing some railroad arbitrations in Chicago, through designations by the national mediation board, as everybody who had left the state mediation board had done in their first year of private practice.

In my first year, I didn't experience the trauma of some of my friends. One colleague told me that in his first year as a full-time arbitrator there had been a horrible month in which he got not a single inquiry about a new case. Absolutely a blank! That never happened to me, even in the first month.

Another friend of mine had left the mediation board for private practice, ecstatic. Labor and management people around the board told him, "Oh, that's great! We need you! It's just wonderful! We're going to set up this permanent arbitratorship for you," and so on. I'm cynical and skeptical about such things and used to say to him, "Don't believe it; don't count on it. I'm sure you're going to do well, but don't count on these promises." Unfortunately for him, I was borne out.

One thing about arbitrators is universally true: because of the nature of the profession, they want above all else to be wanted—not by one side, but by both sides. It is the final encouragement for the successful arbitrator; being wanted by both sides has come true. Of course, there are always some people who can't stand an award that you've issued and drop you for one reason or another. Many arbitrators have been dropped frequently, have lost chairmanships and permanent rotating panels, a dozen or more times. And they are still too busy. Well, I became too busy within a few years.

Early in the 1970s I was asked to be a special arbitrator under the U.S. Steel and United Steelworkers of America contract. Their arbitration system is very structured, with a chairman of the Board of Arbitration, a permanent board and offices, four or more staff arbitrators titled assistants to the chairman and working full-time on salary. The volume of cases is such that the chairman and his staff can't keep up with them, so they ask certain people (many of them are among the best-known arbitrators in the country) to act as special arbitrators. All awards must be countersigned by the chairman of the Board of Arbitration; in other words, he has the right of objecting to an award, or its phrasing, submitted to him by the staff or special arbitrators.

The variety of steel cases was fascinating. Theirs is a very well-developed grievance procedure. Minutes at various grievance steps are recorded in rather detailed factual manner by the company and presented to the union; the union can take exception to anything in the minutes, but if they don't, the minutes become unchallengeable thereafter. Parties can't put into arbitration new testimony that controverts the final minutes. The minutes are introduced in evidence at the arbitration hearing; testimony may amplify it. Or perhaps something new will be introduced that is relevant enough to go into the record, may be more explanatory than the tightened-up minutes, and thus helpful to the arbitrator. Of course so structured a system can be used only where there are long-standing permanent relationships. But there are many of the latter in other industries that don't use a sophisticated arbitration system.

U.S. Steel has, everyone agrees, among the hardest cases in the country, ones that can be the most complex in contractual interpretation. Many steelworkers' contracts, particularly in basic steel, have a provision (Section 2–b in U.S. Steel) which is essentially a "past practice" clause. If something has become an effective condition of employment (assuming it's not changed by the contract, even if not stated explicitly therein), it's embedded in the relationship and enforceable. That goes especially for crew size, which is so important in steel. If a crew of three people has been the established practice, the arbitrator can't change it. There is an exception that requires careful analysis; if conditions change (as mechanization of work formerly done by hand), the practice then goes out the door, because the new structure is no longer the basis for the old practice.

Some of the arbitration cases involve very substantial dollar amounts. Even an overtime grievance involving $11 or $12 for one employee could have implications running into hundreds of thousands of dollars for hundreds of thousands of employees. In U.S. Steel the awards are first reviewed by the chairman. Sylvester Garrett, who was the first chairman and served for about 25 years, is one of the most brilliant arbitrators in the United States. I've described him to union and management people as "a national treasure" for both sides. He could recall (by case number—and there were thousands and thousands of cases!) what was done and said in prior cases, and what the decision was and why. Even where my formulations in a particular case were right, if he had a suggestion his formulations were better, and a better award resulted.

During this period I also became umpire of Reynolds Metals and of National Can Company and the steelworkers union for their plants throughout the country. Both umpireships were very, very interesting. (These were sole-umpire designations outside the Board of Arbitration in the steel industry, although the contracts and procedures had many similarities.) In 1977, after a bout of illness, I gave up all of the steel work and cut back on other designations outside New York City to minimize out-of-town travel.

My approach to decision making in arbitration is the same in all industries and all locations: to be particularly painstaking in preparing the opinion, which ultimately leads to the decision. I am not a believer (as apparently are many decision makers in all walks of life) in coming to a conclusion after hearing the evidence and then writing an opinion to fit it. (I understand that even some Supreme Court justices approach their decision making that way in some cases.) What I try to do is divorce myself of any emotion. For example, it is difficult to take an action that the evidence dictates if pity is one of the considerations. Arbitrators are bound to observe the contract; it leaves no room, for example, for an arbitrator generously bestowing some largesse. If there is to be mercy, it's really the function of the employer; the arbitrator's function is to make a decision on the merits of the case.

Of course I consider mitigating circumstances as part of the substantive matter in a case. For example, if an employee is discharged for insubordination and the proof is absolute that he did refuse to perform an assignment and the company has a practice of discharging employees who refuse to perform an assignment—if that is all you look at, you have absolutely no option.

Insubordination per se is inexcusable, but insubordination provoked may be different, just as self-defense may be justification for a violent action. What I mean is that you look at evidence of all the circumstances which are relevant to the case. And based on them (and I do mean *all* of the circumstances, one of my main goals being to make sure I learn all of the facts), then decide the case based on those facts, no matter where it leads.

I've found over the years that being dispassionate is really the only way to come to a decision that meets the parties' expectations. They may love to win a case because an arbitrator is hard-nosed or because an arbitrator believes in greater leniency than the contract would seem to allow. But both sides really share the view of what they want in contract interpretation from an arbitrator—they want the contract enforced. I think an arbitrator should pursue that course. Parties who lose a particular case may be disappointed. But if the explanation is given as to why they lost the case, it's accepted. (I must say that I get a warm feeling when I find that on the evidence a discharged employee, one with long service or a family or other problems, should be reinstated. That kind of reaction comes only after what might be called coldly appraising a case.)

Making decisions is difficult since many of them are unpleasant, unfavorable, and unappetizing to one side or another. When I make a decision based on the facts and the facts alone, what counts is the evidence. The case may be presented well, it may be presented poorly, but I take everything into my consideration. When I have done that, I feel I have done my best. I have carefully considered, I've labored over it (maybe too much). But when I come to a conclusion, I don't see any way I could have come to another one. Not I. Perhaps you could. Perhaps someone much brighter than I could have perceived things I haven't seen. But if you come to me for a decision, this is my best. And I have felt over the years that I can be relaxed about it after the case is over. I don't worry about it; I don't think, "Oh, should I have done this or that?" I've given my all, once, and there is no more I can do. My philosophy is that this is "a world I never made." It was made for me by the parties, in their contract, in the evidence they had in a particular case, and so on. And I base my award on the evidence, to the best of my ability.

I remember having a big disagreement once with a psychiatrist I met on vacation in a discussion about impartiality. He didn't believe that anyone *could* be impartial. He felt everyone is the product of his environment, which I am inclined to agree with. But as far as detaching myself in any given case, I'm sure I do that. The psychiatrist felt that was not possible, but I think arbitrators (like judges) can and must be impartial.

Some arbitrators feel that strictly using burden of proof as a basis for making an award may be too formal. That of course is the sine qua non in court decisions: someone always has the burden of proof. It may shift from time to time in the course of a hearing, but when it comes down to who wins or who loses, it's *the* determinant. For the arbitrators who think that's not the way to do it, that you are just supposed to listen to everything and come up with a practical decision, I always have the question: "What happens when there is essentially a standoff?" One example (an oversimplified one) is where there are only two firsthand witnesses, both acknowledged to be credible, with testimony exactly antipodal. What is an arbitrator to do? Assuming the arbitrator finds no reason to question either witness's testimony, who wins? Does the arbitrator say, "Well, it's a tie. So take back your case. I can't make a decision"? (Which is what he should do in good conscience, rather than simply take a guess or toss a coin.) When a prizefighter is challenging the champion and the referees mark the rounds half for the challenger and half for the champion, it's a dead heat. The challenger doesn't become the champion, because in order to acquire the championship he must win. That keeps the champion in his position, and that's a good way of resolving the dead heat. But in arbitration there must be some way to decide, and it really is the way that the courts have found, and I think that's the practical way. Even in a court case involving discharge, the employer would have the burden of proof ordinarily.

As I first learned in *Richardson on Evidence* many years ago, this aspect of burden of proof reverses opening-order in arbitration hearings on discharge cases. In my earliest years as an arbitrator at the New York State Mediation Board, a lawyer might automatically say to the union at the beginning of a discharge hearing, "Well, you brought the case, so you go ahead." (I've even had unions which went ahead.) I used to try to settle this between the lawyers because not only in connection with burden of proof, the hearing is backwards if the union opens. Obviously it can't have the burden of proof because it doesn't know necessarily all the reasons why the employee was discharged. The only one who knows that, and can prove it, is the employer. But in those early days, when I was naive and the attorneys were bright and wanted to make points, I wasn't sure just what to do. I did know enough to know that people who bring cases usually have the burden of going forward. But they don't in certain kinds of cases, and dismissal is one of them, whether it's in court or arbitration.

As for the rules of evidence, like many other court rules, they can aptly be followed—in part at least—by arbitrators. There is so much common sense in what we think of as "technical rules" that arbitrators in many cases would do well to follow the rules of evidence. I say "many cases," because it would be disastrous if arbitrators tried to pattern themselves after judges.

Another aspect of this general problem is hearsay. Everyone knows that hearsay is admissible in arbitration in ways totally inadmissible in court. While I admit hearsay, I admit it because it may be helpful in explaining something, but not for its own intrinsic merit.

A classic example of the admission of hearsay (and other objected-to testimony) is the arbitrator's ruling that "I'll take it for what it's worth." In my earliest years I may have done that. But I was told a story years ago by a management attorney who represented many big clients in very important cases. When an eminent arbitrator accepted something "for what it's worth," this attorney didn't know what kind of credit it would be given. "The result was," he said to me, "that I had to put in evidence to contest the hearsay, to make sure that we demolished even that. It took two full days." I must say that frightened me. While I still admit hearsay, explaining why, and what its limitations are, I never have said since then that "I'll take it for what it's worth."

In one case, only hearsay was offered by the employer, a major New York library. It was an unsavory kind of case, involving a custodian who was dismissed for allegedly mishandling young women (high-school students working part-time in the library) he encountered in the basement. The only testimony was hearsay from the one or two librarians whom these four young women had confided in. That was all; no witness's credibility could be tested, no way to determine if there were any conspiracy among the young women for any reason. When the union was objecting to the hearsay evidence as such, I suggested that I would receive it but that of course it has very limited weight. Usually there is no way in which hearsay could lead to discharge.

The library, or its eminent counsel, said that the young women wouldn't come in to testify, they were too embarrassed; but they would be subpoenaed. Another hearing date was set, and the subpoenas were issued. It turned out that one young woman was in California, another was ill, another's parents refused to let her testify. (I forget what was true of the fourth young woman.) The employer's case finished on that posture—no other witnesses, not even witnesses attesting to anything in the employee's record that might lend some weight to the hearsay testimony. The union rested its case with no witnesses, not even the grievant. I found in favor of the grievant and reinstated him. I felt there was nothing else I could do as an arbitrator.

Lo and behold, some time after that I was told that the library's attorney (who also represented libraries throughout the United States) was going around on cases or even speech making, telling library managements that in New York City there was an arbitrator who holds that it's perfectly all right for a guy (a library custodian) to "feel up" young girls. Perhaps that's one way to become famous! (I don't know that he ever mentioned my name. Let's hope not.)

Apart from hearsay, arbitrators often receive testimony that could be deemed incompetent, irrelevant, or immaterial. But after all, arbitrators are not expected to be classical comprehenders of quality of evidence. They are expected to be able to determine, when they mull over a case, what's good evidence and what's bad—even though they may not, like a court, be able on the spur of the moment to rule things out. They certainly can't know the subtleties of the rules of evidence in various jurisdictions, which may differ. But most important is that one of the very, very limited reasons for vacating awards is the arbitrator's failure to hear evidence pertinent to the controversy. On the other hand, nothing happens if an arbitrator takes in everything, including the kitchen sink. It asks for possible *vacatur* if an arbitrator tries to act like a court, and rule on evidence like a court, and happens not to have the court's expertise. Perhaps even the most expert attorney serving as arbitrator may rule out something which a judge may find was germane and should have been received, though the judge might not have permitted it in his own courtroom. A great arbitrator and law professor, Dean Harry Shulman of Yale Law School, once said that the problem is not that the arbitrator will hear too much but that he will hear too little.

When the hearing seems to be drawn out as a result, I might take a second look at materiality or relevance. But my personal experience is that the argument over immateriality and incompetence may take much longer than having the question asked and answered. Which leads me to say that an arbitrator who bases his rulings on irrelevant, immaterial, incompetent evidence, hearsay, and the things to which objections may properly be made, is not long for the profession. Arbitration has gone a long way beyond the day when, if a third party were needed to settle a dispute between a little factory and a little union, they called in a clergyman and said, "What should we do? Who's right and who's wrong?" Being possessed of perhaps superhuman wisdom but maybe short on the ordinary kind of wisdom, the clergyman gave it his best, and both parties were satisfied. But that no longer is true.

For example, credibility is always an important consideration in arbitration. It can rarely be determined simply from witnesses' demeanor. I don't believe that the failure to look someone in the eye shows that person is lying. Nor does being fidgety or perspiring suggest absence of candor; what it may show is merely nervousness. It's surprising how many people who have no particular personal interest in a case become nervous and ill at ease when they're called to the witness stand and asked to swear that the testimony they give is true. Not only that, but many people are upset at being the focus of attention; they are not used to talking in what is essentially a public forum, even if it's only to answer questions. Many witnesses (even if they are prepared, as I imagine most are), feel that they must answer every question put to them, even when the truly accurate answer is, "I don't know." They try to placate the questioner, particularly the cross-examiner who asks leading questions, even though they simply have no personal knowledge for a reply. On the other hand, the practiced liar is confident, smooth, urbane, looks one in the eye, doesn't fidget, and meets all the criteria sometimes assumed for the truth-teller.

There is usually hard evidence that can help establish who is credible and who is not. Generally it's far more reliable than the amateur psychologist's (perhaps the professional's too!) evaluation. That is true even for lie detector tests; there are enough cases showing such unreliability in lie detectors as to place their standing in doubt for determining credibility. There are indicia that may be used. But again, unless supported by objective evidence, they're hardly a barometer of certainty in distinguishing the truthful from the un-truthful witnesses. There are such things as hesitant answers on cross-examination, compared with the smooth answers given on direct; the witness has usually been thoroughly prepared for direct examination, while what is asked on cross-examination may not have been anticipated.

I had a remarkable case which was determined by credibility. A witness, who was a supervisor, gave clear and quite credible answers to questions involving an employee's request for reclassification. The witness's description of the work being performed seemed thoroughly truthful and accurate, even though it was quite contradictory to the evidence that had been given by the grievant himself. When the union attorney got up to cross-examine, he began by saying, "Mr. Arbitrator, I would like to have this witness testify under oath." I was about to say that "You can't change the rules of the game, nobody else has testified under oath." Before I could say it, the company attorney said, "It's perfectly all right with us. Go right ahead." I was not going to interfere with their mutual desires, so I administered the oath.

When the witness began answering questions, he answered each question not in contradiction of the grievant's answers but in contradiction of the answers the witness himself had given earlier on direct examination. Not only was his credibility on direct put in doubt, he was even more convincing as a sworn witness than he had been as an unsworn witness. Since his testi-mony on cross-examination was credited in full, the case was won by the grievant. Later the union attorney explained that he had learned from his witnesses that this supervisor was a very devout individual. While he might be casual about how he answered questions unsworn, under oath he would never give anything but the truth as he best knew it. I must say that was the only time I have seen hard examples of the oath having any practical effect.[2] We know that in many cases it is probably being violated, where there are direct conflicts between one side and the other.

Apropos of what goes on in arbitration hearings, another comment I would like to make extends from experiences on the impressions an arbitrator can give. I have always felt that it was important not only for an arbitrator to be impartial, unbiased, fair, but perhaps equally important to *give* that impres-sion. It usually is more true for unsophisticated parties, like employee griev-ants or employer witnesses, than for the attorneys or sophisticated managements.

Long ago I had a case involving a UAW plant where the union put in its case first (since it was the grieving party), and then the company began putting in its case. After a short while, the management representative (who was not an attorney) said he wanted to make an objection: management was aware and objected that the arbitrator had taken very copious notes (there was no stenographic record) when the union was presenting its case, but when management was making its case, the arbitrator was taking far fewer notes and sometimes took none at all. I explained that when I take notes it's to become familiar early with the evidence. Many facts are not disputed; many times witnesses for the other side are asked questions which are rather parallel to those asked by the first side. And if I know the facts there is no reason to repeat it in my notes. I'm not sure that I convinced them that the note taking did not mean, "The award would be in favor of the union, so why take notes for the company." It gave me pause and did lead me to feel that I should be busily note taking when *both* sides are up.

A second case, just the reverse, happened only a few years ago, with a different union and a large electrical equipment plant. The day after the hearing the union's lawyer telephoned to tell me (sort of for my own good) that his committee had spoken to him after the hearing and were unhappy because they noticed that when the company asked questions on direct, I took copious notes, but when he cross-examined, my note taking was much less. (He assured me *he* knew that had no adverse meaning.) I explained that if cross-examination doesn't reveal anything particularly different, I may ease up in note taking. But the comment made me conscious anew of the importance of appearance as well as substance. It convinced me that the *procedure* of note taking has a value beyond the need to have as accurate a record as one can without a stenographic transcript.

In still another case, the company lawyer was not very experienced. His cross-examination of virtually every witness was a repeat of questions already answered on direct. If the witness had been asked on direct, "Are you employed in this department?" the company lawyer would ask on cross, "Did you say you worked in such-and-such a department?" Obviously there need be no extended note taking, conspicuous or otherwise, of such redundant questioning.

Each situation and contract has its own interesting characteristics in arbitration. I find that the Paraprofessional Grievance Panel has especially intriguing ones. It's a tripartite arbitration board with representatives from the New York City Board of Education and the teachers union (which represents the paras), and headed by a neutral. I was the first neutral chairing the panel and have headed it continuously since its inception around 1970. The Paraprofessional Grievance Panel is unlike the Board of Education panel for teachers, which consists of a single arbitrator drawn from a rotating permanent panel of neutral arbitrators. The paras themselves were largely women who primarily had been homemakers or working in rather menial jobs. Many had relatively little education, which was not inappropriate for paraprofessionals. But early in the collective-bargaining relationship the Board of Education and the teachers union set up a a career training program with release time for taking educational courses, reimbursement for tuition costs, and summer stipends for extensive education training. The result was a dramatic upgrading in the paras' educational level. Many completed high school, and many went on to college and qualified as teachers. It was great to witness the paras' achievements and upgrading over the years as a result of the encouragement and assistance of their union and the Board of Education.

There were numerous discharge cases in the early years. Many of the paraprofessionals had little work experience and weren't accustomed to the discipline of work, let alone the discipline of how to comport themselves generally at work. Administrators treated paraprofessionals as they would treat professionals. They would be kind and speak cautiously when lateness or absence occurred. (There were very few problems with theft or fighting; people must instinctively know that their jobs are on the line when they engage in that.) But kindliness (as I had occasion to say a number of times in arbitration awards) may do a disservice to employees. It may not be helpful. Cautioning, counseling in kindly fashion, is a good thing to do. But if it doesn't work, then there really must be discipline, and very serious discipline including discharge if the misconduct continues. I used to award suspensions after written warnings did no good. But I learned that paras can't be replaced by substitutes the way teachers may be; it would result in the classroom staff being shorthanded. So administrators try to hold on to the paraprofessional every day as long as possible. The result is that when the kindliness fails to stop absenteeism, for example, and principals are absolutely fed up, they say, "Okay, we've had it." (There had been numerous cases where supervisors were fed up, justifiably, after absences and latenesses reached 40 percent or more of a para's work time.) The supervisors would say, in effect, "We've been nice to you, and it didn't work. You're fired!" The paras are astonished, saying, "You were so nice to me. How come you fired me so suddenly?" With perfect truth the discharged para could say, "I'm not doing anything differently than I was doing before!"

And it's all because administrators weren't sufficiently stern. They should have told the employee in writing, with a copy to the union, "You're being warned. If this continues, you face discipline including discharge." If absenteeism continues, even at a lesser rate, the warning can be repeated; and if attendance is still not satisfactory, there is nothing to do but sustain the discharge. But if administrators don't issue plainly written warnings, they get a discharge reversed by the Paraprofessional Grievance Panel. The Board of Education became very active in making this known to administrators, and it has had an effect. Employees too have learned that the Grievance Panel must sustain discharge if conduct warned against is not corrected. The result has been more warnings and fewer discharges.

The problems tend to be somewhat different for faculty in colleges and universities. Academic freedom was the issue in a case with somewhat unusual circumstances. The state college (not in New York) was innovative in its programs; the grievant was a professor who had been granted permission to teach a course he had proposed on group encounter techniques in human sexuality. (This was during the heyday of such activities.) Occasional sessions met in his home; it was permissible and not unusual for faculty members to do so. The administration knew nothing of particular interest about the course as taught by this professor until it learned the class was meeting in the nude, with the professor and his wife (the teaching assistant) also in the nude.

The course included such features as "confidence building": students would stand, one behind another, and the one in front would free-fall backwards to be caught instantly by the one in back (presumably fortifying his or her confidence in mankind or womankind). When the college heard how the course was being taught, it considered the methods highly inappropriate; it even expressed the view that townspeople in the surrounding community would be outraged if they knew what was happening at the college. The administration ordered the professor to bring the class back to the campus and conduct classes with everyone fully clothed. This was done. Simultaneously the professor filed a grievance, claiming violation of his academic freedom because he was not being permitted to teach in the way he wanted. (Part of his defense was that nudity was voluntary with all the students, and the possibility had been suggested to them at time of enrollment.)

Both the union and the administration offered expert witnesses on academic freedom. The union claimed that academic freedom was obviously being violated, saying that the administration had referred to the attitude of the community and that certainly was not the controlling factor in how the college faculty members must comport themselves. My decision as arbitrator was that academic freedom had not been violated; freedom was not necessarily absolute license, the professor's conduct exceeded normal bounds of behavior, his actions were improper. While faculty members may have been permitted to bring students into their homes for class sessions, there was no absolute right to do that regardless of how the class is conducted. The administration's disapproval of the professor's conduct was not dictated by possible community pressure. There were no sound academic reasons to permit a course whose content was purposely concealed; the grievant acknowledged he acted surreptitiously to some extent, feeling that the college president would be better off not knowing how the class was conducted because he would undoubtedly object to it. The course description in the college catalogue made no mention of features which would be considered relatively bizarre even by the most enlightened. Consequently the award sustained the college's denial that the professor had suffered a violation of academic freedom.

A somewhat unusual sex discrimination case came before me in 1974 when the *New York Times* was charged with sex discrimination by the Newspaper Guild, on behalf of four young copy boys. Violation was alleged of a clause prohibiting discrimination on account of sex. Assignments to the night shift excluded four young copy girls (whose job functions were the same as copy boys) and were restricted to males. The reason given by the *Times* was that the Times Square area was dangerous at night, particularly for females (although female reporters and other employees did work nights). The newspaper had the contractual right to make assignments solely at its discretion, but even discretionary rights cannot be utilized in violation of a contract clause. Other evidence, as well as the newspaper's acknowledgment, established that the copy girls were kept off night shift solely because they were females—not for any other reason. The *Times* felt that it was appropriate under the circumstances to restrict night work to the males, who presumably could better cope with an emergency.

My decision held that the nondiscrimination clause must apply and sustained the copy boys' grievance. If it came to a question of personal feelings (if I had a daughter, or if my niece were involved), I would be delighted if the consideration given by management kept her from being in Times Square at three o'clock in the morning. Yet as arbitrator, presented with the parties' nondiscrimination clause, I had no alternative except to enforce it. And I like to believe that I would enforce it in the same way against my niece, if she were the subject of the arbitration.

8

MEDIATING AND ARBITRATING
Benjamin H. Wolf

For almost four decades Ben Wolf mediated and arbitrated disputes in the public and private sectors. His skills were honed at the New York State Labor Relations Board from 1941 to 1950, and at the New York State Board of Mediation from 1950 to 1963. He was called upon frequently to mediate in the public sector after enactment of the Taylor Law in New York State and the New York City Collective Bargaining Law.

After leaving the New York State Board of Mediation in 1963 to become a full-time arbitrator, he arbitrated many heated disputes, including the strike of New York City caseworkers in the early 1960s, and the complex "chart" revisions involving shift schedules for the New York City police force in the mid-1980s. (The impasse panel designated by the Office of Collective Bargaining consisted of Walter Gellhorn, George Nicolau, and Ben Wolf.) Wolf served in major umpireships and many permanent panels, including airlines, publishing, public schools, textiles, universities and colleges, state mental institutions, and others. His skill as a mediator was often utilized in impasses over new contracts for state, county, and municipal employees. He was on the board of governors of the National Academy of Arbitrators in 1971–73.

Wolf was an individual with far-ranging talents—in music, painting, chess, computers, storytelling, sensitivity for people—all of which enhanced the talent he exercised as an arbitrator and mediator up until his death in May 1991.

After graduation from Cornell University Law School, I was admitted to practice in April 1933. That's the time when the banks closed, when Franklin D. Roosevelt was inaugurated for the first time. It was just impossible for a struggling lawyer to make a living. I tried, and went on until my first daughter was born in 1938. Then we had to have money so the family could eat. I took a civil service job with the New York State Department of Labor, enforcing the minimum wage law. From there I went to the New York State Labor Relations Board, which did essentially the same work as the National Labor Relations Board.

Being a labor relations examiner at the SLRB [State Labor Relations Board] meant screening cases to see whether there was a prima facie case for the board to handle. But part of the screening was to try to dispose of the cases without the necessity for board action. I was fairly adept at settling cases before they got to the board. Thinking back on it, that was probably the reason why I was not so successful as a lawyer in private practice: I was pretty good at seeing both sides of the question, and clients don't like that! They want you to be one-sided, all for them and nothing for the other side; if I would tell my clients how the other side might fare, they didn't like that. But it's certainly fitting for a neutral, and that's what I was at the State Department of Labor and the State Labor Relations Board.

Certainly that was the case at the New York State Board of Mediation, where I went in 1950. The staff there was a unique group, not only because we were both mediators and arbitrators, but because we worked together very closely. We would mull over and discuss whatever problems each of us had in our cases and put our heads together on how they had been (or could have been) solved. What varying points of view there were! Every day was a "seminar" in labor relations; it was invaluable training. As a matter of fact, it was the only training; there was no formal training for the staff. On my first day, after just one hour, someone poked his head into my office and said, "We need a mediator," and pulled me out. There I was, a full-fledged mediator after one hour! But we managed.

The Board of Mediation was one of the few agencies where staff did both mediation and arbitration. (It was different in the Federal Mediation and Conciliation Service; federal mediators were not permitted to arbitrate.) One theory in labor relations is that mediators should not arbitrate and arbitrators should not mediate, that these are two different skills and they shouldn't be mixed. This is quite true many times, but on occasion the two skills work in tandem. Sometimes mediation comes to a point where the only way out is to arbitrate, and the parties are willing to go to arbitration if they trust the arbitrator. If you are a good mediator, they trust you. Very frequently the parties would say to me, "We'll go to arbitration if you are the arbitrator."

That happened years ago in a dispute between the Newspaper Guild and a small foreign-language newspaper. (This was right after the *Brooklyn Daily Eagle* closed down because they refused, or could not pay, their employees what the Manhattan newspapers paid.) The Newspaper Guild insisted that Brooklyn papers ought to pay whatever Manhattan papers were paying because all the papers were in competition with each other. The general increase at issue was $4 per week the first year and $3 the second. After meeting with representatives of both sides, I learned very quickly that the newspaper could not pay what the Newspaper Guild was asking. I asked the employer if he could pay $3 the first year and $4 the second year. His answer was, "$3 is better than $4, and I can probably afford that. But the second year, that is definitely bad." I went to the Newspaper Guild representatives and they said, "$3 the first year, provided they pay $4 the second year. That would still be within the framework of the Manhattan formula."

So I had an agreement on the first year. But how would we settle the second year? I said to the employer, "Would you arbitrate it?" The employer said, "We would arbitrate it only if we could trust the arbitrator. If you are the arbitrator, we would submit to arbitration the second year." And when I asked the union, they said the same thing. (They figured that an arbitrator would certainly give them whatever the Manhattan formula was because that was the comparable wage in existence.)

We settled the pending strike, not only by mediation but by the parties agreeing I was to become the arbitrator. Of course, I was in a pickle; I had to arbitrate the second year. But you always left that for "tomorrow." Actually I never had to arbitrate it. By that time, a year later, the heat was off, and the union and employer agreed to some other arrangement for the second-year wage adjustment.

If I had had to arbitrate, I would have arbitrated it as any arbitrator would have: on the merits. Although in interest arbitration, there is no such thing as "the merits." You really have to find out what is proper and acceptable. In impasses (that is, disputes over what the new contract should be) there is a tandem relationship between the function of the mediator and the arbitrator. When public employment became the vogue more than 10 years later, the people who were able to function both as mediators and arbitrators (now called "med-arbs") were quite in demand.

My involvement with public-sector arbitration began with a teachers' representation issue, a few years before the Taylor Law. The United Federation of Teachers had consolidated its position with the New York City Board of Education and was looking to expand beyond New York City. They decided to try to organize New Rochelle; it seemed a likely candidate. And they did. They presented a petition to the superintendent of schools, saying that they represented the teachers and wanted to bargain for a contract. He didn't believe them, and said he would like to find out whether they really represented the teachers. In those days all teachers, department heads, all supervisors, superintendents, were all members of the National Education Association, which was a professional organization. The New Rochelle superintendent felt sure that everyone would choose the NEA [National Education Association], not the UFT [United Federation of Teachers]. He was about to propose holding an election. Fortunately he consulted the school board's attorney, Morris Lasker (later a federal judge). Lasker told him that anything he did would be wrong because it would be something conducted by the employer—and that was not the way to handle a labor-relations dispute. He suggested instead that they get someone who knew something about arbitration, mediation, elections, and the State Labor Relations Board. He suggested me, and I agreed to handle the matter.

In consulting with both groups I found that the UFT group wanted a very narrow unit of classroom teachers, whereas the NEA wanted a broad bargaining unit including the superintendent. That's what they had already. NEA did not want to negotiate a contract; all they wanted was an index. An index is a mathematical relationship between all the jobs, so that whatever salary increase the superintendent got, could mathematically be translated for all other school positions.

When I asked NEA how they would settle disputes, they said, "As we always do. By consensus." My decision required an election to determine the bargaining unit, and I enlisted the aid of the League of Women Voters of New Rochelle to act as electors. We ran the election very successfully, and the NEA won. I had also provided that if the losers wished to contest it, the following year they would have a chance to petition again and there would be another election. That's what happened the following year. The UFT petitioned again, and this time won.

A few years later the Taylor Law was passed and the Public Employment Relations Board was established to administer it. Bob Helsby (PERB's first chairman) asked me to head the first fact-finding board in a dispute between the Triborough Bridge and Tunnel Authority and its union. (The union was part of District Council 37 [DC 37], American Federation of State, County and Municipal Workers, which was headed by Victor Gotbaum. He had spearheaded a protest against the Taylor Law at Madison Square Garden, at which unions and other employee groups had protested the "unfairness" and the "one-sidedness" of the Taylor Law.) I asked Helsby if the parties themselves had selected me. He said no, he was not going to go that route, PERB was going to select the fact finders. "Well," I said, "that makes it tough. However, if that's the case, we've got to make sure that this is a blue-ribbon panel." And it was. Abe Stockman and Bob Feinberg[1] (both top-notch arbitrators and eminent lawyers) were the other appointees to the three-man fact-finding board.

Then the problem was how to get DC 37 to come to the hearing. I called Julie Topol, who was DC 37's general counsel. He protested that it was a "star chamber" proceeding, and he saw no reason why the union should participate; it was an "unfair" law, and so forth. "But," I asked, "do you think that I would be biased?" He said, "No." "What about Abe Stockman and Bob Feinberg?" Same answer. I said that "at worst, the fact-finding is only advisory. It is not a binding decision. Take a chance." He finally agreed to participate.

When the three fact finders met, we had to agree on procedure. Abe and

Bob felt we had to have a record. And since we were fact finders, we would have to find facts. That was fine with me, and I knew they would make sure we had a good record. I conceived my job on this board was to see if the dispute could be resolved. So I would interrupt the proceedings anytime it seemed as if we could work out some solution, and we went along that way. We did work out resolutions for all the problems except one. This was what kind of grievance procedure there should be.

The Triborough Bridge and Tunnel Authority was headed by Robert Moses.[2] He couldn't see why his employees wouldn't take *his* decision as the best possible one. He was willing to go along with hearing what a third party might possibly say, which would be advisory arbitration. But he would not go for binding arbitration. When the panel made its decision, we recommended binding arbitration. That portion of our report was written by Abe Stockman; I think it is a little gem. I am told that when Robert Moses read it, he said, "You know, they're right!" And he accepted it. So PERB's first fact-finding report (in a case that started with such reluctant participants) was accepted by the loser on the one issue that mattered most.

After it was over, the president of the union, Tony Mauro, called me. He said, "I didn't think that we would get a fair shake when we started. Then, when I saw how the hearing was going, I began to worry about the decision. But then, when I saw the decision, I thought management will never accept this. And then the decision came down, and they accepted it; I was delighted. You know, the Taylor Law works!" I told him it is not just the law, it is the people who administer it. (Just a personal footnote: Stockman and I were classmates at Cornell College [now University], class of 1930. Some three decades later, I wrote a note to the *Alumni News* that in the first fact-finding case under the Taylor Law the class of 1930 was represented by two board members—no other class can boast as much!)

In the early years I gave PERB as much time as I could, but restricted my work to Westchester, where I live. (By 1963 I had left the State Board of Mediation and was a full-time arbitrator.) Most of the cases involved teachers. I must have had something to do with 39 of the 41 or 42 school districts in the county—and there was only one strike that wasn't prevented.

The Taylor Law procedures were somewhat different in New York City, where the city and its unions were under the jurisdiction of the New York City Office of Collective Bargaining. In one particular case, I began as mediator at the request of Herb Haber, who headed the city's Office of Municipal Labor Relations. Caseworkers in the Social Services Department had seceded from District Council 37, set up their own organization, and struck the city. It was a pretty vicious strike. (The *New York Times* that morning had a photograph of the welfare offices, showing file cabinets toppled over and papers strewn on the floor. In a bizarre act, the strikers had poured glue into the locks of all the desks.) Herb had called me around four o'clock in the afternoon, and

I got to the city about six o'clock and met with the caseworkers. There was a membership meeting at eight o'clock that night, and they wanted me to mediate the dispute (the whole contract was involved!) in the two hours before the membership meeting. I said, "I have heard of instant arbitration (bench decisions rendered immediately after the hearing is concluded) but not instant mediation. It is kind of difficult. I'll do the best I can." Of course we could not possibly resolve all the issues in two hours.

The meeting kept going all night. The union kept asking for a mediator's proposal, which I kept resisting. A mediator's proposal, you have to understand, is something a mediator will propose at the end of the mediation—when he knows what it will take to bridge the gap, and the parties are ready for it. He voices their unspoken yearnings for some kind of compromise. So you have to be pretty careful that you have it right. I was not prepared to do that yet, even though during the course of the night I learned that the caseworkers wanted $25 a year more than the hospital-care investigators. Traditionally salaries had been the same for both jobs, and that was one reason why the caseworkers had broken away from DC 37. They thought that they were entitled to more than the health-care investigators. (This is like the firemen and the cops, and the problems when *they* want to get away from wage parity.) So $25 didn't seem like much, did it?

At one point the union proposed to the city that it sweeten the pie by a special allowance to compensate caseworkers for working in ghetto neighborhoods where it was dangerous. But so did teachers and police and other city employees. By eight o'clock in the morning the union president begged me to issue a recommendation. Finally, because we were all tired and wanted to go home, I said I would. When the union president read the recommendation I had dictated to the secretary, she complained that it was the same as the city's last offer. I told her I had no basis for recommending more. "What would it take to enable you to give us more?" she wanted to know. I said I would need the facts and figures. "You are proposing fact-finding," she said, "and we went on strike because we did not want fact-finding!" My answer was, "You made a mistake."

Subsequently she proposed fact-finding to the union governing body. They almost mobbed her, but she got it through. (I understand that some caseworkers went after her, and she escaped through a side door. One of the reporters shoved her into his car and drove off just in the nick of time.) So it was agreed that the strike would end, fact-finding would begin, and I would be the fact finder.

Collective bargaining for public employees needed a new approach because, without the right to strike, other ways of resolving disputes had to be available. Arbitration was one answer, but compulsory arbitration always had a bad name, both with employers and unions. The New York City Collective Bargaining Law was devised to overcome that. Called the "finality law," it empowers the impasse officer to make a decision (which is arbitration), but also obliges him to be a mediator as well (because he must consult the parties on each issue before he frames the result). The finality law also avoids forcing an arbitrator upon the parties. It permits the union, as well as the employer, to choose the arbitrator. It has to be a mutual choice. That takes the curse off arbitrator selection, and gives the union more confidence in the results. When the finality law began to be used in New York City, I had the honor of being chosen to arbitrate six of the first seven cases. I guess the parties had confidence in me as a "med-arb." That was my contribution, I think, to the beginning of public-employment relations in this area.

There may be differences between med-arb in the public and private sectors. But I would go at the problem pretty much the same way, whether it was the private or public sector. The techniques are the same, regardless of who the employer is and who the union is. The process has to be one in which both sides learn what their own proposal means. Sometimes parties make a proposal without fully appreciating its significance. The debate which is part of the mediation process (and the arbitration process also) begins to show them the real meaning of what they are asking. They have to learn what the other side's needs and proposals mean, and how vital those needs are to the other side. They have to begin to adjust to each other. They simply cannot be one-sided; they are both in the same boat.

One of the stories I frequently told in mediation is an old Yiddish story about immigrants who are in the hold of a ship. A storm hits, and the ship begins to rock back and forth very violently. One immigrant says (first I'll say it in Yiddish, and then translate it), "Oy, gevalt, der shif gait arunter! (The ship is going down!)" The other asks, "Ess ist dein shif? (Is it your ship?)" They didn't realize that they were part of the ship, they were on the ship. When I get a bargaining group unconcerned that the employer is going broke, they may think, "The hell with him! Let him go broke!" But they are on that ship together.

Mediation skills can be helpful in some aspects of arbitration in the private sector too. I continued to use those techniques during the years I was impartial chairman in the men's shirt industry, under collective-bargaining contracts between individual manufacturers and the Amalgamated Clothing Workers Union. The employers were not in an industry trade association but were represented by the same legal firm, Drechsler and Leff. (Drechsler was a fair-minded management attorney who had spoken in favor of the union shop during hearings on the Taft-Hartley Act. He readily conceded the union shop in order to remove friction over union security and then deal with unions from that point on.) Even without an industrywide collective-bargaining contract, there were similar contracts for all the large manufacturers (Cluett Peabody, Manhattan Shirt, Hathaway, Gant, et cetera).

In most disputes neither side was willing to risk a full open arbitration before the impartial chairman. Before they went into the arbitration, they wanted to know where they would come out. And so there was a preliminary hearing, sort of a pretrial conference, at the offices of the employer or the union, in which we discussed the issue informally. There I could get my licks in and tell them how I felt. And if they felt that was not quite right, I would listen to how they wanted to modify the decision. And if I thought they had a point, we would modify it. At any rate, we would come out with an agreement on how the decision should end. Then we would hold the arbitration. It sounds kind of terrible that it should have been handled in that particular way. But I found it worked very well simply because I was able to mediate so many of the disputes, as well as arbitrate.[3]

An example of this was a wildcat strike at Manhattan Shirt's plant in Charleston, South Carolina. (This was very early in the civil rights movement.) The black members of the bargaining unit (about 40 percent of the union were black) had walked out, in violation of the agreement's "no strike" clause. When I inquired why they had gone out and why the other union employees had not, I learned that it was because of the discharge of a black production worker who had falsified his time record and taken a day off and got paid for it. The reason black workers felt so strongly about his discharge was that a week before a white worker had falsified her production record and was only given a week's suspension. The black workers felt that this was unfair. They promised that they would stop the strike if I came down immediately to decide the case. I agreed to do so.

Before leaving for Charleston I met with the attorneys for both sides and pointed out that if the white woman had been suspended, they have to do the same for the black man. Management was very unhappy about this. We then set out for Charleston. (A jet was chartered to get there and back the same day, more quickly than was possible with regular commercial flights.)

I arrived at the hearing, which was held at the union hall. It was crowded with black members. On the periphery were a number of ministers. (I learned later that they were members of the Southern Christian Leadership Conference who had just been successful in organizing the hospitals in Charleston and were looking to see how this case would come out. I can imagine what they were thinking as they faced this northern, white, Jewish arbitrator. What was he going to do to their southern, black, Christian brethren?)

After listening to the evidence, I retired to consider my decision during the lunch break. They were all waiting anxiously when I came back and began to give my decision, off the bench. It went something like this: What the man had done was stealing, just as if he had gone into the cashier's cage and put his hand into the till. There isn't an employer who wouldn't be justified in firing him for that. And there isn't an arbitrator who wouldn't sustain such a firing. However, if the employer has a different standard, that standard has to be applied. The standard was set the week before when the white woman was put back to work. I said the same standard had to apply to the black man. So my decision was that he could only be penalized with a week's suspension. "However," I said, "the employer does not have to continue that kind of standard if it does not wish to." I turned to the manager and asked, "Do you want to change the standard?" He said, "Yes," and I said, "All right. From now on, anyone who steals will be subject to immediate firing."

Now came the question of damages. I said that there is no doubt that the employer had suffered damages, and they have a contract banning strikes. Who was going to pay for the employer's strike losses? The international union didn't know anything about the strike. Even the local union was opposed to the strike; it was only the black members who had struck. I said that it would not be the first time that members of a trade union were personally assessed damages for an illegal strike, telling them about the famous Danbury Hatters case and others. Faces in the audience were becoming tortured. When I felt that the screws had been applied sufficiently to convey the seriousness of wildcat strikes, I turned to the plant manager and said, "This is the fourth or fifth time I have come here because of a wildcat strike. You never asked for damages before. You let these people think they could walk out with impunity. If you want to change that standard, you can do it only from now on. Do you want to change the standard now?" "Yes," he replied. I told the assembled group that henceforth workers who strike in violation of the contract can be subject to damages. The wildcat strike ended that day. I am told that they never had a wildcat strike after that, down there.

9

DISPUTE RESOLUTION IN THE PUBLIC SECTOR
Arvid Anderson

A peacemaker by profession and temperament, Arvid Anderson was on the firing line for 40 years in pathbreaking government agencies. From 1948 to 1967 he was executive secretary and commissioner of the Wisconsin Employment Relations Board. His tenure spanned a turbulent period in labor relations.

In 1967 he was selected as director of the newly established New York City Office of Collective Bargaining and chairman of its tripartite board, governing labor relations under a new and comprehensive collective-bargaining statute for public employees. Profound changes, including final and binding interest arbitration for municipal employees, were implemented during the 20-year period of Anderson's leadership. He helped resolve myriad labor problems in the turmoil of the city's near-bankruptcy and a succession of long-simmering labor crises. "Though he has spent most of his professional life in a balancing act as the impartial middle man in heated labor-management confrontations, the 60-year-old son of a carpenter has never fallen from the scaffolding," was how he was described by a New York Times *reporter in 1982.[1]*

His federal appointments included membership on the Foreign Service Grievance Board (1977–80) and the Pay Advisory Committee of the Council on Wage and Price Stability (1978–80). He was chairman of the fact-finding panel in 1981 for the contract renewal of the U.S. Postal Service and the Mail Handlers Union, and he has chaired several presidential emergency boards under the Railway Labor Act in airline and railroad impasses.

Since retiring from the Office of Collective Bargaining in 1987, he has been a very active arbitrator on the national scene in both the private and public sectors, including airlines, transit, schools, newspapers, and major league sports.[2]

In 1986 the American Arbitration Association awarded its Distinguished Service Award for Arbitration of Labor Management Disputes to Anderson. In 1987–88 he served as president of the National Academy of Arbitrators.

One of the things that you can say about this kind of career, one does not get bored. The basic process is very exciting and interesting. There seems to be a willingness of the parties, finally, to look at the idea that maybe they can use reason rather than muscle, that maybe there is something to the notion that the power of persuasion can be as effective as the persuasion of power. Seeing those concepts fulfilled, in grievance and interest arbitration and in mediation, brings enormous satisfaction.

Over the years interest arbitration has been growing, maybe not as fast as I might like. We've had it in New York for about 12 years. About 20 states now have interest arbitration or have had. (A few were declared unconstitutional. I know of no jurisdiction where an arbitration statute has been repealed, with the possible exception of Massachusetts. That was an unusual circumstance; a repealer of the arbitration proviso was attached to enactment of an unrelated proposition.) The strike has virtually disappeared wherever interest arbitration has been employed. New laws are just starting in Ohio and Illinois. The Ohio law provides interest arbitration for a substantial number of essential employees, involving many more than police and fire fighters. The Illinois law doesn't have full-scale interest arbitration, but it is permissible in some circumstances.

So I see the likelihood of interest arbitration expanding. Not because arbitrators have any special wisdom, superior to all other mortals. They don't. But if they know something about the collective-bargaining process, they can be part of the system of adjudication. Reason can be substituted for trial by combat. Just as the judicial system solves a lot of our problems, a less formal system can solve some problems in labor relations.

If one accepts collective bargaining, it is premised that you have either the right to strike or interest arbitration. The legislatures are generally unwilling to grant public employees the right to strike. The interest-arbitration process helps parties make up their minds in collective bargaining because if they don't decide their dispute, somebody else will decide it for them.

In this city we've had effective interest arbitration, although there has not been tremendous reliance on the process. We've had interest arbitration to resolve the question of whether policemen should be paid more than firemen. We've had interest arbitration to determine the working conditions and pay of nurses, and sanitation workers, and medical interns and residents. We had a major interest and grievance arbitration combined, involving the question of wage deferrals, which could have easily led to a strike. In the last 12 or so years there have been about 50 interest-arbitration cases. They don't receive the same visibility as a strike because the dispute gets settled.

I don't know that interest arbitration will always work. You can't guarantee that there will never be a strike in a free society. (Poland is demonstrating you can't even guarantee that in a closed society.) Is interest arbitration something the parties are willing to live with? There has been some unhappiness from time to time, but consider the alternatives. Basically the answer is yes. If it were no, the laws would be repealed, or there would be no calls for new legislation extending interest arbitration. Is there a perfect answer in resolving impasses? No. Is the strike the perfect answer? No.

In my view, collective bargaining in an imperfect society is the best device now of matching employers' needs and employees' desires with some system of fairness. I submit that collective bargaining and interest arbitration are consistent with our democratic institutions. With interest arbitration available as the final step, the parties are induced to use collective bargaining to solve their problems short of arbitration. If they were too happy with arbitration and thought it was the "magic bullet," there could be an overwhelming demand for interest arbitration. That would chill the bargaining process. On balance, interest arbitration hasn't had that result.

When I was a 15-year-old living in Hammond, Indiana (which is really South Chicago), that was only a streetcar ride away from the scene of the Little Steel strikes, which were occurring against the Republic Steel Corporation in Chicago and also against Inland and Youngstown Corporations in East Chicago and Indiana Harbor. I had taken a streetcar ride because there was mass picketing and all kinds of excitement both the day before and the day after May 30, 1937.

You will recall from labor history the tragic death of 10 strikers who had been shot, 7 in the back and 3 in the side, by the Chicago police. (I can still see Phil Murray, then the head of the Steel Workers Organizing Committee, later to be head of the CIO, along with then Bishop Shiel of Chicago, saying that 10 men would picket that plant forever. Thereafter, annual memorial services were held in memory of the strikers.) That day, which became known as the Memorial Day Massacre, was a most traumatic event, which had a lot to do with the ultimate enactment of the full-scale Wagner Act. And it persuaded me that there must be a better way to settle labor disputes than with confrontation and muscle and guns.

Later I studied labor economics at the University of Wisconsin and also received my law degree there. The professors I studied with principally were Edwin Witte and Selig Perlman in the economics department, Nathan Feinsinger in the law school. Selig Perlman, a direct disciple of John R. Commons, was a preeminent labor historian. Edwin Witte, an outstanding academic, also taught by his example as a mediator and dispute settler.

The other great influence in my education was Professor Feinsinger. He too was an outstanding academic, but preeminently an excellent mediator and arbitrator. He had played a very prominent role both in the development of the Wisconsin Employment Peace Act and the Wisconsin Labor Relations Act (which was a Little Wagner Act), and was the Wisconsin Employment Relations Board's first general counsel in 1937. In World War II he was an official with the National War Labor Board, and later was with the Wage

Stabilization Board. He played a very major role in national dispute settlement involving steel, airlines, railroads, and shipping.[3]

Feinsinger, along with Ed Witte and others, conducted an interdisciplinary seminar. He would bring in guest lecturers from the psychology and economics departments, from the labor movement and from industry, and some mediators (including the late sainted Will Davis of New York State).[4] All of these experiences stimulated my desire for a career in labor relations.

There was a progressive tradition in Wisconsin. The state had been a leader in workmen's compensation and unemployment compensation laws. Ed Witte had his hand in those laws. The pioneering social legislation was spurred by the LaFollettes[5] to some extent, but not solely. The Little Wagner Act was passed in Wisconsin in 1937 and amended in 1939 by the Wisconsin Employment Peace Act. (The Taft-Hartley Act of 1947 was virtually the same as the Wisconsin [Employment Peace] Act as amended in 1939. And much of the Landrum-Griffin Act of 1959 came from the Wisconsin Act.)

The 1939 Wisconsin Act was enacted because there had been a series of violent strikes, particularly affecting the agricultural industry. Efforts to organize workers at dairy plants and canneries had mobilized the farm constituency who, in cooperation with Wisconsin industrialists, persuaded the legislature to pass the [Wisconsin] Employment Peace Act. It was a law which was bitterly denounced by organized labor. Nevertheless, it was very broad in scope and included mediation activities.

When I completed law school, I was offered an opportunity to be the executive secretary of the Wisconsin Employment Relations Board, which meant that I was the professional staff of the agency. Feinsinger and Witte encouraged me to do it. It offered the opportunity to learn mediation and collective bargaining firsthand. I primarily devoted myself to labor mediation at the agency and also served as trial examiner in drafting findings of fact and conclusions of law. And since the law permitted the parties to request the agency's officers as grievance arbitrators, that's how I started my arbitration career.

I was twenty-six, quite young, when I went to work for the agency in 1948. And I stayed there (except for a brief military stint in the Korean War) for about nineteen and a half years, until October of 1967.

In 1959 the Wisconsin [Employment Peace] Act was amended to give public employees the right to bargain collectively, a declaration that Wisconsin was the first state to make. There was no administrative mechanism attached to the right, but the encouragement speeded labor organization among teachers, policemen, firemen, and municipal employees, particularly at the blue-collar level.

City and county hospitals became highly organized and lobbied for a collective-negotiations bill. One was enacted in 1962 and subsequently amended in 1967 (and then again in 1972) to cover state employees. It provided fact-finding and the possibility of mediation and grievance arbitration. Wisconsin was the front-runner among the states in the enactment of public sector collective-bargaining laws. (We had about five years' experience with fact-finding under Wisconsin law by 1967 when I came to New York City as chairman of the Office of Collective Bargaining.)

Meanwhile, there was a great deal of activity both in the private and in the public sector. The Kohler strike was a bitter struggle between the United Automobile Workers and the owners of the company, a family of self-made industrialists who were paternalists in outlook and totally disavowed the notion of collective bargaining. The UAW essentially lost that strike, but didn't lose representation rights.

Among other tough strikes was J.I. Case, a very large farm machinery manufacturer. Again the UAW was up against a strong-willed company and there was violence on the picket line. The company complained that sheriff's deputies were not protecting nonstrikers as they crossed the picket line, and demanded the National Guard be called in. Governor Gaylord Nelson asked our agency to see if that was called for or whether some mediation could be used. The sheriff finally called on the city of Racine for police help in opening the picket lines. It was a tough situation, but preferable to calling in the National Guard.

The governor then accepted our recommendation for a special fact-finding panel and named a distinguished panel of labor experts, chaired by Nate Feinsinger, with Reynold Seitz of Marquette Law School and Edwin Young, chancellor of the University of Wisconsin. The governor asked the panel whether they had a plan for ending the strike. Feinsinger looked at the governor (who had been in his classes at the university) and said, "No, but I'm going to act like I do." That phrase stuck with me, in terms of the notion that mediators may not have a single correct solution but have to exude confidence that—with some persistence, persuasion, imagination, and sensitivity to the parties' needs—solutions can be found in difficult disputes. In this very difficult strike the question of union security was involved; eventually a form of modified union shop was negotiated.

When the city of Milwaukee negotiated its first collective-bargaining contract with the American Federation of State, County and Municipal Employees, I assisted as one of the mediators. The agreement came after a 39-hour continuous session. The process was new to public and union representatives. They both knew how to be good advocates, but they weren't adept with compromise. Of course our own experience was still limited in public sector negotiations.

One difficulty was finding out who was calling the shots for the employer. The city's legislative body had a great deal of authority, unlike most municipalities. Yet much of the negotiation was being carried on by the city attorney's office and the mayor's press secretary. So there was a question of who was in charge. That experience not only educated us but emphasized the problem in the public sector of finding out who the decision makers are and getting them to the bargaining table.

The contract involved nonuniformed employees, not police or firemen, and not teachers. But the possibility of a strike by white-collar people, and by employees who maintain the water supply, sewers, and hospitals, was a matter of great concern. Happily the dispute was resolved peacefully. We made some contributions to that, as mediators, and sensible leadership came to the fore in the city council and the union. But negotiations for that first contract were very difficult.

The high visibility of that dispute and a number of others affecting public employees in Wisconsin, and all the activity under Wisconsin's pioneering statute, were elements in the invitation for me to go to New York City in 1967 when the New York City Collective Bargaining Law and the New York State Taylor Law were being enacted. Whether to accept the invitation to head the Office of Collective Bargaining in New York City[6] was a very difficult decision because I was thoroughly happy in Wisconsin. My family was happy there. But making a contribution to the collective-bargaining process in New York offered an exciting challenge because I believed that if collective bargaining could be made to work in New York City in the public sector, it could surely be made to work anywhere in the country.

At that time New York City had already had a strike by welfare workers in 1965 and had just survived the strike by transit workers in 1966. Subsequently there were strikes by teachers, welfare workers, marine engineers, and more strikes by teachers. There were some real real problems; it was a time of great unrest.

I was very hesitant about coming to New York because I figured that there were a lot of New Yorkers with a great deal of experience; many, I felt, were considerably more intelligent than myself. If there was a reason why they weren't asked to do this, or weren't willing to do it, why should a country boy from Wisconsin do it? But I was told that I could have as public members on the tripartite board such eminent neutrals as Saul Wallen and Eric Schmertz, arbitrators in whose ability and integrity I had total confidence. And I was able to choose two key deputies[7] whom I also knew well: Philip Feldblum was the general counsel of the New York State Labor Relations Board and one of the ablest labor lawyers I've ever known, and Eva Robins[8] was a top-notch mediator with the New York State Board of Mediation.

The exciting part of the Office of Collective Bargaining was that we were engaged in something new. We had the cooperation of the parties; the agency wouldn't be running the whole show. The parties really had an investment in the dispute-settlement process and wanted to make it work. They felt they knew enough about collective bargaining and could do a great deal on their own. That's proved to be the case, although there was an awful lot for neutrals to do.

One consideration in fashioning the New York City Collective Bargaining Law was that if the city didn't do something on its own, the state would. Whatever suspicions the city's labor-management community may have had about each other, they were convinced that whatever came down from Albany [the state capital] would be less to their liking than a structure devised by themselves. Over a long period of time a distinguished advisory committee worked in very close cooperation with the Corporation Counsel's office and the Municipal Labor Committee. (The advisory committee[9] was headed by arbitrators Saul Wallen and Peter Seitz, Harvard law professor Vern Countryman, Father Carey of Xavier Institute, and aided by Jesse Simons, who was representing the American Arbitration Association.) The Municipal Labor Committee is a unique voluntary association, headed by Victor Gotbaum of District Council 37, Barry Feinstein of the Teamsters, representatives of the Communications Workers of America, and of unions representing uniformed forces in police, fire, corrections, and sanitation.

The gentleman who was committed to really doing something about a law on collective bargaining for city employees was Mayor John Lindsay. Because he came into office on the threshold of the transit strike; that was his initiation as mayor. He was convinced that some mechanism ought to be adopted to deal with these kinds of problems. Therefore he was supportive of a city law, although he didn't have any great control over the Metropolitan Transit Authority, anymore than the present mayor does. Perhaps the mayor then had a little less.

One of the early challenges to resolving impasses was that there was no mechanism for arbitration. That was highlighted in the sanitation strike (which occurred about six weeks after I came to OCB). The sanitation workers went out in a classical demand: they wanted the same settlement that had been negotiated with the police and firefighters. As with so many public employees, the concern was not whether what had been offered to them was fair and reasonable, but "How does it compare with what the next guy is getting?" If the next guy is going to do any better, then whatever they've been offered is no good. This was certainly true here. John DeLury, the leader of the sanitation workers' union [Uniformed Sanitationmen's Association, International Brotherhood of Teamsters], didn't want a strike but wound up with one, a real tough one. And we, at OCB, were in the middle of it.

It quickly became apparent to us (I was aided in that mediation effort by Dean Walter Eisenberg of Hunter College) that what was at stake was not the difference between $400 per year per employee and $425 ($400 being the city's offer to sanitation employees, and $425 being what the city had granted to police and fire employees). The total dollar-cost difference between the parties was something like $250,000. We had narrowed the dispute further to less than 1¢ an hour on an annual basis (in terms of what the difference between them would cost), by deferring certain effective dates of the settlement. The matter could have been settled at virtually no greater cost to the city than its own offer.

But a settlement was nowhere to be had because the dispute had escalated into a symbol between Mayor John Lindsay and Governor Nelson Rockefeller to demonstrate who could be the most effective in dealing with strikes by public employees. There had been a welfare strike, a transit strike, a teachers' strike, and "it was time to show these fellows," so to speak. The fact that the Republican nomination for president was coming up later in the year was apparently not forgotten by the mayor and governor. Rockefeller was resisting the calls to bring in the National Guard. Harry Van Arsdale, president of the Central Labor Council, and Joe Trerotola, head of the Teamsters Joint Council, both declared that not a truck would roll in the city if the National Guard were called. So it was a very serious time.

The legislature was called into session, and the governor was persuaded to form a special fact-finding panel to make recommendations. The panel recommended $425 per year per employee, which would have cost about $400 because of deferred effective dates. The city rejected the panel's recommendations.

But what was ultimately significant was that the governor then convened a second session (of what he called the Taylor Commission) to make recommendations for amendments to the New York City law. The report produced a legislative mandate that the city come up with a plan for finality. The mayor submitted a report. Then we eventually fashioned, with the help of the unions and the city, the present scheme of interest arbitration which has been the law since 1972.

The sanitation strike was ultimately settled by voluntary arbitration. Vincent McDonnell[10] served as the arbitrator, and the figure $425 was confirmed by his award.

The long-range significance was the development of interest arbitration in the city and the state as a reasonable alternative for the right to strike, strikes being prohibited in the Taylor Law. Interest arbitration now applies throughout the state for police and firefighters, an event unlikely if the city of New York had not adopted interest arbitration for its municipal labor force.

Enactment of the city law gave considerable emphasis to grievance arbitration also. For a long period of time there was a notion that government could not be held accountable for its labor contracts. (A breakthrough came around 1967 in a Wisconsin case involving the city of Rhinelander, which challenged an arbitration award reinstating an employee who had been terminated. The Wisconsin Supreme Court found no reason why the political subdivision could not be held accountable for a labor contract in the same way that it could be held accountable in arbitration for performance of construction contracts and disputes arising thereunder.) We still had some of that in New York City, until specific provisions encouraging grievance arbitration were spelled out in city statutes. OCB developed rules with the parties for grievance arbitration, and for resolving disputes on arbitrability, and for panels of arbitrators. That was a signal contribution to arbitration.

Interest arbitration often may result in a "laying on of hands" for what the parties' bargaining has already done. In med-arb there is an opportunity to combine the skills of mediation and arbitration. The med-arb role tends to slide into adjustments and compromises.

Emanuel Stein, about 1980.

Walter Gellhorn (center) with Marshall Breger, chairman of the Administrative Conference of the United States, and Antonin Scalia, associate justice of the Supreme Court and former ACUS chairman, at a reception on 14 June 1988 honoring Gellhorn's 20 years of service as an ACUS councillor.

President John F. Kennedy signing Executive Order 10988 establishing the first system of labor relations for federal employee unions. Government officials and labor-management representatives at the signing included Secretary of Labor Arthur Goldberg and Postmaster General Edward Day. Ida Klaus (left) was the consultant to the task force of cabinet members whose recommendations led to the executive order in January 1962.

Arthur Stark in September 1956, en route by subway to chair a grievance hearing under the collective bargaining contract between the New York City Transit Authority and unions representing subway and bus employees. Stark was named by Secretary of Labor James P. Mitchell as the first impartial adviser on grievances under the contract.

Israel Ben Scheiber, about 1965.

Milton Friedman, Arvid Anderson, and Daniel G. Collins in April 1982, when the *New York Times* identified them as "3 Men Who Hold Keys to a Transit Settlement." Designated by the state legislature to arbitrate the impasse between the New York City Transit Authority and the city's 35,000 subway and bus employees, they succeeded in resolving the issues and averting a strike. *Don Hogan Charles/NYT Pictures*

Benjamin Wolf (second from left) with fellow board members Abram Stockman and I. Robert Feinberg listening to an unidentified witness at a hearing in 1963 involving the Triborough Bridge and Tunnel Authority and the American Federation of State, County, and Municipal Employees, in the first fact-finding board established under the New York State Taylor Law.

Irving Halevy, in private capacity as chairman of the Mark Foundation, a charitable trust, presenting Mount Sinai Medical Center in New York City with the foundation's donation for a pharmacological research laboratory, 1970.
Mike Zwerling

Eric J. Schmertz in Harlem for a hands-on observation of firefighting when he was impartial chairman for the New York City Fire Department and the firefighter unions, 1970. *NYT Pictures*

Thomas G. S. Christensen, about 1960. *Fabian Bachrach*

George Nicolau, 1988 recipient of the American Arbitration Association Distinguished Service Award for Arbitration of Labor-Management Disputes, holding the crystal owl present- ed to honorees. *Courtesy of American Arbitration Association*

Robert Coulson, American Arbitration Association president, briefing reporters in 1989 on the $833.2 million award in the commercial arbitration under AAA auspices that concluded the six-year software dispute between IBM and Fujitsu. *Courtesy of Arbitration Times*

Irving Bernstein,
about 1993

10

UNDERSTANDING BOTH SIDES
Irving Halevy

Irving Halevy was professor of industrial relations at Fairleigh Dickinson University in Teaneck, New Jersey, from 1949 until he retired from the faculty 36 years later. The faculty and students voted him the University Distinguished Service Award in 1976; he was the only faculty member ever selected for this high honor. His colleagues and students relied on his capacity for understanding and reconciling opposing views, electing him to the presidency of the University Council and then the presidency of the University Senate. (The council consists of administration and faculty representatives; the senate comprises representatives from students, staff, faculty, and administration.)

Since the early 1950s he has arbitrated widely in the private and public sectors, frequently in interest arbitrations involving police and firefighters in New Jersey and in Florida (where he now resides).

Halevy studied at Columbia University, earning a B.S. in industrial engineering and an M.A. in industrial relations.

What I'm about to say is in terms of my orientation towards arbitration and general philosophy of cooperation instead of conflict in the work place. My father, I think, had the greatest influence on me, when I begin to think back on my early life. He was born in Russia, and the anti-Czarist movement there influenced his attitudes to injustices occurring in the old country. When he came to New York City in 1907, he went to Cooper Union.[1] He discovered after a while that it was difficult to get a job, especially if you didn't speak English with the appropriate accent. He experienced prejudice, and his feeling of outrage was conveyed to my brother and me.

My father bought a chicken farm in Toms River, New Jersey. He was not really a farmer but thought that being close to the land made a contribution to the purposes of society. It would be the best place to raise his children,

115

he felt, and the best place to find some fulfillment for himself. It didn't turn out too well. We were living in a community which he felt was anti-Semitic, and my father and mother felt ostracized. He experienced again that feeling of being an outsider, and the environment was not conducive to a happy, gratifying existence. In 1931 our house was burned down, and my mother and father decided to leave Toms River. (We lived six miles away from where the Ku Klux Klan allegedly had its eastern headquarters. While it was never proved that the Ku Klux Klan burned down our house, that was the impression left with us.) Unfortunately we had a parting of the ways ourselves. I had a dog which my folks decided to give away, very much against my wishes. When they did it anyway, I left home.

In Toms River I used to caddy during the summer at Cranmoor Manor Golf Course. There I met the vice principal of DeWitt Clinton High School situated in the Bronx. He had said to me, "If you ever come to New York City, you must attend our high school."[2]

At that time I thought like a "rube": Toms River has *a* high school, New York must have *a* high school. The high school that I thought one went to in New York was DeWitt Clinton! So I set out for DeWitt Clinton. I was 15 at the time I left home in 1931. I had no money, I had no job, I had no ideas as to what I wanted to do. I only knew that I was going to strike out for myself, somehow or other. The entire world seemed to be in that position, so I didn't feel completely an outcast. This was at the beginning of the Great Depression.

I went to the Bronx and saw a little sign, "Boy Wanted," in the window of a grocery store. I walked in and got the job for $6 a week, working from six in the morning to ten at night, six days a week. I needed a half-day off during the week in order to go to school, but the owner of the grocery store and I did not get along and had a parting of the ways. (This was around May 1932. I was living in the Bronx, in a very small room for which I paid $2 a month.)

Then I heard there were jobs in Coney Island, at a place called Feldman's Restaurant, out in Brooklyn at the other end of New York. So I went out there. About 100 men were standing on line. I got on line, too; this was about five o'clock in the morning. The door to the building was opened around eight o'clock, and the first four people on the line were selected. Everybody else was told to leave. I walked from the restaurant to some tennis courts I had noticed from the Brighton Beach El (the elevated subway I rode to the restaurant). An elderly gentleman was brushing the tennis courts, and I walked onto the courts, picked up a rake and began to work. Some four or five hours later, the gentleman who owned the courts (a Mr. Reynolds) walked up to me and asked if I wanted a job. He asked where I lived. I told him I had no place to live. He said, "What are your plans?" I said that I didn't have any plans. He said, "Why don't you come and live with me and my wife?" So for the next couple of years I lived with the Reynoldses, taking care of the tennis courts, and resumed my education. I finished high school at DeWitt Clinton High School (going back and forth everyday by subway, between Brooklyn and the Bronx).

During the winter I had a job in a radio factory. We worked for 30¢ an hour, for as many hours as we possibly could. I would start at about four o'clock in the afternoon; I'd wind up at two or three o'clock in the morning. (There was no such thing as premium overtime pay; 30¢ was the rate for every hour.) The conditions were about as bad as they possibly could be. We attempted to organize the place, and when the employer found out, he discharged us. This was my first labor-management experience. (It was years before the National Labor Relations Act, and also before Section 7A of the National Industrial Recovery Act [NIRA], which Franklin Delano Roosevelt put through in 1933, legalizing unionization. Two years later the Supreme Court declared NIRA unconstitutional.) When we were discharged, we had no place to go. And so we just took our discharges and went along.

By 1933 the New Deal (as the FDR years were known) had started various social developments and different kinds of programs. One was the National Youth Administration, where I went to register for employment. I was given a job at WNYC (New York City's municipally operated radio station), as a general helper. I was one of the young amateurs writing programs and performing in them. (For example, "Return of the Founders" was a program with biographical sketches of New Yorkers like Peter Stuyvesant and Peter Cooper. We would write biographies in dramatic form and then take the parts ourselves; we had no professional actors. If somebody was missing, others would have two parts or more.)

During this period I thought that I wanted to become a playwright, and decided perhaps I ought to get some experience. So I shipped out to sea. I worked for $30 a month, "four hours on, four hours off," as an ordinary seaman. We lived in fo'c'sles below deck, under pretty bad conditions. I wrote my first play, called *Glory Hold*, about conditions of seamen and attempted to get it produced. But I was never successful. (I was influenced by the kind of socially conscious, realistic plays written by Eugene O'Neill, Clifford Odets, Maxwell Anderson, Irwin Shaw.) I became very active in the newly formed National Maritime Union, which was trying to replace the International Longshoremen's Association (a union considered relatively corrupt). I did travel around the world as a seaman, and pretty much began to understand that what was happening in the United States was comparatively good compared to what was happening throughout the world in places I saw firsthand, particularly South America, Central America, parts of southern Europe. We weren't alone in our problems living through the Depression.

Another influence at the time was Franklin Delano Roosevelt. He was a great hero of mine. It seemed to me that he represented the real political conscience of the American people, and I supported the ideas that he was expressing.

When I returned from maritime service, around 1937, I met a fellow by the name of Herman Brickman; he was the impartial chairman in the laundry industry. The laundries were commercial power laundries, both linen supply and family laundry; it was a very big industry in New York at the time [home washing machines not yet being available]. (Brickman was also an ad hoc arbitrator, but most of his activity was as the impartial chairman.) He would handle two or three arbitration cases a day. The newly organized laundries had lots and lots of problems. I would sit in with Brickman on these cases and became familiar with the arbitration process. Eventually I became sort of a clerk for him. He would say to me, "Here's my decision and here are the facts. You write it up." Then he would edit it and issue his award.

Those were the earliest influences for me towards arbitration: questions of social conscience; my involvement in trying to organize fellow workers; and (thirdly), the business of arbitration itself, the arbitration process which I was able to watch. As a young man, I saw the world as black and white, with labor always right and noble, management always wrong, and capital itself as evil. To a large extent that sort of represented things that were said politically in those years and the way that people were raised and developed during the Depression.

But I wasn't thinking about becoming an arbitrator myself. I had a number of different jobs, tried out a few things, and none were very successful. None lasted very long. I really wanted to be a writer, but it wasn't easy to get established as a writer and raise a family. (I was married in 1940 and have four children; now I have eight grandchildren. My wife was still a student at Hunter College when we got married.) I did a half-hour program on radio station WOV, called "Labor and Management on Parade," where labor-management cases were arbitrated on the air. Herman Brickman was the arbitrator. The program, which I originated, was much like the present-day television program, "People's Court," where a judge decides cases. But my radio program didn't turn out to be as successful.

In the early part of 1943 I was drafted. I was very convinced that World War II was a proper war; it had my complete enthusiastic support. My last tour of duty, in the latter part of 1946, was to return Germans from China back to Germany. These were individuals, many being held for trial as war criminals, who had escaped from Germany after Germany lost the war and managed to reach the Far East.

When my military service was over, I went to see Brickman. He suggested that I take a job with a company as a personnel director. And I did, with Ever-Ready Label Corporation in New Jersey; it was one of the largest label-printing concerns in the country at that time. Eventually I was made a vice president. My own relationships with the employees were very good. But the general attitude of the union was very antagonistic to the employer. (The union was the United Office and Professional Workers, a CIO affiliate; later it became District 65 of the Retail, Wholesale, and Department Store Union.) The employer was attempting in every way to remedy relationships with the newly organized employees, but was very unsuccessful.

I began to see the other side of the labor situation, began to see that all management weren't necessarily devils and that all workers weren't necessarily saints. And while there were social moves and directions at work in each of these situations, I came to realize that individuals had to be judged individually to a large extent, and situations had to be handled individually. I became a much more balanced individual in that sense. I began to see the possibility of working out methods that perhaps would be suitable to both employees and employers. And I began to think in terms of accommodations that would be helpful in identifying the interest of the employee with the interest of the employer, and having mutual purposes served as a result of these techniques.

I was very impressed with the ideas of George Shultz, whom I heard one day at a Columbia University symposium. (I had earned a B.S. in industrial engineering and M.A. in industrial relations at Columbia University.) Professor Shultz was in the industrial engineering department at Massachusetts Institute of Technology and subsequently became professor of economics at the University of Chicago. (He is currently secretary of state in President Reagan's administration.) Shultz was very much interested in developing means to reduce conflict in the workplace and have employees exert some influence. I saw this democratic industrial approach as a way to correct abuses caused on the one hand by management's insistence on exercising its prerogatives, while the unions were flexing their muscles to achieve their goals, mainly through force of power.

In the 1950s I was introduced to the idea of so-called shared-productivity plans. (The plans were known by the names of their founders, as Scanlon, or by the names of companies which adopted such plans, as Nunn Bush or Armour.) The goal was to share the benefits of increased production with the workers and develop some mutuality of interest.

We introduced the Scanlon Plan in Ever-Ready Label Corporation. To some extent this shared-productivity idea was successful, but at the same time it did not handle all of the differences that exist between individuals. There naturally are antagonisms which arise in a variety of ways, no matter where the arena happens to be. It can happen in a family, and it can happen in a plant.

My own life experiences have made me acutely aware of such antagonisms, and they remain in my consciousness. More than 30 years ago I, along with two lawyers, was representing the New Jersey Laundry Association in negotiations with three unions. We were in the eleventh hour of talks with the Teamsters Union, which was demanding an additional $1 per day in base wage rates, as well as increased commissions. This was a period when most power laundries were in serious straits because of the advent of household washing machines and dryers. Small nonunion laundries were springing up; their coin-operated washers and dryers attracted customers who formerly had used commercial laundries. The decline in use of commercial laundries was so extensive that the demands of the union went beyond the "ability to pay" of most New Jersey Laundry Association members.

Our committee was given an ultimatum: "Either meet the union demands or prepare for a strike." The lawyers and I huddled in our room. It was after midnight and the contract had expired. We talked about whether we should contact the owners at this hour so that they could prepare to shut down their boilers. We knew that the industry couldn't take a strike, and it couldn't pay the increase demanded by the union. I said to my associates, "Let me try to talk to the union committee once more. What have we got to lose?" And they agreed, although they didn't think it would do much good.

I knocked on the door outside the room where the union committee was meeting. One of the officers came to the door and asked what I wanted. I told him I would like to speak with the head of the committee. He came to the door and asked if I was there to make an offer. I said I didn't have an offer, but wondered if he would extend me the courtesy of allowing me to speak to his committee. He said, "You can talk to them, but you're wasting your time and ours unless you meet our demand." I told him that "I feel I've got to make one more effort before we let the situation get to a strike." He called the committee to order and invited me to speak up.

There must have been 30 or more men on the union committee. I said something like this: "Fellows, I don't want you to think that just because I'm here that means I can meet your demands. I just thought that I ought to tell you something that's on my mind and leave it up to you.

"We all grew up in the Depression. I know a kid who left home at the age of 15. He got a job for $6 a week, working in a grocery store 7 days a week and 12 hours a day, with a half-day off to go to continuation school. One day he got a better job for $10 a week and room and board, and so he went to live with strangers.

"Well, he got homesick, and he wrote his father a postal card, letting him know where he was staying. His father appeared one day at the place where the kid was living. Father and son had not seen each other for a long time. They made small talk with the lady of the house, and the father invited the boy to go for a walk with him. They sat down on a park bench, and the boy was about to tell his father how miserable he felt and how much he needed to go home—when he looked down and noticed how beat-up his father's shoes were, with holes in them. He realized then that he couldn't go home, that his parents couldn't take care of him, but that he would have to try to send money home to his parents instead.

"Well (I concluded to the union committee), this industry has holes in its shoes. You route salesmen are going to have to go out and make more money through your commissions and increase the business, and help support the laundries which helped you out until now. That's all I want to say."

I left the room and went back to my committee. Pretty soon there was a knock on the door, and we were asked to join the union committee. The head of the union said, "We're withdrawing our demand for an increase this year because we recognize this industry has holes in its shoes. We're going to do our best so we can come back next year and get what we think you'll be able to afford."

Around that time, 1951 I think, I was offered a position at Fairleigh Dickinson University in New Jersey as assistant professor of industrial relations (I had been teaching some evening classes), and I decided to take it. I thought I would like to teach and write and arbitrate; those were the things that interested me. I found that I was acceptable for the American Arbitration Association's panel of labor arbitrators as a result of some unions and employers endorsing me as someone they might use in arbitration. Although I didn't do very much arbitration at the beginning, it developed. As time went on, I became more knowledgeable, I became more experienced and became more acceptable.

When the New Jersey collective-bargaining law for public employees was amended to provide interest arbitration for police and firemen, I was frequently designated as mediator and arbitrator in such impasses. One was personally memorable. In 1974 I was called upon to arbitrate a dispute between the Jersey City Policemen's Benevolent Association [PBA] and Jersey City. (I was scheduled for open heart surgery at Cleveland Clinic the following day.) After successfully mediating the dispute, following a full day of discussions, I adjourned the proceedings.

On the front steps of City Hall, one of the PBA committee members stopped me and thanked me for my efforts. He asked if I had made any arrangements for blood for the heart operation; the police maintained a blood bank, he said, and would be happy to donate their blood. I told the officer that all the necessary arrangements had already been made and thanked him for their consideration. That evening I suffered a heart attack and was taken by police ambulance from my home in New York City to St. Luke's Hospital. Among the questions asked was whether I had made arrangements for blood. I replied that I had, at Cleveland Clinic in Ohio—but come to think of it, I had been in Jersey City that day and the police had offered blood from their blood bank. The operation took place that night. Approximately a month later I received a note from the Jersey City PBA, asking how it felt to have policemen's blood flowing through my veins.

11

ROLES FOR NEUTRALS
Eric J. Schmertz

An arbitrator and mediator for more than 30 years, Professor Schmertz is a public member of the New York State Public Employment Relations Board since 1991, and on the board of directors of the American Arbitration Association since 1987. He was appointed to three presidential emergency boards under the Railway Labor Act, and arbitrates nationally in both the public and private sectors. Permanent designations include impartial chairman for New York Bus Service and the Transport Workers Union, and the rotating panel for General Electric and the International Union of Electrical Workers [IUE].

He was assistant vice president and director of labor tribunals for the American Arbitration Association from 1952 to 1960, executive director and public member of the New York State Board of Mediation from 1960 to 1968, public member of the New York City Office of Collective Bargaining from its inception in 1968 until 1980. He was commissioner of labor relations of New York City in 1990–91.

Schmertz's mediation skills and endurance are frequently enlisted for difficult contract negotiations between government units and uniformed services or other public employees. He has served as mediator and/or fact finder in crucial impasses involving public employees in New York, Pennsylvania, Illinois, and Massachusetts.

At Hofstra University in Hempstead, New York, he holds the Carlough Chair in labor law, teaching subjects in which his firsthand experience is extensive: labor law, collective bargaining, and dispute settlement. He pioneered in adding alternative dispute resolution to the law school curriculum. Formerly dean of Hofstra University School of Law (1982–89), he has been on the faculty since the inception of the law school in 1970.

People ask me how one gets into the labor arbitration field. Those interested in becoming arbitrators, young arbitrators, students, others who have an academic interest in arbitration—all ask the same question. I give them all the same answer, and I believe it seriously and strongly: that is, that one should become immersed in the fringes of the profession before actually launching an arbitration practice.

In my case that meant not only studying labor law and the arbitration process in law school, but also professional activity in labor relations. It turned out that I spent an equal amount of time, a little over two and a half years, on both sides of the bargaining table: with a labor union (the American Federation of State, County and Municipal Employees) and subsequently as a labor relations director for the Metal Textile Corporation, a subsidiary of General Cable Corporation. This was back in the 1950s.

In between the time that I worked for a labor union and for an employer in a labor relations capacity, I was at the American Arbitration Association in an administrative capacity. In those years the AAA [American Arbitration Association] administrators were known as tribunal clerks; they're now called tribunal administrators. I rose through the ranks in AAA to assistant vice president for labor case administration throughout the United States. Though I was not yet dealing substantively with arbitration as an arbitrator, I was on the fringes of that.

When I decided that I wanted to become an arbitrator (and that was in my early years at AAA), I was very mindful of one of the essential aspects of an arbitrator's career. That is, of course, his acceptability to both sides. And acceptability turns in significant measure not only on intelligence and integrity, but also on impartiality. It seemed manifest to me that one of the ways of gaining impartiality in a demonstrable sense was to spend virtually an equal amount of time on either side of the bargaining table.

Between 1960 and 1962 I was the director of the New York State Board of Mediation (and thereafter served as member of the board until 1968). That got me a little closer to the substantive practice of labor arbitration; for the first time I began to take on some arbitration cases in my official capacity, but not yet in a private capacity. When I finished as director of the Board of Mediation, I launched my own private practice of labor arbitration. One never knows (and I think this is true of all arbitrators) just what's going to happen when you announce to the labor relations community that you're a labor arbitrator.

I started by combining work as an arbitrator with what I then thought was going to be a temporary career, teaching at the university level. I was appointed assistant professor in the School of Business at Hofstra College, thereafter to become Hofstra University. Fortunately my arbitration practice became substantial, virtually immediately. I took on a full caseload and did some teaching in the School of Business in the evenings, from 1962 until 1970 when Hofstra established its law school. I became one of the founding professors in the law school and dean in 1982.

So I merged a substantial amount of labor arbitration practice with two other activities useful in arbitration: academic work and some government service. That blend, I found, is the formula for success in labor arbitration. New arbitrators who have not had the advantage of peripheral jobs on the fringe of arbitration probably have to be a little more patient about gaining acceptability.

I'm still an arbitrator. The profession has been very exciting, very rewarding for me. It affords an opportunity to use certain abilities and at the same time to enjoy a kind of autonomy that a person in a salaried position, or a representative of one side or the other, is unable to enjoy. I like the autonomy, the ability to be as free of institutional pressures as one could conceivably be. This has been the most satisfying and the most productive kind of work that I could have done.

While I arbitrate in both the private and public sector, there was a period when a lot of my activities were in the public sector. I was a public member of the Office of Collective Bargaining of the city of New York for some dozen years, from its inception in 1968. During those years I was also the impartial chairman between the city of New York and the two firefighter unions (the Uniformed Firefighters Association and the Uniformed Fire Officers Association).

Those were the years when public sector collective bargaining was in its infancy. Unions were just beginning to be recognized, and their labor relations with the city of New York institutionalized under a new collective-bargaining law in New York City. The difficulties and the growing pains, the confrontations and the patterns (the things that have to be established in the early years of a new labor-management relationship)—all these were at the forefront of the activities. A lot of things we did were unprecedented. I think we broke a lot of new ground.

At about the same time I was also serving in somewhat like an arbitrator capacity as a hearing officer, almost like a judge, in discipline cases under the civil service law for the New York City Transit Authority. Once a week I would be at the Transit Authority. At other times I would be at the Office of Collective Bargaining, as a board member, or serving as impartial chairman between the city and the firefighters' unions. On other days I was in private arbitration cases. At the same time I was doing some teaching at Hofstra law school. So I had a busy week, but one that was stimulating.

I enjoy the public sector work. In grievance arbitration it is quite comparable to the private sector. The arbitrator is called in to adjudicate a dispute arising out of the application or interpretation of the collective-bargaining agreement during the agreement's term. That's tremendously important work.

But on top of that, or in conjunction with that, the public sector involves interest arbitration. The strike is prohibited by legislation, generally speaking.

The alternative to the strike over terms and conditions of employment, not just disputes arising out of interpretation of the contract, is frequently arbitration. I have found that the most exciting part of arbitration. More demanding, more challenging, more satisfying when there is a resolution.

The almost 12 years that I spent as the impartial chairman between the city of New York and the two firefighting unions involved virtually every conceivable aspect of neutral activity. I'd handle grievance arbitration, mediation of new contract terms and conditions, and fact-finding and compulsory arbitration when the parties could not agree on new contract terms. I played all those roles, depending upon what I felt was needed at that particular time, and indeed what developed in terms of the relationship between the parties.

I did it despite the fact that then (and even now) there is a general view amongst arbitrators that one doesn't mix mediation of a dispute with arbitration of a dispute, with fact-finding, with counseling and playing an advisory role in the same dispute. I may be "a minority of one," or in a small group that thinks otherwise. I think that a good sophisticated neutral can and should be prepared to shift gears at any minute—provided the parties agree, provided the parties want it, provided the parties understand what is going on—and provided that the neutral doesn't impose a process that the parties don't understand or don't want. But if they do understand and they do want it, I think it's perfectly proper and indeed quite productive and constructive for a neutral to be prepared to start as a mediator, for example, and transform himself into a fact finder for advisory decisions, and/or transform himself into a binding arbitrator, and to combine the activities.

Is that a matter of personal preference? In part. Some neutrals find the varying roles are manageable, and some are comfortable in them, and some are not. I think that too many of my arbitrator colleagues have confined themselves just to grievance arbitration. When something comes along which requires intensive mediation four or five days around the clock, or fact-finding for new contract terms, or a different role as a neutral—they have not the time to do it or the experience or the interest. And I think that's unfortunate because it means that some of our best arbitrators, with the greatest experience and the best minds and knowledge of this field, have in a kind of myopic way confined themselves just to one phase of dispute settlement.

I discount the notion that a neutral can not play a variety of roles with the very same parties under the same collective-bargaining relationship. I think that the arbitrator can mediate as much as he can and get some things resolved by mediation. (That's what I've done in firefighting and in the nursing-home industry.) Some things are not necessarily amenable to mediation but remain in impasse. Things that can be mediated so that the parties themselves find solutions—fine! Other things ought to be decided by fact-finding or by an advisory opinion from a neutral or by binding arbitration.

The very same person who has been mediating all the disputes could transform himself into a fact finder or an arbitrator to decide the remaining issues.

That happened extensively in the public sector between the city of New York and the firefighters. I suppose I was able to do that because it was a new relationship. The parties were just getting started under a new collective-bargaining law, and they were feeling their way. But they were intelligent enough (and, I think, imaginative and venturesome enough) to respond to my suggestions as a neutral that certain things be mediated and others dealt with on an advisory basis or in arbitration or fact-finding. And to let their impartial chairman play all of these roles simultaneously or consecutively, or any way that he, with their agreement, found to be effective.

I remember being criticized about my impartial role for spending time unilaterally with the fire commissioner, talking about problems arising under the contract. Or spending time, without the city's participation, with the leadership of the unions or their executive board. And it was not totally unusual for me to counsel the fire commissioner and/or the union that certain planned moves, particularly during the city's fiscal crisis, would or would not violate the contract.

Basically, those who criticized said, "You can't act in an impartial consultative capacity with one side or the other and then serve as a neutral in the event that your suggestions are rejected and a dispute arises that you have to arbitrate as the impartial chairman." I found that was not true.

Let me give an example. In the late 1960s New York was on the brink of a firefighters' strike, and I was the mediator in contract negotiations. The basic dispute involved the question of how many firemen should be on a fire truck, manning it. The union was insisting, for a whole variety of reasons, that at least five firefighters be on a vehicle at all times. The city did not have a basic objection to five, generally speaking. But it was beginning to feel the impending fiscal crisis and wanted to be certain that if the economics turned sour and employment had to be reduced systemwide, that the number of firemen on each vehicle could be reduced. The union adamantly opposed this because it was convinced that the city would reduce manning under the guise of a fiscal crisis when there was no fiscal crisis.

That was resolved by suggesting contract language which was ultimately accepted by both sides. The language went something like this: there should be five firemen on each vehicle, except that in times of bona fide fiscal crisis the city would have the right to reduce the manning, but would not do so if the reduction constituted "a subterfuge." *Subterfuge* is a very loose and subjective word, but it saved the day and was acceptable to both sides. Of course I knew what they had in mind.

A few years later a dispute arose as to whether or not a proposed reduction of firemen on a fire truck was a subterfuge. An outside arbitrator, who had not been involved in those negotiations, would not (in my opinion) have any idea of the real meaning of subterfuge in that setting. One could run to the dictionary and hear testimony from the negotiators about what they had in mind when they agreed to the contract language.

The fact of the matter was that I was still impartial chairman. Whatever *subterfuge* means generally, I knew what it meant in this setting because I was the one who proposed that language to the parties, as the mediator at the time. I knew exactly what was agreed to and exactly what was intended. One could not get (in my opinion) a better interpretation of some critical language except from the very person who was involved in the impartial capacity during negotiations.

I could give example after example after example, where the very same neutral who can move from mediation to fact-finding or arbitration and to advisory consultation throughout the collective-bargaining relationship can play a very instructive and useful role. It can be far more effective than just bringing in an outsider each and every time a dispute arises.

I did the same type of work with the same kind of approach in the taxicab industry and in the nursing-home industry. Both were industries in chaos. Taxis are privately owned, but the industry is quasi-public because it is franchised and fares are regulated by the city and the state. The industry had never had a union before, and in 1968 I was the first impartial chairman.

Working conditions at the various garages were totally different. There was no comparability, no parity, no stability, no standards. If the impartial chairman had confined himself just to arbitrating disputes arising under the collective-bargaining agreement, he would have done his job. But I was asked, and readily agreed, to take on cases submitted by both sides which had as the objective the standardization of the taxicab industry for conditions of employment and wage rates. They would get that through arbitration by the submission of cases in which the arbitrator would look at the conditions and the standards and make binding determinations which would bring about standardization. Apparently that is not the role of the traditional arbitrator, and it's not even the role of the traditional impartial chairman. Yet I think it is more the role of the impartial chairman than it previously was.

Let me give an example from the nursing-home industry. Every time the private nursing homes in the New York metropolitan area negotiated with the Service Employees Union, they always reached an impasse. There was always a threat of a strike because the employers would never make a wage offer. The reason was because employers' income came overwhelmingly from Medicare and Medicaid reimbursements by the federal government and the state of New York primarily. The state fixed rates that the nursing homes could charge Medicaid patients, and the state would pay those rates on behalf of such patients. If the rates were high enough to cover not only costs and a reasonable profit, but also to pay a wage increase to union employees, there was no difficulty renewing the contract. But if the rates were just enough to cover costs and a little profit (or maybe no profit, depending on who was right or wrong in that debate), wages could not be increased in the new contract unless the state was prepared to raise the Medicaid reimbursement correspondingly.

But the state was not a party to the contract and was not at the bargaining table. There was the union, and there was the employer. The union made a wage demand, and the employer made no counteroffer. In that setting a mediator could mediate until he was proverbially blue in the face, but could never, never achieve a resolution. The employers could not pay money they didn't yet have and did not know that they would get. They were not prepared to do that. And the union was not prepared to take a contingency contract, meaning a wage increase only if the industry was reimbursed for it by the state.

The underlying problem was the reimbursement process. As a consequence of scandals and improprieties engaged in by nursing-home operators, there was a raging battle between the industry and the state on whether or not the state supplied enough reimbursement to cover legitimate costs. The state said, "Yes, we do. We give you plenty of money. You must be stealing it or operating inefficiently. Not only do we give enough money to do what you have to do, but there is even enough to pay a wage increase to the union."

The industry would respond, "No, you are wrong. The rates are too tight. You haven't accounted for this or that. You haven't made adjustments to counter inflation. And we're choking economically on the reimbursement rate."

It was apparent that the industry and the union could never settle the wage issue unless there could be a resolution of the basic underlying problem, which was the state's reimbursement schedule to the industry. It was more a dispute between the industry and the state than a dispute between the industry and the union. The industry was prepared to pay a reasonable wage increase which at least took care of increased living costs. But it took the position that it simply did not have the money to do so.

The industry may have been correct or they may have been incorrect. They may have been telling the truth or they may not have been telling the truth. But it was impossible in the course of wage negotiations between the employers and the union to assess whether the industry or the state was right on the adequacy of the reimbursement rate. In that situation I engaged in a most major transformation. Instead of confining myself to mediating or fact-finding or even arbitrating between the nursing-home industry and the union, I approached the state of New York.

I said, in effect, "Whether you are at the bargaining table or not, the state of New York is an essential participant in this setting, realistically. If you want to avert a strike which could be very damaging to the public interest and the patients, we've got to work out something that can permit a determination on whether the reimbursement schedule is enough to accommodate legitimate costs, including the cost of improving the wage structure." The state ultimately agreed. It didn't want a strike; nobody wanted a strike.

My suggestion was that the foundation of whatever wage increase was agreed upon by the industry and the union would be an understanding that an employer could appeal to a special forum if the existing reimbursement rate wasn't enough to cover the cost of the wage increase. If the employer were able to show that its reimbursement rate was indeed too tight, the special forum would be able to order the state to pay more in reimbursement to accommodate the wage increase.

The state and the industry set up a new arbitration forum, called the Labor Cost Review Panel. It was a tripartite panel, with one designee named by the state and one by the industry; I served as chairman. Employers could complain that their reimbursement rates were inadequate and get more money. Conversely and very importantly, the state could claim it was overpaying. If the state could prove that, the panel had the authority to take money back from the nursing home and return it to the state. (The panel existed for about four years until it was negotiated away.)

The nursing-home situation arose because of misuse of Medicaid funds by the operators, during the period of scandals. There was thievery going on and fraud. As a result, the government properly tightened up very severely. They wanted to make sure that there wasn't a surplus of money that dishonest operators could steal. I think they tightened up perhaps a little more than the conditions would permit. Something had to be introduced to loosen it up.

Do I have any ambivalent feelings about an arbitrator influencing policy in this manner? Yes. Someone who plays the role that I'm suggesting does influence policy. I do not advocate an arbitrator taking on a policy-making role, substituting his judgment for a managerial judgment. But sometimes I think it has to be done, in unusual settings, as in the public sector where the city's financial crisis had such an impact in public safety matters. The public officials like to say, as the mayor does, "I represent the public interest." And indeed they try to and they want to. But there are times when they cannot because they are also the employer.

The only one at the bargaining table who objectively can see the public interest is the neutral. Perhaps that's presumptuous. I'd rather a neutral not play that role. But nobody else can play it. I don't want to totally overemphasize this, to the point where people think that's the way I handle every case. Overwhelmingly my arbitration cases, and even my mediation cases, are handled in a traditional way, especially in the private sector.

In fact, I claim that I'm more traditional than many arbitrators, and I'm what's called "a strict constructionist." I rarely, rarely in a grievance setting give advice to the parties. I rarely make a recommendation. If there are grounds for a discharge and the employer had the right to discharge, I will always sustain the discharge—even though I think a lesser penalty might have been enough to make the point.

I believe in strict construction of the collective-bargaining agreement which the parties negotiated. I don't know why they negotiated some provisions, but they did. Having done so, it's the arbitrator's job to enforce what was negotiated. It's not the arbitrator's job to legislate new conditions.

When would I advocate the arbitrator playing several roles? When he knows the parties well. When he is serving in essentially an impartial chairman capacity with some continuity, and when it is really a mediation setting, and the problems he is mediating are only manifestations, and it's clear that other things have to be done in order to get long-term solutions.

And finally, and I suppose most importantly, only when the parties are amenable to it. The minute one side or the other says to me, "We'd rather you not play that role, Mr. Arbitrator," I would never, never push any further beyond the traditional arbitrator bounds.

So I take the position that if you have not gotten the authority to go beyond your role as arbitrator and you can't get that authority without the parties being imposed upon, then for heaven's sake don't go any further than the traditional role! Indeed I would insist that you maintain the traditional role. I'd be the first to be sharply critical of an arbitrator who stepped out of his arbitral role without permission, expressed or implied. And when I don't have the authority, I'm amongst the strictest and the most rigid of all arbitrators when it comes to enforcing the terms and conditions of the contract.

The integrity of the arbitration profession is worth noting. There has not been a single instance in which an arbitrator has been accused and proved of having committed misconduct. I know of no situation where an arbitrator has even been accused, for example, of being bribed, or having committed fraud, or colluded with one side to the disadvantage of the other.

This cannot be said for any other profession, including my own profession as lawyer, and including judges. We have had instances of corrupt judges, of judges who have been bribed, of judges who have been corrupted. Now if you compare the arbitration system to the judicial system, and you say that the arbitration system has been going on now for at least 50 years, and there are tens of thousands of arbitration cases each year, and you do have a provision in the statute that an arbitrator's award can be overturned for fraud or evident misconduct or bias and prejudice, and you find among arbitrators virtually no bias or prejudice and no misconduct and no commission of the kind of offenses that we ordinarily find reprehensible—we have an extraordinary profession and persons who are trying very hard to do the right thing.

You know, they say that we're like baseball umpires, the umpire who said,

"I may be dumb, but I'm impartial." Well, I think we are not dumb. I think that the arbitration profession is made up of very bright people, people who are trying hard to do the right thing, and people who have integrity. We haven't got any scandals.

And one of the reasons is that we serve in a "fish bowl." Everything that is done is seen. And we serve on acceptability. We are not appointed by the government, and we don't have lifetime tenure like a judge. We have to "earn our chevrons each day" in each case, like a famous airline. Each situation is brand-new, and each time we are on our best behavior, on our best mettle. And we police our own profession. The parties do, too; when someone does a poor job, he or she is not acceptable anymore.

12

LEGAL CHESS IN ARBITRATION
Thomas G. S. Christensen

Professor Christensen arbitrated in many industries on a wide range of issues, from the early 1960s until his death in November 1992. Four presidents— Johnson, Nixon, Carter, and Reagan—appointed him to presidential emergency boards for airlines and railroads under the Railway Labor Act.

The experience in labor law and arbitration that he brought to his students at New York University School of Law was abundant. From 1948 to 1954 he was confidential attorney-adviser to NLRB member Orrice Abram (Abe) Murdock, Jr., and committee chairman of the chairman's task force on the NLRB. He wrote and lectured extensively on labor law subjects. He was a member of the law committee of the American Arbitration Association and former secretary of the labor law section of the American Bar Association, and he served on the board of governors of the National Academy of Arbitrators in 1975–77.

Christensen was a professor of law at New York University for 30 years, joining the faculty in 1962, and was executive director of the university's Institute of Labor Relations from 1962 to 1972. He shared his keen insights generously with arbitrator colleagues. And for newer and aspiring arbitrators, he was a wise mentor and adviser.

I grew up in Iowa City, a university town. All my brothers and sisters (I'm the youngest of seven) went to the University of Iowa, and most went on to graduate school. I was the black sheep of the family—I became a lawyer. All my brothers and sisters, as well as my parents, were involved in teaching, in one way or another.

When I was about to graduate from the University of Iowa College of Law, I had a placement session which was a short conversation with the dean. When I indicated that I wanted to go to Washington, D.C., and work for the government (this was in 1947, still a period when the New Deal was fresh in people's minds), he said, "Well, good luck. We train lawyers here to practice law in Iowa." So I went to Washington pretty much on my own.

By 1948 I was at the National Labor Relations Board, and worked there for seven years, ending up as what was glowingly referred to as "confidential attorney-adviser" to board member Abe Murdock, formerly a U.S. senator from Utah. I became his legal assistant, basically like a clerk to a judge, but something more.

I liked Senator Murdock enormously. He was one of the two people who probably influenced my life, as far as labor law. He was a very uncommon person. Early in our relationship he made it very clear that he never wanted me to write anything for him that offended my own principles and my own sense of what was right. And he was very adamant in insisting that the both of us worked for the same boss. The "boss" was the United States government and its people. He was a very pro-labor person, placed on the board by President Truman as a labor representative. Yet he was a very independent individual, actually a small-town lawyer in many respects. And he didn't hesitate to take positions that he knew would offend the American Federation of Labor or the Congress of Industrial Organizations (then separate).

When I left the NLRB, I went to Cravath, Swaine and Moore, a preeminent law firm, management oriented. I worked there for seven years and learned an enormous amount. During that period I met someone who profoundly influenced my career, particularly as an arbitrator. His name was Stephen C. Vladeck.[1] An incredibly fine litigator, he represented the machinists' union [International Association of Machinists], which had representation rights for unions at a number of Cravath's clients.

In January 1962 I came to New York University School of Law as associate professor and became a full professor a year later. The teaching offer was due in part to Dan Collins, who had gone back to teaching there (he had worked with me at Cravath as an associate), and to Steve Vladeck, who was very prominent at the law school and a member of the adjunct faculty for many years.

How does my arbitration work influence my teaching? It would be easier to say that my teaching influences my work as an arbitrator. You can't teach well without being eternally curious. And you can't teach well in a field that's as explosive as labor law without constantly keeping up with the field. So teaching brings to my arbitration work (I think) the more informed knowledge of labor laws in general. I'm not at all sure that I would want to be a full-time arbitrator, or exclusively a teacher, writer, researcher. Combining teaching and arbitration is an ideal mix as far as I'm concerned.

There are "many rooms in the mansions" of arbitration, but basically two different types of cases. One is contract interpretation and the other deals with people, not with words as such. The "people" area obviously includes disciplinary actions and other matters of conflict. "Legal chess" is an expression I've used, as have others, for contract interpretation. It is a chess game; you're analyzing words and concepts in a mental process, as opposed to the vitality of dealing with people's problems.

An example that I've used in my arbitration class (as a matter of fact it's the final problem for this semester, a written problem) was the situation in which a large company was going into bankruptcy. It was widely publicized at the time. One division was a profit-making division. (Whether or not that was due to the fact that it was one of the few organized parts of the corporation is only for speculation.)

The president of this huge corporation decided, "I'm going to have to take drastic steps to retrench," and he issued mandates to that effect, including cutting the workforce and reducing wages. Somebody apparently did remind him that you couldn't do that just by a swoop of the pen when you have a union and a union contract. So they began the delicate dance of negotiating with the union, which was aware of the parent company's problems but also knew that they were making a profit and indeed working overtime. So at one point after they'd been talking about this, the company announced that they were simply going to close down the plant, except for certain essential work, for a period of about a week or maybe a couple of weeks.

Now this is both "people" and "legal chess." The argument in that case, as far as the actual arbitration, was whether or not the company had locked out the employees by closing the plant for a short period when there was available work. And the words *locked out* are critical. Or had the company, in fact, simply temporarily laid off most of its employees? Again the word *layoff* is critical, as the contract specifically said the company cannot "lock out" during the contract term. The contract also said the company can, in management of its workforce, "lay off" employees.

So it's "legal chess," to the extent that I had to puzzle out what I would conclude this to be: a lockout or layoff? It was also "people," because beyond all these bits of "legal chess," behind the pawns and queens, et cetera, was the fact that there was a very personal struggle going on. Between an irate union that said, "Look, we've been making money for this corporation!" And a desperate middle management that had orders from on top: "Boy, you cut costs! And you do it by slashing hours and wages!"

I found that case a fascinating one to deal with. And, I must say, in my arbitration class last night I had allowed them to choose which side they wanted to represent. While there's no consistency in the composition of the class, oddly enough they split almost 50–50. And they were almost at each other's throats by the end of the class! I didn't tell them what I ruled (I will, next week) because actually there's no *right* answer.

One other area of considerable importance, particularly in the public sector, forces an arbitrator to adopt new thinking. That's interest arbitration for a new contract, as contrasted with rights arbitration where the question is whether rights in the existing contract have been infringed. In interest arbitration you set up a new agreement for the parties. You decide for them what they're going to have in the way of a collective-bargaining agreement.

Under the Railway Labor Act governing railroads and airlines, one doesn't quite have interest arbitration but there are presidential emergency boards for impasses on new contracts. The president appoints neutrals to a board that hears both sides and comes out with recommendations. That's one step short of arbitration, meaning that the recommendations are not of themselves enforceable. But the process carries a fair amount of public-relations pressure on the parties to accept the recommendations. I've had the pleasure of being on four of those panels; I was appointed by Lyndon Johnson the first time, by Richard Nixon the second time, Jimmy Carter the third time, and by Ronald Reagan the fourth time.

I've also done some interest arbitration in the city of New York, where unions of city employees cannot strike. Impasse panels are appointed, with the authority for binding recommendations. What the impasse panel comes out with is what the parties get.

One of the impasse panels I was on involved firefighters. I served with Michael Sovern, now president of Columbia University, and Eric Schmertz, dean of Hofstra University School of Law. We had a very tense situation because the firefighters' strike was suspended by order of the judge, and we were instructed to come out with a decision by Saturday midnight. (We finally got an extension until Sunday morning.) [The panel's decision was dated 1 November 1973.] Among the things the panel considered [in connection with the financial impact of wage improvements and with the issue of how many firemen were needed to man the trucks] was something new called "slippery water," which is water chemically treated to reduce the friction inherent in a canvas hose.[2] As it was presented to us, use of slippery water would save a great deal of money because fewer firefighters would be handling the hoses.

I can remember going back to my apartment about 4:30 Sunday morning after we put in our panel recommendations which would bind the parties. I was so tensed up I couldn't even sleep. Sitting there on the couch, it occurred to me that nobody had ever told us that they tested slippery water and it actually worked in the sense that they had fewer people on the hoses.

That's what's frustrating and humbling and intriguing about interest arbitration. It's really making somebody else's judgments for them. The neutral has the comfort in ordinary grievance arbitration of being able to say (at least to himself), "The parties set these contract terms. They asked (in effect) for this result." But in interest arbitration they're getting a result that they haven't agreed on.

Arbitration is a fascinating field. I think the encouraging thing generally is that while most of my generation sort of wandered into it (it certainly wasn't my career plan), now more and more people are training for it. And also younger persons and women and minorities. A lot of barriers have broken.

13

LIMITS IN ARBITRATION
Daniel G. Collins

Daniel Collins has been arbitrating since 1968, with increasingly numerous designations. He has been impartial chairman for the New York League of Theatres and Actors Equity since the early 1970s, impartial arbitration chairman for the National Basketball Association and the National Basketball Players League since 1988, and impartial arbitrator for the New York City Transit Authority and the Transport Workers Union and the Transit Supervisors since 1990. He was appointed under the Railway Labor Act to four presidential emergency boards. In the public sector he has handled many interest arbitrations as well as grievances. Since 1980 he has been a public member of the Office of Collective Bargaining.

Formerly he was special labor counsel to the New York City Board of Education (1965–68) and special labor counsel to New York City (1966–68). Since 1961 he has been a full-time member of the faculty at New York University School of Law, where he teaches contracts and labor law, and a seminar in public sector labor law.

He served on the board of governors of the National Academy of Arbitrators in 1983–85 and as secretary of the labor law committee of both the New York City Bar Association and the New York State Bar Association.

In 1956 I came back from military service and went to the Cravath, Swaine and Moore law firm. They then had a very substantial labor practice and represented, among others, the steel industry. I was interested in labor and asked to be placed in the firm's labor department—where I was placed, and then had an opportunity (as part of an ad hoc training program) to visit all the Bethlehem Steel mills and observe some labor arbitrations. I became a labor arbitration attorney for Cravath's clients. After a few years I worked in the firm's corporate department doing international legal transactions.

I left Cravath about January 1961 to come to New York University School of Law as an associate professor, teaching contracts and labor law and also commercial law. (From 1958 on I had taught in the evening program the law school had at the time.)

And then an opportunity arose to become labor arbitration counsel for the New York City Board of Education. (I think the opportunity arose because I was the secretary of the labor committee of the New York City Bar Association and a member of the committee was then the president of the New York City Board of Education.) I did that from about 1964 to 1968, and handled all of the board's cases in labor arbitration. Theirs was one of the first contracts that had a binding arbitration clause; needless to say, it was in advance of the Taylor Law by some years.

By about 1961 Ida Klaus had become the director of labor relations for the New York City Board of Education. An experienced former National Labor Relations Board attorney, she had a lot of other experiences in government; she was the city's labor counsel at one point and had been the consultant to President Kennedy's task force on federal labor relations. She probably was one of the most knowledgeable people on public-sector labor relations at that time. We worked very closely in all of the arbitrations which the board was then engaged in with the United Federation of Teachers.

Subsequently, about 1966 or 1967, I was asked to become special labor arbitration counsel for the city of New York during the first administration of Mayor John V. Lindsay. One of the first cases that I had, although not the first such case, involved the so-called parity proceeding for police sergeants and fire lieutenants. The panel that we appeared before was chaired by a very eminent labor arbitrator, Dave Cole, and contained two nonlabor people: Dr. Buell Gallagher, then the president of City College of New York, and former Judge Charles Froessel of the New York State Court of Appeals.

When the panel finished with their award, the result was that the wage relationship between police and fire officers was changed. I should add that the police sergeants had always received less than the fire lieutenants, and the effort by the police sergeants was to achieve parity. They got half of parity in that proceeding.

But the result ultimately was to upset established relationships throughout the uniformed services in the city of New York. And when the spiral finally came to rest again, I think it's fair to say that it cost the city about a quarter of a billion dollars in terms of pay adjustments, first to the police sergeants, then to the police officers, and then to the firemen, who had parity (by contract) with the police officers, and then back to the fire officers, who achieved a bit more of a gain. And it spiraled around for a while. Needless to say, the sanitation men were involved because they had a relationship to the police and firemen. The transit police had a relationship. The correction officers had a relationship.

It was one of the great lessons of municipal labor relations: that you don't readily upset established wage relationships without expecting it to cost a great deal of money and travail, which it did. I've always thought that panel, which I think was a diligent panel, was nevertheless inexperienced in labor relations and didn't appreciate what the ultimate consequences would be, in the kind of award in this proceeding which didn't involve *all* of the interested parties but only two: police sergeants and fire lieutenants.

We had agreed to the panel, so no one could blame the result, I think, on anybody but ourselves. But one indication of the difficulty with nonlabor relations professionals in that kind of situation arose at the very first meeting of the panel when evidence was presented. Dave Cole, a very well-known old-time labor arbitrator and a man of immense reputation, was sitting as chairman. Gallagher and Froessel were sitting as members of the panel, all neutrals. The first thing that happened was that the attorney for the police sergeants (I think it was Fred Livingston of the Kaye Scholer firm, an experienced labor attorney and an impartial in his own right) made an objection. With respect to certain testimony, he said, "That's hearsay, Your Honor. I object." Although Judge Froessel wasn't sitting as the chairman of the panel, he immediately instinctively responded, "Objection sustained." At which point Dave Cole said, "Oh, Judge, we don't do it that way here."

I think that was our problem, from the beginning to the end of the proceeding. My impression is that Cole understood the relationships, and perhaps the other panel members were less aware of the consequences of deciding to move halfway. At the time there may have been a hundred different unions in the city with probably a couple of hundred bargaining units. Any labor-relations professional would have understood (as I think Cole did) that members of each bargaining unit had certain perceptions of their relationships to other bargaining units, particularly insofar as wages were concerned. As soon as one wage pattern in one relationship was upset, it was inevitable that all those other patterns would begin to fall. It's exactly what they did.

The police officers convinced the panel that there should be some change. And there was. Interestingly, later on the Public Employment Relations Board decided that parity contracts were beyond the scope of bargaining. Too late.

What was my own beginning as an arbitrator? At some point an attorney (whom I had a case against) asked if I'd be interested in being an agreed-upon arbitrator in an industrial dispute. (If my memory is correct, it was a machine company in New Jersey.) With some trepidation I said, "Of course." And since then I've been an arbitrator, a neutral. I never again represented any party in a labor-relations matter. I enjoyed arbitration but was terrified at first.

I remember talking with Tom Christensen, a faculty colleague who was doing some arbitrating by that time. (He had represented the Board of

Education earlier than I. We had shared an office at Cravath as associates; he came there after a lot of experience at the National Labor Relations Board.) When I expressed certain discomfort about how to decide the case and whether or not it would offend the parties and all those things that arbitrators probably worry about needlessly—or perhaps not needlessly—I thought Chris's [Tom's] advice was marvelous. He said, "You should just treat every arbitration as if it's your last." Which I did. (And fortunately it wasn't my last.) I think that's good advice for any arbitrator.

I worried over my first arbitration, and I worry over a lot of arbitrations. Some of them I just worry, trying to think of what the right decision is, and sort of letting percolate everything I've heard and what's in the briefs, and feeling that at some point I will really see the light of day and be comfortable with the position I take. But at the outset I didn't know that and wasn't sure I was ever going to be able to decide the case. Although in retrospect I think it probably wasn't that difficult a matter. I've had regrets about very few cases. Once in a while I have had second thoughts or realize that I went beyond my mandate in some way and perhaps said something in phrasing the award that didn't serve the parties' long-term interest.

In that respect I recall one of the very first arbitrations very early in my career as an attorney. It was before a distinguished arbitrator and involved a discharge. It wasn't something that was open-and-shut, and his decision was perfectly reasonable. But in the course of the decision the arbitrator castigated my client, gave him a long lecture about the way they ran their labor relations. The kind of thing that, I suppose, had been done in the early days, when some major industries had permanent umpires who really gave a lot of advice, which was probably sought after and accepted. Dean Shulman was a classic case.[1] He was given a very expansive role in terms of advice.

In any event, my client didn't like being lectured, and I didn't like the fact that the arbitrator had done it. It certainly left an indelible impression with me as to what I perceived to be the proper role of the arbitrator—which was not like Dean Shulman or like Supreme Court Justice William Douglas in his famous opinion in the Steel Trilogy.[2] I saw a much more restricted role, a much less expansive role for the grievance arbitrator in any event, than Shulman or Douglas did. And I've acted that way in terms of my own arbitration practice. Again it's hard to say whether that's right or wrong. It may simply be right for a period when people's expectations and needs require that, and I perceive that they do. Perhaps in Dean Shulman's day exactly the opposite was required for a formative period when parties were developing basic attitudes towards collective bargaining. By the time I came to arbitration, I had a different view of the arbitrator's role, partly from that one early case and partly from my own intellectual and academic experience.

There are arbitrators today who are able to work with a different view of the arbitrator's authority. I think Dean Schmertz of the Hofstra School of

Law is a classic example of an arbitrator who sees a broader role. While I disagree with that, I think he does it very effectively and it may serve the interest of the parties that he's involved with. Or if it doesn't, they tell him.

By and large I think that the arbitrator is viewed in a neutral, passive way. I think that's a very helpful and probably accurate perception of the role I see for the arbitrator. Dean Theodore St. Antoine of the University of Michigan Law School wrote an article about arbitrators being the parties' agreed-upon "reader." The parties have simply chosen someone to read what they have written, to tell them what they have said. That's a very nice way to look at the arbitrator. Hopefully he'll be able to read.

I'm trying to think of some situations in which I might have had experiences in arbitrating which, if they weren't unique, were at least somewhat unusual. Around 1972 or 1973 I was asked by Actors Equity and the League of Theatre Producers to serve as the "alien umpire" under their contract. I should explain that at that time the contract had two arbitration systems: one for resolution of contract disputes generally, in a standard arbitration clause, and the other for resolution of disputes that arose under the "alien" clause in the contract. The alien clause essentially tracked the language of the U.S. Immigration and Naturalization Act and provided that a nonresident alien actor or actress could only work on Broadway if they were performers of "international renown and distinction" (I think that's the term) or perform services that no resident performer could.

For a number of years the contract clause had specified that a theater critic be the alien arbitrator. But around 1972 I was one of several arbitrators asked to handle such cases. Eventually the parties abolished the distinction between alien and regular arbitrations. Over the years I think I did more of the alien arbitrations than anyone else. I must say the assignment has always struck me as being almost the frontier, if not the fringe, of a labor arbitrator's expertise and appropriateness.

Here is a classic example of this kind of arbitration. Eliza Doolittle in *My Fair Lady* was played by Julie Andrews in the first Broadway production, and it was a great success. She was an alien, a British actress, and played a part that was very demanding in terms of the ability both to sing high C's and to speak with a Cockney accent and also in the "Queen's English."

The second time a production was mounted on Broadway, the producer wanted to bring in an English actress to play Eliza Doolittle. The question was whether or not there was an American that could play the part. The evidence that came in was that in the first production it had been an American who had taken over from Julie Andrews at some point. So one of the successors to Andrews in the part had been an American, without any dire consequences.

It was a very contentious arbitration. I held that under the "unique services" clause it would not be appropriate to bring the English actress the producer wanted. The result was that an American played the part. The production was not a great success. Whether it was for that reason or others, is entirely beyond my ken.

However, some years later a producer determined to mount another Broadway production of *My Fair Lady,* with Rex Harrison coming back, and also proposed to hire an English actress for the part of Eliza. Same issue, same arbitration. The language of the rule hadn't changed much; if anything, it had been tightened up a bit.

The evidence in the second arbitration was essentially related to the "inappropriateness" of my first decision. "All that talk about American audiences not caring about the fidelity of Cockney or Queen's English," the producer said, "was simply not true." They pulled out clippings from all over the United States, where critic after critic said of the American who played Eliza (as per the first arbitration): "Oh my goodness, is she from _____?" (You name your unfavorite city!)

Besides that, the producers brought in the balance sheet to show they lost a fortune. That had happened around the country every time the production had a non-English actress playing the role. There were eight or nine instances, not all of them first-rate productions. But I suppose that's worth something. In any event, I let the English actress in. I decided on the basis of a little bit of hindsight and experience that Eliza Doolittle was a rather unique role in terms of the alien clause.

Ironically the actress that was hired never performed in the part. She developed vocal problems the night before the opening and an American actress played Eliza. It was not a great success. Whether it was a coincidence or the casting, I suppose is very speculative. But that's the only case that I can actually recall reversing myself on the basis of my own lack of foresight. Needless to say, the case got a lot of press notoriety so I'm not telling anything "out of school."

One of the fascinating things about being an arbitrator is that all the contracts are different. I may know something about the theater. Yet when I walk into a steel mill or an electrical plant, I'm fascinated by the process there. Arbitrators have to absorb a fair amount of practical information rather quickly if they're to do the job they're called upon for.

In the private sector, I would guess more than 50 percent of the cases I arbitrate are discipline matters. A lot of those cases are very difficult. "Who said what?" "Who did what?" And yet I've always been struck by what I think is a commonality of perception on the part of the arbitrators. Possibly in part because arbitrators have developed ideas like progressive discipline, "work now, grieve later," doctrines pretty much acceptable across-the-board. Those cases are difficult because they're factual, unlike most of the public sector cases where the questions are, "What does the contract mean?" A whole system of statutes and constitutional law may interplay with the contract to a much greater extent than in the private sector, so that public sector cases become much more complicated and I suppose there's a greater premium on being a law professor or a lawyer. I'm not sure that's what the parties really bargained for when they adopted arbitration systems in the first place in the private sector.

There has been almost no interest arbitration in the private sector. The private sector unions have opposed it; we really have had very little experience with it. In the public sector interest arbitration seems to serve a felt need in many situations, in part because there's no right to strike. I think it works very well within limits. It's not without its problems either.

In grievance arbitration we have the parties' agreement; that's the standard. (Plus a century really of contract arbitration doctrine involved in the judiciary process that may or may not be so appropriate in labor cases or situations.) But in interest arbitration we have very little by way of standards. We put them in the statutes, but that's the theory. Is it really those standards that awards are being issued on? The statutes typically say "comparability, the interest of the public," et cetera, et cetera.

And yet I think Arvid Anderson and others have written that the one factor that's probably the most paramount in many of these cases is the question of acceptability, which in no sense is a standard at all. What really is acceptable? What can the parties each take in terms of an award, in terms of the interests of some ongoing labor-relations relationship?

So I think that the old-time labor arbitrators who shy away from interest arbitration certainly have something to be said for their position of concern about the difficulty of applying a successful consensual system in the private sector (in terms of grievance arbitration which has its standards and has its traditions) in an essentially nonconsensual system in the public sector, where the standards are not clear. And if they're clear, may not be clearly stated, may not be the ones that really apply. So it's a real problem. In certain respects one must approach the interest arbitration process with great trepidation.

On the other hand, I don't see any better alternative in many specific situations to interest arbitration, unless one wants to go to a strike with collective-bargaining "strike rights." Although there's been some academic interest in that, there has not been much public acceptance of that position. And the air controllers' strike indicated the public rather prefers (it seems to me) the strike prohibition and its enforcement. And that's a sobering observation.

14

EXPANDING DISPUTE RESOLUTION
George Nicolau

George Nicolau began arbitrating for the first time in 1970. Since 1980 he has been a full-time arbitrator and a very busy one. Earlier he practiced law (1952–62) as an associate and then as a partner in New York City labor law firms representing trade unions. Thereafter he was deputy director in the Peace Corps (1963–65), deputy regional director in the Office of Economic Opportunity (1965–66), commissioner of the New York City Community Development Agency (1966–68), executive director of the Fund for the City of New York (1968–70), and executive director of the Institute for Mediation and Conflict Resolution (1970–79).

At the institute Nicolau trained hundreds of ordinary citizens, police officers, government officials, correction officers, prison inmates, and others, teaching them the methods and uses of mediation and negotiation. He mediated troublesome conflicts in New York communities (such as the Seward Park Housing dispute in 1974 and the Crown Heights conflict in 1978). He helped establish inmate grievance procedures in correctional facilities in California, Colorado, Massachusetts, New York, and South Carolina.

Nicolau is impartial chairman since 1980 for the American Broadcasting Company (ABC) and the National Association of Broadcast Engineers and Technicians (NABET), and the National Broadcasting Company (NBC) and NABET. Since 1986 he is impartial umpire in major league baseball, serving as chairman of the Major League Baseball Tripartite Arbitration Panel. In 1991 he became permanent arbitrator for the Maritime Service Committee and the Marine Engineers Beneficial Association (MEBA), and the Tanker Service Committee and MEBA. In 1993 he became impartial arbitrator for the National Hockey League and the National Hockey League Players Association, and industry chairman for the League of Voluntary Hospitals and District 1199.

Since 1987 Nicolau has been a public member of the New York City Office of Collective Bargaining. He was chairman of the committee on labor legislation of the Association of the Bar of the City of New York in 1972–75 and was president of the Society for Professionals in Dispute Resolution (SPIDR) in 1987–88. In 1988 the American Arbitration Association awarded Mr. Nicolau its Distinguished Service Award for arbitration of labor-management disputes. In 1992–94 he was vice president of the National Academy of Arbitrators and will be installed as president in 1996.

I came to arbitration by a rather indirect route. Actually I only arbitrated my first case about 16 years ago. But looking back, it probably was foreordained. When the war shattered my dreams of playing second base for the New York Giants,[1] I decided to become a lawyer. The kind of lawyer I always wanted to be was a union lawyer, and I came to New York because I assumed this was where the action was. Michigan was home base; I graduated from the University of Michigan. I came to Columbia University School of Law with the hope that I could work for some unions at the time I was going to law school, and I did. Then for 12 years or so I was a member of one law firm and then another, representing Actors Equity, Communications Workers of America, National Maritime Union, and a host of others, and appearing before the National Labor Relations Board and before a lot of arbitrators. I was intrigued by the arbitration process, of course.

Then John Kennedy was elected president and that turned me in another direction. I wanted to do something else because he was suggesting that we do something grand and good. I joined the Peace Corps staff in 1963, worked with Sargent Shriver (the founding director of the Peace Corps) for a couple of years, traveled in South America and the Caribbean and various other places. I found that introduction to government fascinating. When it came time to go back to New York, I couldn't resist Sarge's call to become the deputy regional director of the Office of Economic Opportunity [OEO] in New York. (OEO administered the federal government's "war against poverty.")

John Lindsay, who had just become mayor in New York, thought enough of what I was doing at OEO to ask me to head the Community Development Agency [CDA], which was a part of the HRA [Human Resources Administration] super-agency.[2] This was an exciting time. Lots of places in the country were burning in 1966, 1967, 1968[3]—but not New York, and I was very much involved.

I left CDA to become the first director of the Ford Foundation's new Fund for the City of New York. Foundations are exempt from city property taxes; the Ford Foundation decided it wanted to make a contribution in lieu of taxes. They thought it made no sense to just simply give money to the city's general revenues, so they decided to start the Fund for the City of New

York. Its focus was to help the city deal with problems that the bureaucracy might not be able to handle: productivity studies of the Sanitation Department and others; things that the City Planning Commission wanted to do and could not necessarily get public money for, but could get private money. The Fund is still going very well.

Then an opportunity came along to come back into the field of disputes settlement. Ted Kheel started the Institute for Mediation and Conflict Resolution. The whole idea was to take the techniques that we had learned in negotiations and mediation and arbitration, and try to apply them to the disputes that communities were having. At that time, in the late 1960s and early 1970s, there were plenty of those. And we thought that it would be useful if we could train government officials and people from the community, like those who were running small agencies, or just people whom we could identify as up-and-coming leaders. Could we train them in negotiation techniques and mediation skills that would be useful in terms of resolving issues? Could we build dispute-settlement systems where they didn't exist? And could we actually mediate some community conflicts? We did.

What we did in some prison systems was an interesting approach. "We" means the Institute for Mediation and Conflict Resolution and another organization which should have credit too: the Center for Criminal Justice, now called the Center for Community Justice, headed by Linda Singer, a lawyer in Washington. Around 1972 we happened to meet at a conference with Allan Breed, the head of the California Youth Authority, which is the state's system for youthful offenders. And we thought that kind of system needed something that could be adapted from industrial society: a grievance and arbitration procedure. If you know any prison wardens or administrators and could conceive of giving them this idea a dozen years ago, it would be something they would consider "off the wall." Not one of the states even had their correctional officers organized in unions, as they are now in many jurisdictions. And there were no grievance procedures for prison employees, let alone prisoners. But Allan Breed was very receptive. (Was this before the riot in New York State at the Attica prison? No, that was in September 1971; these conversations in 1972 were partially a reaction to that event.)

We said, in California, "Why don't we go out to one of your institutions and just simply talk about the idea and see whether it could make sense to administrators and inmates?" There was a lot of skepticism, but they let us try it. And so we did, and were able to build a system that had arbitration at the end—advisory arbitration, but arbitration nevertheless. The American Arbitration Association helped us get a number of arbitrators in the San Francisco Bay Area to donate their time to hear cases not resolved prior to the arbitration step. And, by God, the procedure worked! It's still there. Now an administrator can only turn down an arbitrator's decision if he finds it wholly irrational or contrary to law.

We put an inmate grievance system into New York adult prisons some time afterwards. It's not working as well in New York as it is in California, but it has brought an entirely new dimension to prison life. We had insisted that grievances be heard by a committee with equal numbers of inmates and administrators, on the theory that if they could confront specific problems, they would resolve them by a majority or unanimous vote. People said that would never happen, the vote would always be 2 to 2. But 80 percent of the grievances are resolved that way, and the system of "equal voice, equal vote" is now part of the corrections law in New York and California.

One of my conditions in coming to the Institute for Mediation and Conflict Resolution in 1970 was some time off to arbitrate, and that's when I started to arbitrate. When I left the institute in 1979, it was for full-time work as an arbitrator. It turned out that there is not an industry in which I had earlier represented the union where I have not been selected as arbitrator now. Back in the 1950s I had represented Actors Equity, which is the union in legitimate theater; producers asked whether I would serve as one of the three impartial arbitrators. I said, "Well, Paul, I used to represent the union." And he said, "Yes, I know that. That's why we're calling you, because we've had that experience with you, and we know that you're fair." That kind of reaction has been very fulfilling.

I've had the good fortune to serve as either sole umpire or on permanent panels in arbitration for theaters and television and their various unions, for airlines and pilots (and other unions of airline employees), and major league sports and their players. In each, the salaries are very high, and the contracts are very, very complicated. That is to say, even the basic collective-bargaining agreements are very complicated.

In thinking of sports, I've come to the conclusion that it's practically commercial arbitration. (I'm thinking of situations in basketball and soccer. I was the sole arbitrator between the National Basketball Association and the players for two or three years, and I'm still the arbitrator for the Major Indoor Soccer League and the players there.) This is what I mean: there is a basic collective-bargaining agreement, of course, but every player signs an individual contract which (in the same way as in theater or television) has minimum terms. Things above the minimum are added, depending upon the player's stature and drawing power. These individual contracts are also subject to arbitration by the same arbitrator who arbitrates differences arising out of the collective-bargaining agreement. And some fascinating questions arise that are more akin to commercial arbitration and business law than one would get in a usual collective-bargaining agreement.

Here's an example, from basketball. Under the collective-bargaining agreement there is a provision whereby the player can become a free agent if he's been in the league for a certain number of years. But if he becomes a free agent and tries to market his services to other clubs, the club that owns him presently has a right of first refusal. A club that wants him has to make an offer in writing, specifying what they will pay him, what property they will give him, and what investments they will give him. The club that owns him then has 15 days to match that offer. If they do, they get to keep him. If they decide not to match the offer, then the player can go with the other club.

The idea came from the National Football League, but there the offer only had to be in terms of the salary, without other things such as property, a condominium, stock. So in football the home team's offer would prevail if it were as favorable in salary, even if it were less favorable than the total of everything offered by another team.

When the basketball players came to negotiate this provision in their agreement, they said, "The offers have to be compared with everything—money, property, and investments." And the clubs said, "Some of those things may be hard to value. How can a team that owns you match the offer if it really isn't sure what the condominium or stock (offered by the other team) is worth?" The players said, "We'll let arbitrators decide that within 24 hours." So they put into their agreement a procedure called "valuation arbitration" in which the impartial arbitrators were to decide such questions within 24 hours. Why 24 hours? Free-agency offers can be made within a particular time, after the end of the season and before the start of training. Everyone wanted the time for the arbitrator's decision as short as possible. Twenty-four hours is impossible; it can be relaxed at the arbitrator's insistence, and on certain questions the arbitrator can use independent experts of his own choosing. That kind of provision isn't found in the ordinary labor-relations contract.

The first question brought to arbitration involved an offer by the Seattle Supersonics to Alex English, star player of the Denver Nuggets. Part of the offer was that he could, after the first year, take his very high salary in stock of the Seattle club, which is owned by a closely held corporation. The Denver Nuggets said to the arbitrator, "How much is that worth?" The arbitrator had to decide what the stock of a closely held sports corporation was worth. Not what it was worth today, but what it would be worth two years from now, three years from now, four years from now, and five years from now. It took more than 24 hours to determine that. The investment advisers said, "You can't value this because people don't buy sports teams for the money. Other considerations are at work." I said, "I know that. Still, we have to value this somehow or other." So we did. It's that kind of tough issue that can come up.

There are also issues that involve the law of the state in which the contract was signed. Looking back at opinions issued in some of these cases, I realized how much of Louisiana law I had in a particular opinion. Or, in another, how much I dealt with business cases that were cited by both parties.

There was another kind of issue that came up in basketball arbitration. The parties had borrowed from standard insurance contracts the concept of disability benefits for players if they were "totally and permanently disabled." Standard language, the standard kind of provision. They never thought of what that really meant in terms of the sports enterprise. The first case that arose involved a player for the Baltimore Bullets. He had an injury to his knee, from which no basketball player had ever come back. But he thought of coming back and his team encouraged him to come back (not only his teammates, but also the manager and the owner), and he played part of the season. Then he realized, after talking to his doctors, that he really couldn't make it, and he filed for disability benefits.

The league (not the club, which in effect testified for the player) took the position that because he was playing he was not "totally and permanently disabled." That got into a whole mess of insurance law. I ruled otherwise. In sports, the pressures to come back are enormous because of the investment in the player—so enormous that each league has a Comeback Player of the Year Award. So I ruled that "totally and permanently disabled" did not have to mean instant permanent disability, and to collect benefits a player did not have to remain continuously out of action from the day of his injury. What had to be shown was an injury, and a resultant disability which was enduring despite comeback attempts and was the cause of the player's inability to perform at a level sufficient to remain in the league.

The interesting thing is that for the first time the parties had to focus on what they really meant to establish in their contract, and not just adopt standard insurance terms. In the next collective-bargaining negotiations they came out with an entirely different clause that allowed a medical referee or doctors to determine disability. The question of continuous disability was finessed by agreeing to a reduction of benefits geared to the number of games played during a rehabilitation effort. They created mileposts so everyone would have a fixed standard, and they made a rational system. What had happened initially was that the disability issue came up at the end of negotiations and the parties just adopted standard language. A case like the one in Baltimore required them to focus on specifics.

The first substance abuse case in basketball was arbitrated about four years ago. Basketball now has an entire code involving drug and alcohol abuse; the players and the league agreed on it less than six months ago. But there was no code in effect in 1980. When a basketball player was arrested on drug charges and other charges, I was faced with the issue of whether the club could suspend him indefinitely, pending trial on those charges, because of conduct detrimental to the club.

So here was the situation of off-premises misconduct by what I'll call a "public performer." The issue hadn't been raised before, and there's one interesting phenomenon. You know, we've all had off-premises misconduct cases. But what made this one unique, of course, was the public status of the individual, of the star.

One of the arguments of the league was what I call the "athlete as hero" phenomenon: that the athlete had to be held to a higher standard because every young boy and girl in America looked up to him. And, as a consequence, a club had the right to suspend indefinitely immediately, which they did in this case, without waiting to determine whether there would be a financial consequence to the player continuing or not. Well, faced with the "athlete as hero," it reminded me of the colorful history of Babe Ruth who was one of the great athletes of this country but could hardly have been a model.

Anyway, I decided that, in the circumstances of that particular contract and that episode, that the club could refuse to play this player—but they couldn't refuse to pay him. He had a guaranteed contract. It's the club's choice to play him or not, any night of the week. But they couldn't refuse to pay him on those grounds because they showed no injury whatsoever. And they could show no other reason to me why he should be deprived of that contract guarantee.

Of course the interesting thing about that case (I'm convinced that the decision was exactly right; the individual we were talking about became Comeback Player of the Year!) is that the individual took treatment for alcohol and drug abuse, recovered, became Comeback Player of the Year, and this year was runner-up for the Most Valuable Player slot.[4] And obviously I feel a part of all of that process.

These cases I've mentioned were not easy to decide. Arbitrators understand that. Every once in a while you sit there and say, "Why have they brought me such a difficult case?" And then you say to yourself, "Those are the only kind of cases you get. They settle the easy ones."

Broadcasting is another area where complex issues come before the arbitrator. (Ben Roberts[5] was the first impartial umpire under NABET contracts with the ABC and NBC networks. NABET stands for the National Association of Broadcast Engineers and Technicians. After Ben's death in 1980, I became the impartial umpire.) NABET members are the people who man the cameras, run the switchers, operate all the technical equipment. Obviously they play a key role in broadcasting. Their collective-bargaining contract is a highly complex document, dealing with all varieties of technical equipment.

The broadcast technician's major concern is jurisdiction: "Who operates particular equipment? Does a NABET-represented person operate that equipment? Or can it be operated by someone from another union? Or someone nonrepresented by a union?" There are some intense battles on jurisdiction.

The contract states that only NABET-represented employees shall operate equipment used in transmitting video or audio signals for broadcasting, closed-circuit broadcast, et cetera. NABET over the years has always taken that to mean that once a piece of equipment (such as a switcher that will do the switching from one input to another) is brought into the studio, no one other than NABET employees can any longer ever touch it. And that means literally. One company had decided that when the switcher was not in use and disconnected from the broadcast system, it wanted supervisors to receive some "hands-on" training, just so they knew what this new switcher was capable of doing. The company took the view that if they didn't know its capabilities, they could not fairly judge employees operating it, either to criticize or praise them. Even though nothing would ever be broadcast by the supervisors, this was a very, very hot issue. We went back to some of the early decisions on jurisdiction (Ben Roberts had been such a fine arbitrator) and could see that jurisdiction had to be tied to a function, such as broadcasting or closed circuit. This was not such a function, and I so ruled.

The networks contracts have an expedited procedure, permitting a hearing within 24 hours if it's claimed that something which is going to happen will violate the contract. Generally we don't work that fast, but we've done some expedited cases within 48 hours and I've turned out the decision within that time. I'm authorized under the contract to render an award without an opinion, and follow it later on with an opinion. I've rarely done that. It's just a matter of my own style. I'd rather work all night and get all the reasoning down, and put out the award together with the opinion.

The only grievances that rival NABET's in complexity are ALPA's (that's the Air Line Pilots Association). NABET's major concern is jurisdiction, ALPA's is seniority. Because seniority determines just about everything. Training for upgrading has to be offered in order of seniority. If a pilot on a 727 jet bids for an L-1011 and he is highest on the seniority list, it has to be offered to him. If he qualifies, then it's his. The equipment a pilot flies determines his wage scale; the heavier the equipment, the more he earns. Seniority also determines where a pilot is based, flying routes, vacations, layoffs, recalls. So the pilot's seniority number is extremely important.

There's an important overlay in the airline industry, and that's the Federal Aviation Administration. FAA licenses pilots and sets minimum standards. That has to be kept very much in mind in drug and alcohol cases. They are difficult, difficult cases. It's not the same as a person in a shoe store or a furniture warehouse. A man is piloting a very, very big machine up there, and you have to think long and hard about a case like that.

Are the arbitrator's standards and procedures very different for pilots and athletes than what he must bring everywhere to the practice of arbitration? I don't think so. Some of the cases may be a bit more complicated sometimes, but the arbitrator's function is still the same. The most difficult case is still the discharge of a particular person, whether he's a pilot or a baggage handler or a person who works in a factory somewhere. I find these more taxing than nondischarge cases where an award may shift millions of dollars back and forth. I handle a lot more than these so-called glamour things, and you can't treat any case differently. Every case is important to the parties. It wouldn't be there if it wasn't important to the parties in some way. And you have to respond to that.

One aspect of arbitration which I find intriguing is the difference between being an impartial umpire and being an ad hoc arbitrator. When you're an impartial umpire, you have a different area of responsibility, I think. When you hear an ad hoc case, you may see the parties again, you may not. You will give it the best you can, but you are not part of the continuing relationship. And as an impartial umpire, you are. You not only are concerned about the impact of a particular decision but also the relationship. (The reason I don't want to make too much of this is that sometimes arbitrators think that we are the linchpin of the relationship. That really isn't so.)

Nevertheless there are situations where you say to yourself, "This relationship is not good at this moment in time. Or, this relationship needs some improvement. What can I do? How can I move this thing along? It doesn't seem to be working as well. They're bringing everything to arbitration; the grievance procedure has broken down. The parties aren't taking to each other."

And you find ways (or at least I try to find ways) to deal with that. I did, in a nursing-home situation, where it was clear that the procedure had broken down. The parties were about to bring to arbitration a case that might take a very long time, although it probably could be decided just after a stipulation of facts. I made the parties sit down to work out that stipulation of facts. They suddenly realized that for the first time in six months they were talking to each other again. They took off from that point and started having their normal grievance meetings again. They not only settled that case, but they settled a number since. In the larger scheme of things, that's a small event. But I thought it was something that an impartial umpire should do. You don't see that in an ad hoc situation. You might have some sense of whether the relationship is good or bad, but you have no fine-tuned sense. Whereas as an umpire, you do.

In some situations you see the parties accept what you've done as impartial umpire and apply it in similar circumstances afterwards. Or you may pick up the next contract and it still has your name in it as arbitrator. (That's the good news.) But there's a whole new clause on a subject where one party sought to undo what that foolish impartial umpire did the last time around. I don't know whether other impartial umpires feel as I do, that there are areas of responsibility which an impartial umpire has to very carefully deal with, but deal with nevertheless.

But number one: you can't go around exaggerating your importance. You know you are useful to the parties, but that's essentially it. It's a useful function. You personally are not God, although sometimes your responsibilities are fairly awesome. But the relationship is theirs. You have to look at it and say to yourself, "Is there any way I can probe to find out whether I can be helpful?" If that slight probe meets resistance, you don't deal with it. You can't deal with it. The parties will sense when it's time to deal with it; they may ask for your aid, they may not. But you know although you sit in the center at the table, you are not really the center of things. Once you decide that you are, you're probably heading for a certain amount of trouble.

15

AMERICAN ARBITRATION
ASSOCIATION PROCEDURES
Robert Coulson

Robert Coulson was president of the American Arbitration Association (AAA) from 1971 until he retired in April 1993. During his tenure AAA's membership and activities were greatly enlarged. He emphasized using an expanded range of dispute resolution options—not just binding arbitration but sophisticated negotiating techniques, mediation, fact-finding, all forms of private adjudication, and democratic elections.

A person of unfailing bonhomie, Coulson has been a continuous ambassador of arbitration to a disputatious society in the United States and all over the world, spreading the message of alternative dispute resolution for every kind of disagreement—not only in labor and commercial situations, but also in neighborhoods, families, divorces, schools, and so on.

He has written prolifically and persuasively on alternative dispute resolution. His books include How Arbitration Works, Labor Arbitration—What You Need to Know, The Termination Handbook, How to Stay out of Court, Arbitration in the Schools, Police under Pressure: Resolving Disputes.

Institutionally the American Arbitration Association has long been important in the history of labor arbitration.[1] And Coulson's work significantly advanced the reach and effectiveness of the American Arbitration Association.

I was a graduate of Harvard Law School and after graduating practiced law very briefly in Boston and then in New York. First with a medium-sized firm and later as a partner in a small firm. I found that I was spending a great deal of my time on bar association activities and on nonprofit activities. And I also discovered I was enjoying the administrative part of my volunteer activities more than I was enjoying my law practice. I began to look for a position in the administrative field, but related to the law.

The American Arbitration Association at just that point had gone through a reorganization. It had a new president, Donald Straus; he had a background in labor relations and international relations, but he was not a lawyer. So, he was looking for someone with my background to help him and I came to the association as the executive vice president in 1963.

I'd served as an arbitrator once or twice in commercial cases. In my practice I'd done some work in the collective-bargaining field, representing employer corporations, and so I knew something about labor arbitrations. And I knew something about litigation. All in all, I was very favorably disposed towards the concept of alternative dispute resolution so that fitted my career needs. I must say from hindsight I was extremely fortunate to find my way to the American Arbitration Association.

The association was much smaller then. It was handling probably a quarter of the cases then that it handles now, and in dollars it was a much smaller organization. Until the time that Don Straus became president it was really starved for funds. The membership wasn't very sturdy. There weren't enough cases to generate sufficient operating income, and the association was a more dormant organization than it has grown to be. So, to a large degree I have grown with the AAA and the AAA has grown with me. And it provided a vehicle for a very interesting lifetime career experience in the alternative dispute resolution field.

The AAA's annual budget is running now about $17 million a year. About $1.5 million is membership dues and contributions from members. Almost all of the rest is fee-for-services, the major portion being administrative fees in commercial, construction, and textile cases. And then a substantial amount from insurance cases and from labor cases. About 7 or 8 percent of the operating income comes from administering elections; the Elections Department is a rather substantial part of our work. Then the balance is from educational programs and from publications, and from the rental of films, and a few contracts for demonstration programs that we carry on for foundations or for community groups.

AAA fees in the commercial field are based on a percentage of the amount in issue between the parties. If a claim is filed for a small case, it would be 3 percent; for a larger case, the percentage diminishes rapidly. The same thing is true of a counterclaim. But since some of the cases we handle are in the millions, some of those fees can get fairly substantial.

On the other hand, a case of that magnitude requires us to provide a great deal of administrative backup to provide the services. We have tried to calculate our fee schedule so that each category of case will cover the cost of providing the service. The one category that probably doesn't meet that standard is in the labor field, where basically we are competing against two things. We are competing against the parties' ability to administer the case themselves. And we're competing against a service provided by the Federal Mediation and Conciliation Service and by some state agencies, where they will provide either a list of arbitrators or, in the case of some states, they will provide the services of arbitrators on a gratis basis.

What is AAA's role in the arbitration process? We maintain a panel of appropriate arbitrators, and we participate in initiating the case, which is important because once the case is initiated then if one of the parties decides not to participate there can be an ex parte hearing. So this is a self-enforcing system. In addition, we provide the administrative machinery for exchanging documents and requests. We also have hearing rooms available throughout the country. We train arbitrators, and if an arbitrator (in nonlabor cases, chiefly) has a procedural question during the arbitration, our professional staff can help answer it.

In commercial arbitration, the award is generally one sheet of paper. It simply decides the case. It doesn't give the arbitrator's reasons for the decision. That contrasts, of course, with labor arbitration where arbitrators are expected to, and in fact do, write sometimes lengthy opinions stating the evidence as they heard it and their reasons for reaching a decision.

We have about 3,000 labor arbitrators on our panel. When a case is filed, we will send a list of labor arbitrators to the parties, and they will try to mutually select someone from our list. Or, if they are unable to do so and can't find people in possibly a second list, we will then appoint an arbitrator. Labor arbitrators are delighted to be appointed on cases, because it's their professional work. They charge a per diem fee. They will hear the case and render an award, and then bill the parties for the time they spent on it.

How do people get on our labor arbitration panel? They are recommended by people in the field who are known to us and have a good reputation. We then get from the candidates their background, their education, and a list of people who would vouch for their ability to serve as arbitrators. We have a screening procedure, which is handled administratively. We look at their record, their background.

We are looking for experience, for impartiality, for a knowledge of the collective-bargaining field and of the labor arbitration process. And we then write to the management and labor references that they have given us so that we can obtain an independent judgment from these people as to whether the arbitrator-candidate would be accepted as an arbitrator if we submitted their name on a list. We have about 3,000 on the panel and we add 200 or 300 names a year. Of course, many of the most acceptable and experienced arbitrators have been in the field quite a number of years and are now beginning to taper off, retire, die. There's a constant need to refresh the pool of arbitrators.

There are some people on our panel, about two-thirds of the people, who don't get a case in any one year. Of roughly a thousand that do hear cases, many of them will hear one case, two cases, three cases. Some will hear as many as 30 or 40 or 50 cases.

Those same arbitrators are getting cases from other sources. They may be obtaining cases because their name was sent out by the Federal Mediation and Conciliation Service, or because it was sent out by the Public Employee Relations Board of their state, or they may be serving as chairman or umpire of a permanent panel. And so, it's a very complex market in which they are providing their service.

Usually, when the union files a case with AAA, we will initiate the case and at the same time send a list of labor arbitrators to the parties. Under our procedure the parties strike off the names of people who are not acceptable. Each party does that separately, and then each party numbers the remainder in order of their preference. They send the list back to us, and then we try to appoint the highest mutual preference. We also, however, try to appoint an arbitrator who will be available within a reasonable time. If we are told by an arbitrator that for the next six months that arbitrator is unable to accept cases, we wouldn't appoint that person, we would go on to the next person.

Are the lists made up by computer? No. We are doing it by exercising the best judgment of the regional office that's handling the case. We feel that one important benefit of utilizing the AAA facilities is that the lists that are sent out and the processing of the appointments are done by people who are actively engaged in that activity and who are knowledgeable about the needs and the preferences of the particular parties and about the availability and the competence of the arbitrators on the panel. So we feel there's an element of professional judgment involved in that process that can be useful. We think it would be improper to simply do it through a rotating list—which we could do through our computer, but that's not why we have a computer.

We were established back in the 1920s as a service that was primarily intended to encourage people to use alternative dispute resolution procedures, to encourage people to negotiate their disputes, to use mediation and conciliation, to use arbitration, to use the election process, all of these ways of resolving disputes out of court. And so our administrative services, which are a large part of what we do, are simply to demonstrate how these procedures work. The core purpose of the association is to educate people in how to make use of these alternative procedures.

And, of course, one of the major ways to educate people is to give them something in writing. So our publications are either an attempt to persuade people to use these processes (arbitration, mediation, and the like), or show them how they work, give them practical information about how to process their disputes through these methods. All of our publications are written and issued in an effort to encourage the greater use of alternative dispute resolution.

How would I summarize the advantages of arbitration as opposed to litigation? It depends of course on the type of controversy involved. I will have to generalize. I think that the main advantages of arbitration are that it's a private system. It doesn't involve going to court. It's not a system that's imposed on the parties. They choose it. They can agree with each other that rather than resolve their dispute in court they will create their own system.

They will find a third person who is most likely to understand their dispute and is impartial. Depending on the kind of dispute, they can identify the category of person who is most likely to understand it. That gives the process a finer quality of judgment because the dispute is being submitted and decided by someone who is an expert in that particular field.

In addition, the arbitration procedure can be and usually is more simplified than the traditional court procedure. The rules of evidence are generally waived so that the parties can present the case to the arbitrator efficiently and effectively. The parties can introduce criteria or considerations that might have been barred by the technical rules of court.

It's a private procedure. It's not a matter of public record. It's less expensive because it's simpler. The arbitrator's award is final and binding on the parties. The parties don't get involved in a long process of appealing the award.

Furthermore, there's less paperwork. In arbitration, moving parties file a simple demand, explaining what the issue is. There doesn't have to be pleadings. There doesn't have to be a motion practice. There doesn't have to be a record taken by a stenographer. There is no requirement of briefs. There can simply be an oral presentation by the parties and their attorneys, who present the issues clearly and accurately to the arbitrator.

Should the parties be represented by attorneys? We have a strongly held position that the parties should have a right to be represented by attorneys if that's what they want. We advise parties that they have that right because arbitration is an adversary process. The parties should make a judgment as to whether they need an attorney. In most substantial cases, both parties will be represented by attorneys. And not only by attorneys but by qualified trial attorneys—qualified advocates, because not every attorney is a good advocate.

In labor arbitration, in about half of the cases the union will be represented by an attorney. In about two-thirds of the cases, slightly more perhaps, the employer will be represented by an attorney. That's not to say that there's inequality in representation. If the union is represented by a business representative who is frequently in the arbitration tribunal, they are likely to have a fully qualified advocate. It's not necessary to have a law degree in order to be an excellent advocate. That takes experience, a natural ability, and it takes the skills of effective advocacy.

In commercial arbitration it usually is a question of the magnitude of the case. In the larger cases we find attorneys on both sides. Again, sometimes those attorneys are outside attorneys, trial counsel. Sometimes they are members of the inside corporate legal department. It's up to the parties to make the decision as to how they will be represented.

In arbitration it is not necessary for the attorneys representing parties to be certified or licensed in the particular state where the arbitration happens to be heard. A New York lawyer can go to West Virginia and present a case in arbitration. That's a big advantage to a corporation with an inside legal department which wants to have those people handle arbitrations all over the country. The same is not necessarily true in court.

As one would expect, there are cases where the process gets bogged down in the work habits that lawyers are accustomed to in court. Lawyers will ask for adjournments; lawyers will ask for transcripts; lawyers will sometimes ask to file a brief; lawyers will sometimes quibble and argue about the acceptance of evidence, citing whatever rules of evidence they may be familiar with, federal or state. It is sometimes the case that arbitration gets bogged down, and because of the work habits of the attorneys.

We have tried to deal with that problem in several different ways. In smaller cases we offer expedited or streamlined rules where we have a simpler process for appointing the arbitrator, where we have shorter notice periods, where we eliminate the transcript and eliminate briefs, where we have a shorter period between the end of the hearing and the time the arbitrator will render an award. So, structurally, we have tried to offer to the parties a streamlined or expedited procedure. And this works, in small cases.

Whom would the AAA like to have as arbitrators on its panels? It depends very much on the kind of case. In the construction field, we would want a person who has had a substantial amount of experience in the business of construction. One who is familiar with how the process works, how the contractor works for the owner, how the subcontractors work for the contractor. Possibly somebody with a professional background who understands the engineering or perhaps the architectural elements involved in the job. That kind of experience is vital. We also want somebody who can understand testimony, can understand the meaning of documents and can make an informed decisions as to the issue that is presented to them.

Now, take labor arbitration. We are looking for a person who understands the collective-bargaining relationship, who understands not only the best interests of the firm (or the government employer) from a management point of view but also understands the individual legal rights of the grievant and the supervisor who may be involved. It's a very complicated interrelationship between the people and the firm, between the people and the best interest of the enterprise. Also, it requires an understanding of the collective-bargaining relationship, that is, the contract itself and what went into creating that contractual relationship, so that the decision finally reached by the labor arbitrator will be informed and impartial and will help all of the parties involved in the employment relationship.

Labor arbitration is an important part of the system of self-government between the employer (the management group and the owners of business) and the union. It's a representative process, representing the best interests of all the members of the union and the individual grievant. These are multi-dimensional problems. It takes somebody with experience in labor relations and experience as an arbitrator to understand many of the sensitive nuances of that kind of dispute.

Does AAA have an internal review or policing mechanism? Yes, we do. It operates more along the lines of a quality program, though, than a judicial review program. In every case, when the award is sent out to the parties, we send a postcard asking them to comment on both the procedure and the arbitrator. From time to time we receive complaints about arbitrators. We then counsel with the arbitrator. We try to encourage the arbitrator to improve the level of performance. If we become convinced that an arbitrator is substantially below the competency level that should be appropriate for labor arbitration, we will probably not send out that arbitrator's name again, or at least we will send out the name less frequently. We will be more sensitive to the performance of that arbitrator. There are arbitrators we have stopped sending out. They are still on our panel but we don't send their names out anymore.

Of course, it works both ways. If we get reports from parties that an arbitrator has done an outstanding job, we're more likely to send out that person's name more frequently. Our job, as we see it, is to offer to parties the best possible arbitrators for their cases. And we try to be very sensitive to getting feedback from the consumers of the service.

If we feel that somebody is complaining simply because they lost the case, we will give that complaint less credence. But we often find parties who have won cases saying that although they won they think that the arbitrator was deficient in one way or another.

Reasonably frequently we receive a comment from a party that the arbitrator seemed unwilling to listen, seemed to have his mind made up before the hearing, seemed to be in a hurry. These are the kinds of insensitive actions by arbitrators that sometimes create a bad reaction on the part of the party. Parties want an arbitrator who will listen to the case and not indicate any kind of leaning. They want an opportunity to present their side of the dispute in a thoughtful and an unhurried way. They want their day in court. They don't want an arbitrator to hurry them. They want the arbitrator to listen as if their testimony were believable. They want a thoughtful person with an open mind, appraising the issues that they are presenting. When they don't get that, then we get a postcard.

16

THE HISTORICAL CONTEXT: A SHORT HISTORY OF ARBITRATION
Irving Bernstein

Historical context and perspective are essential for understanding the import of these oral histories from 14 arbitrators. A small group, its members are part of the very small—in numbers—arbitration profession, which is not even the sole profession of all its practitioners. More than half of these 14 arbitrators were variously, and even mainly, professors, lawyers, or administrators of labor law.

Because they functioned in a very special labor relations milieu, during periods of extraordinary social and economic change, the significance of their oral history accounts goes far beyond what this small group achieved in their work as arbitrators.

That context is set forth in Irving Bernstein's illuminating chapter on the history of labor arbitration in the United States. He has exactly the credentials and background for such a survey. His doctorate from Harvard University is in American history. His academic career has been in political science and industrial relations, as a longtime professor of political science at the University of California at Los Angeles and, formerly, as associate director and acting director of the Institute of Industrial Relations. Professor emeritus since 1987, he has continued his scholarly and professional activities.

Bernstein's firsthand experience with arbitration began in 1942, as a hearing officer at the National War Labor Board. Since 1948 he has arbitrated numerous labor disputes and served on various boards, including the Federal Services Impasse Panel (by appointment of the President). A member of the National Academy of Arbitrators for many years, Bernstein was an NAA vice president. He was national president of the Industrial Relations Research Association and founding president of the southern California chapter of IRRA.

Bernstein is the author of numerous books, monographs, and articles on industrial relations, arbitration, and labor and economic history, including A History of the American Worker, 1920–1941 *and a three-volume work consisting of* The Lean Years *(1960),* Turbulent Years *(1970), and* A Caring Society *(1985).*

Recent books are Promises Kept: John F. Kennedy's New Frontier *(1991) and* Guns or Butter: Lyndon Johnson's Presidency *(1995).*

Expertise in industrial relations, arbitration, labor and economic history, and in oral history, are all evident in this chapter. It is even shorter than Professor Witte's 1952 landmark historical survey of labor arbitration but likewise constitutes a noteworthy contribution to understanding arbitration.

The word "short" appears in the title of this chapter for good reason. There is virtually no literature on the subject. In fact, the major work is Edwin E. Witte's 1952 essay "Historical Survey of Labor Arbitration," which is a modest 64 pages in length.

Until about 1900 the word "arbitration" meant what we would now call "collective bargaining," as well as "conciliation" and "mediation." This has caused a good deal of confusion. In the nineteenth century many spoke of submitting disputes to "arbitration," which did not conform with the modern definition. In fact, the term "collective bargaining" was invented by Beatrice Webb in the 1890s. She gave it a precise meaning, and it came into general usage in the early twentieth century. As a consequence, "arbitration" took the sense we now intend. It was just in time.

By contrast, commercial arbitration was accepted much earlier than its labor sister and was soon blessed by the law, both statutory and as a result of litigation. The New York chamber of commerce (its proper name does not survive) promoted arbitration among its members as early as 1768. The Chicago Board of Trade began a similar program no later than 1880. In 1873 Illinois enacted an arbitration statute that served as a model for many other states. The main limitation of these laws was that they were not enforceable unless both parties accepted the award of the arbitrator.

The history of American labor arbitration falls into four periods, though the first is empty: (1) prehistory, from the emergence of unions in the late eighteenth century to the close of the nineteenth, (2) the Progressive Era, from the turn of the century to the end of World War I, (3) the New Deal, from 1933 to the close of World War II, and (4) maturity, from the end of the war to the present.

Prehistory

A number of labor unions during the nineteenth century inserted provisions in their constitutions calling for negotiations, mediation, and arbitration in the current meaning as alternatives to the strike. But employers, evidently unanimously, refused to accept the authority of a third party to make a binding award. From the great railway strikes of 1877 to 1901, a number of states enacted laws calling for the appointment of arbitrators by district courts. In 1886 Massachusetts and New York created full-time boards to "arbitrate," and Ohio and Illinois soon followed their lead. While these agencies handled a substantial number of disputes, only a handful were true arbitrations.

The most important strikes of the era occurred on the railways, leading to public discussion of arbitration as a peaceful alternative in that industry. In 1886 President Grover Cleveland proposed a permanent railroad board for voluntary arbitration. In the Arbitration Act of 1888 Congress stripped down his proposal to an ad hoc all-neutral board when both parties asked for one. It was never invoked during the decade it was in effect. The successor Erdman Act of 1898 covered only train service employees, provided for the mediation of labor disputes, and allowed arbitration by a joint request of the disputants. Prior to 1906 it was used only once, and in other cases the carriers refused even to submit wages to mediation.[1]

The Progressive Era

Arbitration as we know it emerged during the Progressive Era, for several reasons. Despite several secondary dips, the economy expanded dramatically between 1897, when the United States came out of the depression of 1893, and 1920, the end of the period of World War I. Apart from Samuel Gompers, who headed the American Federation of Labor, there were several impressive new labor leaders—notably, John Mitchell, the president of the United Mine Workers (UMW), and Sidney Hillman, who established the Amalgamated Clothing Workers. Union membership grew dramatically from less than 500,000 in 1897 to over one million in 1901, to two million in 1904, to three million in 1917, to three and a half million in 1918, to four million in 1919, and to five million in 1920. Labor unions enjoyed considerable popularity, particularly among leading progressives in the professions, the universities, and in politics—including, critically, those in the White House during the presidencies of Theodore Roosevelt and Woodrow Wilson.

The new era conveniently opened at the turn of the century. In 1902 Governor Murray Crane of Massachusetts personally arbitrated a Teamsters strike in Boston. But that was only a prelude to the great anthracite strike that culminated in 1902. This was the era of hard coal, which supplied virtually all the heating for New England, New York, New Jersey, and Pennsylvania, as well as much of the Midwest. Anthracite was found in northeastern Pennsylvania, and the supply was controlled by a handful of coal-carrying railroads dominated by the Reading. Their managements were bitterly anti-union. Most of the miners were new immigrants from southern and eastern Europe who were illiterate, at least in English, and who worked for very low wages and very long hours, under appalling conditions. Mitchell became president of the UMW in 1899 and launched an organizing drive the next year. But by the time the strike began, fewer than 8,000 of the 144,000 miners were members.

Nevertheless, the men demanded an immediate strike; Mitchell restrained them. He invited the operators to meet in August 1900 to discuss the demands, but they refused. The walkout began on 17 September, and 90 percent of the miners went out. A month later the operators simply posted a 10 percent wage boost and a number of improvements in conditions. Despite the absence of a contract, the union told the men to return to work. By now virtually all of them were members of the union. In 1901 the employers offered to continue the new terms for a year, and Mitchell agreed.

This truce could not last, and on 14 February 1902 the UMW called for a meeting with the operators on 12 March. Again they refused to sit down. The union now published its demands: a 20 percent wage increase, an eight-hour day, and the accurate weighing of coal. The UMW soon reduced its demands to 10 percent and nine hours, but the operators did not budge. On 8 May the UMW offered arbitration of the issues by either a board of five selected by the National Civic Federation or a board of three consisting of Archbishop Ireland, Bishop Potter, and a third person to be chosen by the other two. George F. Baer of the Reading Company, the leading employer, replied that coal mining was a business, not a religion. (Baer, J. P. Morgan's legal adviser in 1901, was made president of the Morgan-controlled Reading Company.) He would soon add what was probably the most infamous remark ever made by an employer: "The rights and interests of the laboring man will be protected and cared for—not by the labor agitators, but by the Christian men to whom God in His infinite wisdom has given the control of the property interests of this country."

The men walked out solidly on 12 May 1902 and stayed out. In June President Theodore Roosevelt learned from the attorney general that there was no way to reach the strike under the Sherman Act. The price of hard coal started to rise in August, and schools in Massachusetts closed in September. Governors and mayors informed him that the coal strike might cause misery during the winter that could invite public disorder. In September Roosevelt explored indirect intervention and was appalled to discover that the operators were determined to smash the union and that Mitchell therefore had no option but to continue the strike. "Of course," Roosevelt wrote Senator

Mark Hanna, "we have nothing to do with this coal strike and no earthly responsibility for it. But the public . . . will tend to visit upon our heads responsibility for the shortage of coal."

Thus, Roosevelt could not stand aside. He decided to act upon what he called

> the Jackson-Lincoln theory of the Presidency; that is, that occasionally great national crises arise which call for immediate and vigorous executive action, and that in such cases it is the duty of the President to act upon the theory that he is the steward of the people, and that the proper attitude for him to take is that he is bound to assume that he has the legal right to do whatever the needs of the people demand, unless the Constitution or the laws explicitly forbid him to do it.

He called on both sides to meet with him on 3 October at the temporary White House at 22 Lafayette Place. That day schools were closing in New York, and the price of the dwindling supply of hard coal had risen to an astronomical $35 a ton. Roosevelt, who had recently suffered a severe leg injury, entered the room in a wheelchair. He pleaded for a quick settlement, basing his appeal on patriotism. Baer did not heed him. Rather, he condemned Mitchell as the sower of "intimidation, violence and crime" and rebuked the president for "being called here to meet a criminal." Roosevelt became extremely angry and vented his wrath on Baer. Mitchell, the only leader who remained a gentleman, urged the president to appoint a commission to *arbitrate* the dispute; the UMW would accept its decision as final. The operators rejected the idea out of hand.

Now Roosevelt was fully engaged, and he adopted a two-track approach: to get J. P. Morgan to force the coal operators to accept arbitration, and if that failed, to order the army to seize the mines.

On 9 October Secretary of War Elihu Root, otherwise the leading lawyer on Wall Street, wrote Morgan a proposal: a commission appointed either by the president or by Morgan to hear the issues and render a solution. The operators would not have to deal directly with the union. The solution would constitute a five-year agreement, and the miners would return to work. Both sides quickly rejected the idea, and there was talk, alarming to Roosevelt, of a sympathetic strike by the far more numerous bituminous miners. He sent Root to New York for a long session with Morgan aboard the latter's yacht, the *Corsair,* on 11 October.

Roosevelt opened the second track the same day by summoning Major General J. M. Schofield, who had compiled a distinguished record during the Civil War, become commander of the army in 1888, and retired in 1895. Roosevelt told the elderly general that he was considering a plan to seize the anthracite mines and that Schofield would be in charge, "under me as

Commander-in-Chief, paying no heed to any authority . . . except mine." As a legal precondition, it was necessary for Governor Stone of Pennsylvania to ask for federal intervention. Roosevelt instructed Senator Quay of Pennsylvania to order the governor to make the request. Morgan was informed of these details, and he passed them on to Baer and other mine employers. The operators, conceding to the inevitable, agreed to arbitrate but insisted on stacking the commission. They named four of the five members; the union would be allowed to pick one, who must be of "pronounced eminence as a sociologist."

Roosevelt trumped this maneuver neatly by increasing the size of the commission to seven. He selected the four from Baer's list and added former President Grover Cleveland, liberal Catholic Bishop John L. Spalding, and, with a laugh, the "eminent sociologist" E. E. Clark. In fact, Clark was the grand chief of the Order of Railway Conductors. The miners returned to work on 21 October 1902.

The Anthracite Coal Strike Commission held extended hearings and rendered its awards on 22 March 1903. The UMW was recognized as a signatory of a three-year collective-bargaining agreement. For many miners wages were raised 10¢ an hour; for many others the daily wage was the same for 9 hours as it had been before, daily hours were reduced from 12 to 9, and checkweighmen were established. The new wage scales were retroactive to 1 November 1902. Perhaps most important, disputes over the interpretation and enforcement of this award would be referred to a bipartite board of conciliation. If the board deadlocked, a judge from the Third Circuit Court of Appeals would make a final and binding decision.

This award was a great triumph for President Roosevelt, for John Mitchell, and for the United Mine Workers. It was also an auspicious entrance for both interest and grievance arbitration at the opening of the new century.[2]

On 28 June 1910 in a packed meeting at Madison Square Garden, the International Ladies' Garment Workers' Union (ILGWU) presented a strike vote in the cloak and suit industry that the workers approved 18,771 to 615. These employees, largely female, were overwhelmingly Jewish, along with a significant Italian minority, virtually all recent immigrants. Their employers, Jesse T. Carpenter wrote, provided "starvation wages, insufferable hours, and inhuman working conditions. They contributed heavily to the evils of sweatshops, speed-ups, homework, and industrial diseases." By their strike, the workers said, "Enough!" Along with substantive improvements, the union demanded the closed shop. The employers in this chaotic industry, who competed ruthlessly by lowering labor costs, refused to bargain with the ILGWU and insisted on the open shop. It would be a long strike in the cloak and suit industry.

A. Lincoln Filene, who ran the Boston department store with his name, sent word to his old friend Louis D. Brandeis, who was vacationing at Bretton

Woods, New Hampshire. The walkout had closed hundreds of shops and idled thousands of workers, and riots and evictions occurred daily. Among progressive groups, Brandeis was the number-one lawyer, as Root was for corporations and the Republican party. Filene wanted Brandeis to intervene, but he declined. "I told him that I would have nothing to do with any settlement of the strike involving the closed shop. That I did not believe in it, and that I thought it was un-American and unfair to both sides." On 21 July the conservative—that is, collective bargaining–oriented—strike leaders indicated that they would agree to "a fair basis of negotiations." Brandeis came to New York on 23 July, by which time 50,000 were on strike.

The next day the strike committee gave him their demands. "All of these officers," Brandeis wrote, "understand fully that under this proposal the closed shop is not a subject which can be discussed." He would urge a preferential union shop. But after tough bargaining, the negotiations foundered over this issue. The employers got an injunction against strikers interfering with those who wanted to return to work. Filene brought in Jacob H. Schiff, the Wall Street banker, and Louis Marshall, the noted lawyer, who persuaded a few leaders on both sides to agree to a comprehensive contract. They needed a name for it. Julius H. Cohen, lawyer for the employers, suggested "treaty of peace." Marshall proposed an alternative. "Why not call it 'protocol'? Neither group will know what it means and it will achieve the result"—thus the famed "Protocol of Peace," which became the name of the agreement signed on 2 September 1910 that ended the great strike.

The protocol established a system of internal government, the key feature of which became the board of arbitration. In 1911 the tailors' and dressmakers' trades also adopted the protocol; in 1913 the waistmakers did so as well. Brandeis, with considerable reluctance, agreed to be the chairman of the board.

The early years of the protocol were stormy, but it survived and became the key stabilizing force in this industry, which had seemed determined to tear itself apart. The arbitrator more than any other who carried the torch lit by Brandeis was Paul Abelson.[3]

There was another great strike in the needle trades in 1910, in Chicago in the men's clothing industry. The labor conditions were similar to those in New York for most of the workers: immigrant labor, but not predominantly Jewish, earning very low wages and working very long hours, under terrible conditions. The exception was the skilled cutters, about 10 percent of the workforce, who were Americanized and enjoyed attractive pay, hours, and conditions. Another difference from women's clothing in New York was that a handful of Chicago firms were large and sold their garments nationally.

The largest firm, Hart, Schaffner and Marx, employed 8,000 to 10,000 workers and was the industry leader in sales, quality, technology, and efficiency. Founder Joseph Schaffner was progressive in outlook but never paid any attention to his employees, who were wretchedly treated by his hard-nosed managers. Trouble began on a small scale on 22 September 1910 and escalated rapidly to a marketwide strike of 35,000 to 40,000 workers a month later. There was a good deal of violence. The Garment Workers Union, a small organization made up mainly of skilled men, had little interest in the destitute immigrants and soon lost control of the strike to a rank-and-file group led by a brilliant and dedicated young immigrant cutter, Sidney Hillman.

Schaffner was shocked and bewildered by the strike and invited a Northwestern University economics professor, Earl Dean Howard, to handle the firm's labor relations. He urged Schaffner to make an offer: an arbitration board of three to hear all grievances and wage demands, with the strikers returning to work without recognition of the union. While there was strong worker opposition, Hillman urged acceptance and prevailed. Workers in the other shops remained on strike.

On 13 March 1911, Carl Meyer, the company's attorney, and Clarence S. Darrow, the lawyer celebrated for defending the underdog and this time representing the union, signed an agreement that included a 10 percent increase for the low skilled and 5 percent for cutters, a 54-hour week with time and a half for overtime, and a board of arbitration for unsettled grievances. They also adopted the Brandeis protocol formula for the preferential shop.

This led to an immense flood of complaints that overwhelmed Howard and led to many brief work stoppages. Darrow, unable to practice law at the same time, withdrew and was replaced by his partner, W. O. Thompson. For a while, Howard and Thompson failed to reach agreement on the third member but succeeded in gradually whittling down the number of grievances. In 1912 they found their man, John E. Williams, a former miner who had arbitrated for the United Mine Workers and the Illinois coal operators. He performed superbly and became the key figure in establishing the renowned Hart, Schaffner and Marx arbitration system.

It was gradually extended to the remainder of the Chicago market and to the other major markets, particularly New York, Rochester, and Baltimore. A number of notable arbitrators gained their first experience in the men's clothing industry. Two became national figures—Professor Harry A. Millis of the University of Chicago, who arbitrated in that city, and Dr. William M. Leiserson, who arbitrated in Rochester, Baltimore, Chicago, and New York. (Dr. Leiserson's service in government and arbitration was preceded and then followed by university teaching, first at the University of Toledo and subsequently at Antioch College and Johns Hopkins University). A generation later Millis would be chairman of the National Labor Relations Board (NLRB) and Leiserson would be on the NLRB board and earlier had been chairman of the National Mediation Board. Sidney Hillman would achieve national stature by building the Amalgamated Clothing Workers, helping to found the Committee for Industrial Organization

(CIO), and serving as an important adviser to President Franklin Delano Roosevelt.[4]

Before Woodrow Wilson became president in 1913, he had long written and spoken on an enormous range of issues, but almost never about labor. Yet in the White House he was vastly more friendly to labor than any of his predecessors had been. American Federation of Labor (AFL) President Samuel Gompers enjoyed easy access to Wilson. Brandeis was the main architect of the New Freedom, Wilson's domestic program. In 1916, in the face of virulent opposition, Wilson named Brandeis to the Supreme Court.

For the new Department of Labor, at the urging of Gompers, the president chose William B. Wilson of the UMW as secretary. The latter then created the U.S. Conciliation Service to assist in resolving labor disputes, mainly by mediation but occasionally with arbitration. The Clayton Antitrust Act of 1914 sought to put unions beyond the reach of the Sherman Act and to reduce the authority of the federal courts to issue labor injunctions. The Eight-Hour Act of 1914 established that limit for women workers in the District of Columbia and prohibited the employment of women at night. The LaFollette Seamen's Act of 1915 set safety and working standards for American sailors.

In 1916 the railroad operating crafts demanded the eight-hour day, with no reduction in pay, and time and a half for overtime for their 400,000 members. The carriers refused these demands, and the unions called for a strike. Concerned about the national impact, Wilson himself intervened at a meeting at the White House on 13 August at which he proposed the eight-hour day and no overtime premium. The unions accepted, but the railroads refused. On 28 August 1916 the president appeared before a joint session of Congress to urge passage of an eight-hour bill. Congress adopted the Adamson Eight-Hour Act on 2 September, the day the strike was to begin. In effect, this was compulsory arbitration by the federal government to prevent a strike of the critical train service employees.

U.S. entry into World War I in April 1917 transformed the nation's labor relations system. Gompers became a member of the Council of National Defense, and labor was represented on the Emergency Construction Board, the Fuel Administration, the Food Administration, the War Industries Board, the president's Mediation Commission, and several agencies involved with the navy's civilian labor relations.

In April 1918 the National War Labor Board (NWLB) was established. There were five labor and five employer members, and two for the public— the liberal Frank P. Walsh and the conservative William Howard Taft. In effect, the board became a compulsory arbitration agency. Unions gave up the right to strike, and employers conceded the lockout. In return, the NWLB would issue decisions specifying the resolution of disputes. While these awards were not legally enforceable, public opinion against work stoppages was so powerful that few dared to challenge the board.

In its brief life, the NWLB enunciated policies that would have a significant impact on the future of labor relations. Workers had the right to bargain collectively through representatives of their own choosing. They could not be discharged or otherwise discriminated against because of union membership. The status quo on union security continued for the duration of the war. Union wage rates, where established, would be paid, and "the living wage" was granted to those at the bottom of the wage scale. The eight-hour day became a flexible standard. The board heard 1,251 disputes and made awards affecting 1,100 establishments with 711,500 employees. Interestingly, Assistant Secretary of the Navy Franklin D. Roosevelt handled the navy's extensive labor relations program. This gave him the opportunity to learn about unions and labor relations, knowledge that would come in handy later.[5]

The New Deal

During the 1920s employers wiped out the gains labor had made earlier in the century. Even worse, the Great Depression swept away many more unions. By 1933 there were fewer than three million union members. Collective bargaining and arbitration barely survived.

The tide turned dramatically with the coming of the New Deal in 1933. Labor found an even better friend in Franklin Roosevelt than it had had in Woodrow Wilson. Section 7(a) of the National Industrial Recovery Act in 1933, the 1934 amendments to the Railway Labor Act, and the keystone, the National Labor Relations Act of 1935, reintroduced the principles of the wartime NWLB and gave them enforcement teeth. John L. Lewis launched the Committee for Industrial Organization in 1935 to organize the mass production industries, and the American Federation of Labor responded with its own organizing campaigns. The result was a great increase in union membership and collective-bargaining agreements. During World War II the rate of gain increased significantly. By 1940 there were over 8 million union members, and by 1946, almost 14 million.

Following the fall of France in 1940, the United States launched a massive rearmament program to assist Britain and to build its own defenses. The enormous increase in federal expenditures caused a rise in employment and stimulated the inflation of prices and wages. This led to a marked increase in the number of strikes, which threatened the defense program.

Roosevelt therefore issued an executive order on 19 March 1941 establishing the tripartite National Defense Mediation Board to resolve disputes in the defense industries by mediation and voluntary arbitration. Between that date and 12 January 1942, when the board closed down, it disposed successfully of 96 of the 118 disputes it received. It failed in 4 and sent them to the White House. The president seized the North American Aviation and Air Associates plants—that is, the army took them over and imposed settlements of the strike issues. The same procedure was used with the navy in the shipyards of Federal Shipbuilding. In the captive mines case, Roosevelt ordered arbitration and the employers reluctantly accepted an award of the union shop. The remaining 18 cases were referred to the successor agency.

FDR revived the Wilsonian formula for wartime labor policy. Shortly after Pearl Harbor, he called management and labor leaders to the White House and got them to agree to these principles: no strikes or lockouts for the duration, and a second National War Labor Board to solve disputes in which collective bargaining had failed. By executive order on 12 January 1942, the NWLB was created, and it inherited the mediation board's unfinished docket. Though its authority was misty, the parties accepted its "directive orders" in the overwhelming majority of cases.

The NWLB program depended upon the arbitration principle in three ways. Its basic procedure—hearings of disputes over the terms of agreements and orders to resolve them—was a system of compulsory interest arbitration. To a much lesser extent, the board designated arbitrators directly to render final and binding awards in grievance cases. Finally—and in the long run most significant—the board's policy was to require the insertion of grievance procedures concluding with arbitration in collective-bargaining agreements.

On 1 July 1943 the board issued a broad policy statement that *all* strikes, including those arising from grievances, must be prevented. Thus, parties to collective-bargaining agreements had to recognize a patriotic duty to "install adequate procedures for the prompt, just, and final [arbitration] settlement of day-to-day grievances involving the interpretation and application of the agreement." NWLB ordered such grievance procedures in its cases. The result was an enormous increase in grievance arbitration by the end of the war in 1945.[6]

Maturity

Because the oral histories in this book are for the most part devoted to arbitration experiences in the period since World War II, this final section sketches only a few of the key developments of this time.

First, at the end of the war there was a sharp increase in both the demand for and the supply of arbitrators. The latter came largely from the now defunct NWLB—both the four original and distinguished public members (William H. Davis, George W. Taylor, Wayne Morse, and Frank Graham) and the far more numerous members of the national and regional boards and staffs. (WLB alumni who came to be regarded as outstanding arbitrators included Benjamin Aaron, Gabriel Alexander, David L. Cole, G. Allen Dash, Nathan Feinsinger, Robben W. Fleming, Sylvester Garrett, Walter Gellhorn, James C. Hill, John Day Larkin, Jean T. McKelvey, Arthur S. Meyer, Harry H. Platt, Ralph T. Seward, Harry Shulman, William E. Simkin, Emanuel Stein, Abram H. Stockman, Saul Wallen, and others too numerous to list here.)

Together these individuals constituted the "War Labor Board generation" of arbitrators. They handled the heavy load of disputes that employers and unions entrusted to arbitrators jointly selected by the parties, either directly or from panels of qualified arbitrators maintained by designating agencies such as the American Arbitration Association and the Federal Mediation and Conciliation Service.

The post–World War II generation of arbitrators was called upon in multitudinous ad hoc arbitrations. Mostly from their ranks came the so-called permanent arbitrators (such as umpires and arbitration board chairmen) who headed the numerous industrywide and companywide arbitration systems that companies and unions established in steel, auto, aluminum, rubber, coal mining, iron ore mining, airlines, et cetera. These were very sophisticated systems, each with distinctive and innovative procedures and concepts. Variously included were such techniques as expedited arbitration for simpler cases, internal publication and indexing of all awards, and prescribed rules in case presentation. Very active arbitration systems flourished at Bethlehem Steel, Ford Motor Company, General Electric, General Motors, U.S. Steel, and many other major corporations.

The War Labor Board generation of arbitrators set standards for private arbitration practice—integrity, a sense of public responsibility, quality of performance, and procedural flexibility—one means by which arbitration became a quasi-profession. Historically, the great professions—religion, medicine, the law—have defined themselves in two ways: by requiring specialized education and testing for entry and by upholding standards for performance. Arbitration, however, is unlike professions in which entry is governed by certification and controlled by institutions or professional associations. Arbitration is open to anyone jointly agreed upon by the parties to an arbitration, namely, the employer and the union representing the former's employees.

In 1947 the former WLB arbitrators formed the National Academy of Arbitrators. It established standards of arbitration experience and of acceptability to both management and labor to qualify for membership. NAA issued a code of ethics for arbitral conduct: the "Code of Professional Responsibility for Arbitrators of Labor-Management Disputes" (originally titled, in 1951, "Code of Ethics and Procedural Standards for Labor-Management Arbitration") was initiated officially and approved by a committee of the American Arbitration Association, the National Academy of Arbitrators, and representatives of the Federal Mediation and Conciliation Service. To enforce the code, NAA created a committee on professional responsibility with a grievance procedure whereby those who wished to complain about an arbitrator's behavior could file a grievance and be heard. NAA's regular meetings and published proceedings provided a forum for the exchange of information and viewpoints about the arbitration process and arbitral determinations. NAA also encouraged on-the-job training so that an inexperienced individual could learn arbitration under the supervision of a seasoned practitioner.

Additionally, shortly after the war a number of prominent universities established educational, research, and degree programs in industrial relations, with a significant emphasis upon collective bargaining and arbitration. The most comprehensive program was at the New York State School of Industrial and Labor Relations at Cornell University, which offered both undergraduate and graduate degrees including the Ph.D. Many other universities created more modest programs—prominent among them, the University of California at Berkeley and at Los Angeles, Illinois, Michigan State, Wayne State, Wisconsin, Iowa, and Minnesota. In addition, law schools expanded their courses in labor law, including collective bargaining and arbitration. Many young people were trained to enter the expanding field of labor relations. Some later became arbitrators.

But the main replacements for the War Labor Board generation (as its members retired or accepted fewer cases or died) were individuals who had acquired expertise in arbitration and mediation at government agencies, such as state and local labor agencies, and/or as staff arbitrators in industry or company arbitration systems. Also entering the ranks of arbitrators were professionals from colleges and universities and related fields such as law and economics. Many of them arbitrated only on a part-time basis. Others embarked on second careers as arbitrators as they retired from their first careers or chose to move into arbitration.

Both the government-agency and the second-career groups had professional contact with the former WLB arbitrators. Many of the latter moved into governmental labor agencies and universities after the War Labor Board went out of existence.

Adding to the importance of arbitration, from the late 1940s onward, was the seal of approval that labor arbitration received from the highest authority in the land, the Supreme Court. In 1960, after a recent history of judicial intervention in the arbitration process, the court unanimously affirmed, in the Steel Trilogy, the legal integrity of arbitration. Sam Kagel summarized the principles enunciated in these three interrelated cases:

The court clearly separated the role of courts and arbitrators in cases involving arbitrability and enforcement of awards.

On arbitrability: The courts are limited to finding whether there is a collective bargaining agreement in existence; whether there is an arbitration clause; and whether there is an allegation that a provision of the agreement has been violated. If the arbitration clause is broad enough to include the alleged "dispute," then arbitration must be ordered.

On enforceability of awards: If the arbitrator stays within the submission and makes his award on his construction of the contract, then the award must be enforced.

In either arbitrability or enforcement cases the courts are not to get into the merits of the cases; they are not to substitute their judgment for that of the arbitrators; they shall not refuse to act because they believe a claim frivolous or baseless.[7]

Around 1970 the labor movement in the private sector moved into a steep and prolonged decline. There seem to have been two reasons for this. The first, and doubtless the more serious, was a profound transformation of the American economy as the result of rapid technological change, foreign competition, mergers, and downward pressure on prices and wages. The other was an unfriendly National Labor Relations Board, particularly during the Reagan and Bush administrations. There was a resulting severe drop in union membership and the loss of contracts due to the disappearance of many unionized firms in declining industries. Arbitration fell off in such industries, notably in steel. The Board of Arbitration in steel experienced a declining caseload after years of high-volume arbitration activity that had kept a corps of outside arbitrators busy in addition to the board's own staff arbitrators.

At the same time, though starting somewhat earlier, there was an increase in collective-bargaining agreements and union membership in the public sector, as well as in service industries, notably hospitals. The legislative model at all levels of government was the National Labor Relations Act, with adaptations to public employment. This development emerged in the cities during the 1950s. Liberal mayors, particularly Joseph S. Clark, Jr., of Philadelphia and Robert F. Wagner, Jr., of New York (the son of the author of the National Labor Relations Act), established little NLRAs. The states followed. At the urging of Secretary of Labor Arthur Goldberg, President Kennedy early in 1962 issued an executive order establishing a collective-bargaining system for the federal government. This program received a statutory base under President Carter with the enactment of the Federal Service Labor-Management Relations Statute as Title VII of the Civil Service Reform Act of 1978.

The result of this proliferation of laws was to encourage collective bargaining, including arbitration, in the cities, counties, and states, as well as in the federal government. One consequence was a large volume of arbitration involving all levels of government and unions representing government employees. In the U.S. Postal Service alone, thousands of grievances came to arbitration annually.

A similar expansion in arbitration, though of much less magnitude, occurred in professional sports. In baseball, football, basketball, and hockey club owners negotiated collective-bargaining agreements with players' unions. They contained arbitration provisions that were frequently invoked.

Throughout the 1990s the extent and nature of labor arbitration have been changing, as has the legal and social framework within which modern arbitration was launched.[8] Change being a constant in society, arbitration too will undoubtedly have to deal with it.

APPENDIX
Methodology

This book is an unanticipated by-product of the oral history of arbitrators that I began working on in 1983; interviews were completed in 1984 and transcripts in 1985. At that time few labor arbitrators had been interviewed for oral history purposes, and transcripts of such interviews as existed were in private reference collections.[1]

It seemed to me then—and still does now—that oral history is a particularly appropriate method for eliciting useful and interesting firsthand accounts from arbitrators, without violating the necessarily confidential nature of their work and without inhibiting transmittal of knowledge enriched by experience.

Arbitration is essentially a private process, fashioned by the parties for their needs. Hearings are not open to the public. Transcripts are not usually made; when they are, they are ordinarily available just to the arbitrator and the management and labor representatives. Arbitration awards go to the parties and are written for the grievants as well as their representatives and antagonists. Most awards are unpublished and may be published only with the consent of both parties.

There are sound reasons for the confidentiality and discretion that underlie the arbitration process. But one consequence is that the arbitrators, who perforce become increasingly knowledgeable over the years, do not—and should not—disclose much that they learn in their professional work.

Oral history interviews should not be a vehicle to tell tales out of school. But there is a valid distinction between maintaining confidentiality and suppressing insights arising from hands-on activity. Well-designed oral history interviews can enable arbitrators to share their accumulated experience without breaches of confidence and without gossip. Such firsthand accounts are prime sources in arbitration history as well as in labor relations and law. Beyond the interest such material has for students of dispute resolution, it is especially valuable to those who actually use the process and are directly affected by its operations.

In recounting the oral history project's implementation, the basis for selecting the 14 individuals interviewed should be noted. No claim is made that they constitute a formal statistical sample. Yet the mix among the 14 is characteristic of the profession. (The group is "skewed to high-level experience and distribution," as I noted in chapter 1, concluding that these arbitrators' notable experience in arbitration and related fields, plus their personal characteristics, resulted in their knowing "things worth saying, worth being heard.")

In conducting the oral history project, I had the advantage of personal knowledge and experience in arbitration, dating back to the National War Labor Board in 1942. I selected for these interviews arbitrators whom I have known and esteemed for many years. To some extent I know their histories in arbitration, either because we worked together or talked about some of these matters over years. I had a fairly good notion of where to find the "gold," but the oral histories unearthed a richer vein than anticipated.

What I had anticipated accurately was that these arbitrators would be fluent and articulate as interviewees. As for speaking vividly and extemporaneously, that was no problem for these expressive individuals. But focus as well as fluency is necessary for good interviews, especially when time and resources are limited. That is why this oral history project was designed to evoke focused interviews that would draw on the depths of the arbitrators' experience.

The project sought to preserve the experience and insights of a noteworthy group of highly experienced arbitrators. It involved substantial time and interest from the 14 colleagues who agreed to work with me on the project, and it was facilitated by the two oral historians who were generous with their professional expertise and by the 10 law students who assisted in the interviews after completing intensive training for interviewing. I interviewed five of the arbitrators (Gellhorn, Nicolau, Scheiber, Stark, and Stein), and the law students interviewed the others.

Work on the project was on a pro bono basis, with everyone fitting time for the project into demanding personal schedules. The interviewees, and myself, were active arbitrators; some were professors with heavy teaching responsibilities as well. Interviewers were divided between third-year law students, some with part-time jobs, and graduate law students, many of them practicing lawyers.

The project yielded 14 transcribed oral histories, totaling some 700 typed pages. Following publication of this book in 1995, the unabridged transcripts will be deposited for reference use in five libraries: the American Arbitration Association's Library and Information Center on the Resolution of Disputes in the AAA's national office in New York City; Columbia University's Oral History Collection in Butler Library in New York City; Cornell University

School of Industrial and Labor Relations' Martin P. Catherwood Library in Ithaca, New York; Hofstra University School of Law's library in Hempstead, New York; and New York University's Robert F. Wagner Labor Archives in New York City. In addition, the transcripts will be catalogued in The Library of Congress, *National Union Catalog of Manuscript Collections*.

An article based on the oral history interviews was published after they were transcribed: Clara H. Friedman, "Arbitrators in Oral History Interviews: Looking Back and Ahead," *Employee Relations Law Journal* 12, no.3 (Winter 1986–87): 424–48.

The project also yielded, serendipitously, this book. The interviews were so effective and interesting that I was encouraged to produce a book for a wider audience than will refer to the transcripts.

From the beginning of the oral history project, an understanding of oral history's value was fostered, as was good rapport among all participants in the project. The project was launched with a meeting at the American Arbitration Association of virtually all the 25 participants. After explaining the project's aims and methods, I introduced Elizabeth Mason, a longtime oral history teacher and practitioner on the Columbia University faculty and the assistant director of Columbia University's pioneering Oral History Office. Her exposition of oral history and her answers to questions from the arbitrators and law students left the group with an appreciation and enthusiasm for the significance of the oral history we were undertaking.

Later the students were provided with a packet of pertinent readings in oral history procedures and responsibilities.[2] I had compiled these from leading oral history sources, grouping the material by oral history purpose, interview techniques, and interviewers' obligations. The packet directed attention to candor as "the forte of good oral history, a candor emanating from the rapport which the interlocutor, each in his way, was able to establish with the respondent."[3]

The importance of listening was explained in the packet: "The interviewer should be someone who can sit quietly and listen. . . . An interview is not a dialogue. The whole point of the interview is to get the narrator to tell his story. Limit your own remarks to a few pleasantries to break the ice, then brief questions to guide him along. . . . Don't worry if your questions are not as beautifully phrased as you would like them to be for posterity. . . . Don't use the interview to show off your own knowledge, vocabulary, charm or other abilities. Good interviewers do not shine; only their interviews do."[4]

Next the students participated in a day-long role-playing session at New York University, suggested and hosted with verve by Debra Bernhardt of New York University's Robert F. Wagner Labor Archives. Students, working in pairs consisting of one Hofstra Law and one New York University Law student, interviewed each other, alternating as interviewer and interviewee, using a specially prepared scenario[5] as well as improvising their own.

The written scenario posed questions on matters the students might have to deal with during the upcoming interviews with the arbitrators, such as: "How do you begin the interview?" "What do you do when the arbitrator refers to an acronym you don't know?" "What do you do if the interview is coming to an end and the arbitrator has not covered every topic expected?"

We noted during the role-playing that in the upcoming interviews it was not appropriate to practice prosecutorial skills and pepper the arbitrator with insistent probing questions. Students were advised that the most effective role for the interviewer was as facilitator, interested listener, relaxed and relaxing host. The student's responsibility was to move the interview from one topic to another without cutting off the narrator and to pay attention to technical details, from working the tape recorder to getting the correct spelling of unfamiliar names mentioned by the arbitrator.

Before the students went off to their assigned interviews, I briefed them individually on the arbitrator's background and the scope of the interview. Similarly, the arbitrators were briefed on their interviewer's background. Background information came from brief résumés all participants had been asked to provide earlier. Students were also given one or more of the arbitrator's awards, and any other relevant writings by the arbitrator.

I also used the résumés as an aid in the interview assignments, looking for congenial matching. Thus the student who was a triathlon competitor and a labor relations attorney in the U.S. Army was asked to interview the arbitrator who was a skilled sailor and ice-hockey player; the rapport between those two was immediate. Another student who aspired to a career at the National Labor Relations Board interviewed the arbitrator who had been a high-ranking NLRB official; the interviewer became so absorbed in questions on the arbitrator's NLRB career that the interview lasted far longer than expected.

Not every student/arbitrator match was so felicitous. One student, who interviewed the arbitrator heading the office where the student was interning, was in such awe of the arbitrator that he could hardly keep the interview going. Another student became very interested in an incidental—and not really important—comment by the arbitrator; the student's extended questioning on this point used up the cassettes brought to the interview and crowded out an anecdote I had particularly asked the student to get from the arbitrator during the interview.

But on the whole, rapport between arbitrators and their interviewers (including the two cited above) was good and the interviews went well. In the individual postinterview feedbacks, the students told me with evident sincerity how much they admired and respected the arbitrators they had interviewed.

In the individual briefings that preceded the interviews, each student was advised of the scope and focus of the interview. That had been worked out earlier when I conferred with the arbitrators individually on what would be covered in the interview. We agreed that the interview would start with an account of the circumstances that led the person to a career in arbitration, and the rest would deal with important aspects of the arbitrator's particular experience and insights. The interview topics were thereafter jotted down in brief checklist format.[6] One copy went to the arbitrator as a reminder of the interview's parameters, and another copy went to the student as a guide to the direction the interview was likely to take.

The checklists did not preclude the arbitrator from adding or deleting topics during the interview and did not specify details or emphases. The checklists merely served to avoid omitting important matters and to forestall unintended digressions. The checklists did not chill spontaneity at the interview, being very broadly stated. The students were asked to avoid stilted questioning by becoming familiar with the scope of the interview but not trying to memorize questions in advance.

The checklists were helpful in adapting to everyone's time constraints. Initially the goal was one interview of about one hour's duration for each arbitrator. But that turned out to be insufficient; all the interviews continued for several hours, and some were full-day sessions, with a few going for a second day.

After the interviews were concluded, each student telephoned me to report how the interviews went and whether different training could have prepared them better. Arbitrators also provided similar feedback. The students and the arbitrators reported that the interviews went smoothly, and that possible problems mentioned in the training sessions did not occur.

The fact is that the students trained extensively for the single interview each conducted. They considered it a good learning experience and enjoyed being part of the project. Listening to the interview tapes, I found that many conducted their interviews with great skill, and that none were inadequate for the task. Undoubtedly they would have become even more skillful interviewers if additional arbitrators could have been interviewed. But our project did not have the time or resources to expand the number of arbitrators in the interview group or to assign the students to more than a single interview.

The next step was to have the taped interviews transcribed—a task complicated by the poor technical quality of the equipment used during the interviews. Our cooperating law schools were not able to provide adequate equipment, and the personal equipment many of the students used as an alternative was mostly inadequate also. None of the students reported difficulties in using the equipment, but I personally had some problems. During one interview I pushed the wrong button and erased a long segment—which the arbitrator later repeated for me, graciously and brilliantly.

Many of the arbitrators had thought their personal secretaries would be able to transcribe their interviews, but that turned out to be unfeasible. Results were poor in most cases where the arbitrators' personal secretaries or outside transcribing services did the transcripts. Much of what was said during the interview was incomprehensible to the transcriber or was garbled by the transcriber.[7]

Virtually all the tapes had to be retranscribed in a time-consuming and costly manner. I listened to each tape, fortified by direct knowledge of the arbitrators' and students' vocabularies and frames of reference, and had my own personal secretary transcribe the tapes, checking with me throughout as necessary.

If good taping equipment had been available for the project, as well as professional transcribing facilities, the project would have been completed in far less time and with much less work. As it was, each transcript my personal secretary produced went through at least two typings—apart from typing that might have been done by the arbitrator's secretary or outside transcriber. After her first typing, there was at least one more to correct spelling and conform punctuation with meaning. Whether the arbitrator said, "I made the decision?" or "I made the decision!" required my listening to the tape.

But at the end of the long and tedious transcribing, the transcripts read the way the arbitrators had spoken and were faithful to the arbitrators' meaning. Each arbitrator received for review a copy of the final typed transcript. For those arbitrators who had seen earlier inadequate transcripts of their interviews and been appalled by them, the review copy relieved their forebodings. Arbitrators were urged not to polish the transcripts during the review process, in order to maintain the authenticity of the interviews as oral history. Notwithstanding that extensive polishing and editing are usually second nature for arbitrators, they limited themselves to such emendations as correcting misspellings, dates, and the like. They did not reformulate their utterances, and they left their spontaneity intact.

The material that I subsequently selected for publication in this book was taken directly from the transcripts. Sections of particular interest were chosen and abridged as necessary to meet the book's space limitations. The style and substance of the arbitrators' accounts were not revised, polished, or rewritten. Interviewers' questions were deleted for the book, not being an integral part of the text, although the questions had been necessary to "prime the pump" during the interviews. The words in the book are the arbitrators' words, although the book has fewer words than were spoken during the interviews. Each chapter reads as a seamless whole, even though the material was put together from what had been said at greater length.

The arbitrators' voices remain distinctive and recognizable in the book, as in the interview transcripts. They sound as if they are in their offices, talking to the readers, sharing experiences of their long and honorable careers in arbitration. That individuals like these have flourished in arbitration helps us understand arbitration's notable achievements and its still great potential.

Would it have been possible for such vivid and engaging communication to emerge from the oral history project without as much advance preparation, conceptualization, and demands upon the participants? Perhaps—but it seems to me that the painstaking work throughout the project stimulated the participants to bring their best to this undertaking and to communicate usefully and memorably.

Notes and References

Chapter 1

1. In earlier years the term "arbitration" encompassed mediation and collective bargaining, but nomenclature has changed and contemporary arbitration has a separate and distinct meaning. Arbitration and mediation are now regarded as different processes. In Witte's 1952 "Historical Survey of Arbitration", he noted that "tracing the beginnings of labor arbitration in the United States is difficult because the term 'arbitration' was long used with a meaning different from its present connotation. Its earliest usage included collective bargaining" (Edwin E. Witte, "Historical Survey of Labor Arbitration," Labor Relations Series [Philadelphia: University of Pennsylvania Press, 1952]. Taylor, in his preface to Witte's survey, praised the "attention given to the problem of nomenclature. . . . In the very early days the term 'arbitration' connoted collective bargaining and agreement making. Later it became synonymous with 'mediation' and 'conciliation.' The association of the term with the bringing in of an outsider with power to decide is relatively recent."

In the year before Witte's survey, Sharfman differentiated arbitration from other "ancillary procedures": "Arbitration is frequently used as a generic term embracing all the procedures commonly followed in which outsiders, generally government officials or agencies, assist in effectuating peaceful settlement of labor-management controversies. It is obvious, of course, that the essence of arbitration is the actual determination, with findings that are binding, of the matters in dispute. . . . In all the ancillary procedures short of actual arbitration, therefore, negotiation by the parties, is both the primary and finally conclusive step. These procedures, including conciliation or mediation and investigation or fact-finding, where at most only recommendations are presented to the parties, must be sharply differentiated from the arbitration process, where disputes are actually decided by individual arbitrators or arbitration tribunals." I. L. Sharfman, "Free Enterprise, Collective Bargaining and the Arbitration Expedient," *Proceedings of Fourth Annual Meeting of Industrial Relations Research* (28–29 December 1951), 144.

Fleming in 1965 capsulized the current meaning of the term "arbitration": " 'Arbitration,' as used at the turn of the century, usually meant what we would now call 'negotiation.' Since the basic problem of unions was then one of recognition, their primary concern was one of sitting down with the company to discuss contract terms. The limited umpire systems which existed grew out of great strikes, though the systems were intended to deal with continuing problems. . . . Grievance arbitration was growing rapidly at the time World War II came along. . . . By the end of the war grievance arbitration was not only widely used, it was widely accepted. . . . As of 1964, 'arbitration' in the industrial context clearly means grievance arbitration. With rare exceptions . . . it is voluntary and applies only to the meaning and interpretation of collective-bargaining agreements." R. W. Fleming, *The Labor Arbitration Process* (Urbana: University of Illinois Press, 1965), 29, 30.

The present meaning of "arbitration" was similarly defined in 1983 by Nolan and Abrams: "Only relatively recently has labor arbitration been defined as the voluntary, private adjudication of disputes arising under a collective bargaining agreement by a neutral third party. For most of the nineteenth century, 'arbitration' was interchangeably described as negotiation undertaken in a conciliatory spirit, adjudication by a joint labor-management body, and referral to a neutral third party. Disputes over the terms of new agreements were not distinguished from those concerning the interpretation of existing contracts." Dennis R. Nolan and Roger I. Abrams, "American Labor Arbitration: The Early Years," *University of Florida Law Review* 35, no. 3, (Summer 1983).

2. Being an attentive listener is essential for an arbitrator, to ensure hearing everything said for the record, and to assure the parties that they are getting a full and fair hearing. Arbitrators generally take this responsibility very seriously, even when presentations are long and convoluted or repetitive. Listening (and comprehending and note taking) is not as easy as it looks. On point in this connection is the story Harry J. Dworkin of Cleveland told me many years ago. Early in his distinguished arbitration career, Dworkin's wife (who was on faculty at an Ohio university) sat in at an arbitration hearing he held out of town. The hearing went on all day. Later Dworkin's wife commented to him privately, "I don't understand why you come home from hearings all tired out. All you do all day long is sit and listen!"

3. In large part the interviews constitute living history, albeit many of the individuals and events recalled by the arbitrators may not be familiar to some readers, especially students and even professionals relatively new to arbitration. Individuals and events mentioned in the interviews are significant in the development of arbitration, although details on them are not easily accessible in standard sources. Thus, it seemed to me useful to identify them in the endnotes. Readers who are interested will have access to more details than the arbitrators could appropriately provide in their interviews; readers who are not interested can skip the footnotes. In any event, the endnotes do not interfere with the flow of the arbitrators' observations and, to some extent, flesh out other notable figures and events in labor arbitration.

4. The reference is to Robert Coulson, president of the American Arbitration Association for over 20 years. He was called upon at times to serve as an arbitrator, as in 1975 when the Office of Collective Bargaining appointed him—along with Walter Gellhorn and Emanuel Stein—to chair the arbitration board in the contentious pay-parity dispute between the city of New York and the police union.

5. The influential nature of the labor arbitration profession is implicit in the finality of labor arbitrators' awards on matters of import in the workplace. Considering

the volume of labor arbitration cases annually, the number of active labor arbitrators is small, absolutely and relatively. The number of labor arbitration cases from all sources—including the American Arbitration Association, the Federal Mediation and Conciliation Service, and direct appointments by the parties—was estimated as 55,000 in 1986 by Mario F. Bognanno and Charles J. Coleman, eds., *Labor Arbitration in America: The Profession and Practice* (a project of the Research Committee of the National Academy of Arbitrators and the NAA Research and Education Foundation) (New York: Praeger, 1992), 94.

Currently the number of mainline labor arbitrators in the United States is about 630, "mainline" denoting arbitrators who are members of the National Academy of Arbitrators. (NAA members are generally considered well-established arbitrators who handle more cases than non-NAA members. The 1994–95 NAA membership directory lists 678 arbitrators, 40 of whom practice in Canada.) This is an all-time high in NAA membership, and also in the number of recognized arbitrators. Back during the Great Depression there were only one or two dozen experienced arbitrators in the entire country. (Nolan and Abrams, "American Labor Arbitration," 413.)

Not every mainline arbitrator handles large numbers of cases. Arbitrating is a part-time activity for many NAA members; only 43.5 percent of NAA members practiced arbitration full-time in 1986. Bognanno and Coleman, *Labor Arbitration*, 49.

The caseload is not evenly distributed among mainline arbitrators: "A comparatively small number of arbitrators handled most of the cases . . . the busiest 10 percent of the U.S. arbitrators decided about half of the 1986 cases." Bognanno and Coleman, *Labor Arbitration*, 95–96.

Even taking a more expansive view of the number of labor arbitrators and including arbitrators who are not NAA members, one must conclude that labor arbitration is still a very small profession. "In 1986 there were approximately 3,500 arbitrators in the United States and about 600 of these (17%) belonged to the NAA." Bognanno and Coleman, *Labor Arbitration*, 8.

The estimated number of arbitrators—3,500—far exceeds the number called upon with some frequency by management and labor to arbitrate their disputes. But even if there were 3,500 arbitrators, that number is miniscule compared with statistics for the number of lawyers—some 77,000—and judges—about 38,000—in the United States. U.S. Department of Labor, "Current Population Survey" (1993 figures), *Statistical Abstract of the United States.*

The number of actively utilized arbitrators is difficult to estimate. It is more realistic to begin with the 630 figure based on NAA membership than with the 3,500 estimate, which includes non-NAA members (of whom only a small portion arbitrate full-time and/or frequently). Even the 630 figure has to be reduced by half, or probably much more, because many NAA members are inactive, either by choice or because of infrequent selection. "More than 20 percent of the people listed as arbitrators received no cases in 1986. Many of these, however, said that they did not want cases. They indicated that they had removed themselves from the active ranks of arbitrators. . . . But about 9 percent stated that they wanted cases but didn't get any in 1986." Charles J. Coleman and Perry A. Zirkel, "The Varied Portraits of the Labor Arbitrator," in Bognanno and Coleman, *Labor Arbitration*, 38, 39.

Being listed on designating agencies' arbitration panels or even holding membership in NAA does not necessarily betoken active utilization as an arbitrator. "FMCS and the AAA reported that a large number of arbitrators on their rosters do not decide any cases; more than 20 percent of the arbitrators in the NAA study did not decide a single case in 1986." (Charles J. Coleman, "The Arbitrator's Cases: Number, Sources, Issues, and Implications," in Bognanno and Coleman, *Labor Arbitration*, 91, 92.)

Over the course of years changes occur in caseload distribution and arbitrator status. Some non-NAA arbitrators become NAA members, some part-time arbitrators become full-time arbitrators, some less active arbitrators become more active, and some newer arbitrators move into the front ranks of the profession. The reverse also occurs; some arbitrators retire or cut back on caseloads. At all times there may be arbitrators who fall out of favor with some parties; parties are free to stop selecting them (if they are ad hoc arbitrators) or to not renew their appointments (if they are permanent umpires) if there is dissatisfaction with any particular award. Whether or not dissatisfaction with an award derives from significant shortcomings in the arbitrator may be immaterial to the arbitrator's continuing acceptability.

Analysts of arbitration generally conclude that "entry into and advancement in arbitration is difficult" (Joseph Krislov, "Entry and Acceptability in the Arbitration Profession: A Long Way to Go," in Bognanno and Coleman, *Labor Arbitration*, 82). Many factors, including chance, influence whether an arbitrator—even a highly qualified one—will be sought after by designating parties. "The would-be arbitrator chooses a hazardous path. A large number of people seek entry, but some are never called. Many enter the field and never build a large caseload. Most arbitrate on a part-time basis, many contentedly so, while others hope for the extra cases that will enable them to 'go full-time.' Finally, there is a quite small group that works at this profession full-time and makes an excellent living" (83).

Nevertheless, arbitration continues to be a profession to which many able and even illustrious individuals aspire. And arbitration continues to be an activity in which most practitioners find great satisfaction and take deep interest, whether it is their full-time endeavor or an assignment they can undertake only occasionally.

Chapter 2

1. Louis Brandeis, U.S. Supreme Court Justice from 1916 to 1939 and closely associated with Chief Justice Oliver Wendell Holmes in judicial opinions, was earlier an attorney distinguished in public interest advocacy. He was a pioneer in labor arbitration. In 1910 New York City garment employers and the International Ladies' Garment Workers' Union asked Brandeis to help them settle the general strike that had shut down the industry (consisting typically of exploitative sweatshops). Brandeis formulated what became known as the Protocol of Peace, which ended the strike, and he designed an arbitration system that opened up a new era in industrial relations. From 1911 until 1916 he implemented the system as the public member of the Board of Arbitration in the women's garment industry.

2. Arbitration issues and problems are the subject of papers discussed at annual NAA meetings. Published in annual volumes by the Bureau of National Affairs, the NAA proceedings are a major source for users and students of arbitration. Topics included in a recent volume indicate the range and depth of the proceedings: "The

Future of Labor Arbitration: Problems, Prospects and Opportunities," "Arbitration of Medical and Health Issues," "The Changing Character of Labor Arbitration," "The Arbitration of Statutory Disputes: Procedural and Substantive Considerations," "Arbitration and the Courts," "Functus Officio under the Code of Professional Responsibility: The Ethics of Staying Wrong," "Investigatory Due Process and Arbitration," "Ten Commandments for Labor and Management Advocates: How Advocates Can Improve the Labor Arbitration Process," and "The Use of Hearsay Evidence by Arbitrators." *Arbitration 1992: Improving Arbitral and Advocacy Skills*, Proceedings of the 45th Annual Meeting, National Academy of Arbitrators (Washington, D.C.: Bureau of National Affairs).

3. The "Steel Trilogy" refers to the U.S. Supreme Court decisions in 1960 in three cases involving the United Steelworkers of America versus American Manufacturing Company, Warrior & Gulf Navigation Company, and Enterprise Wheel & Car Corporation. The court held, in favoring arbitrability of labor disputes and enforcement of arbitration awards, that an award, in the words of Justice Douglas, "is legitimate only so long as it draws its essence from the collective bargaining agreement."

4. Governor Edison, a public figure in his own right, was the son of Thomas Alva Edison, the famed inventor.

5. David L. Cole, a lawyer from Paterson, New Jersey, was a nationally known mediator and arbitrator who was appointed by every president from Franklin D. Roosevelt to Richard M. Nixon to resolve labor disputes in coal mining, railroads, airlines, maritime, and other industries. He was the first chairman of the New Jersey State Board of Mediation (1943–45), a public member of the National War Labor Board in the New York region (1943–45), president of the National Academy of Arbitrators in 1951, head of the Federal Mediation and Conciliation Service in 1952, and the first "no-raid" arbitrator in the AFL-CIO program to resolve jurisdictional disputes. "His emphasis upon the mutual needs of the parties rather than upon their differences was always the touchstone of the Cole approach," said Robert Coulson, president of the American Arbitration Association, when Cole died in January 1978. *New York Times*, 26 January 1978.

6. Paul R. Hays was a professor of labor law at Columbia University School of Law until 1961, when he was appointed to the U.S. Court of Appeals, Second Circuit, on which he served until his death in February 1980. Judge Hays had been on the board of the New York State Board of Mediation (1940–44), a public member of the National War Labor Board, New York region (1942–43), and an arbitrator for 23 years. In 1964 Hays expressed very critical views of arbitration, dissenting from the U.S. Supreme Court holdings in the Steel Trilogy cases: "Labor arbitration is a private system of justice not based on law and not observant of law. There is no reason why it should be able to call on the legal system to enforce its decrees. Moreover there is affirmative reason why the courts should not lend themselves at all to the arbitration process." Paul R. Hays, *Labor Arbitration: A Dissenting View* (New Haven, Conn.: Yale University Press, 1966), 113.

Hays also dissented from Justice Douglas's view that "the ablest judge cannot be expected to bring the same experience and competence to bear upon the determination of a grievance, because he cannot be similarly informed." The Supreme Court's view of arbitration was apparently based upon the work of Harry Shulman and Archibald

Cox, Hays opined, and he agreed that Shulman and Cox were indeed "the equal of the 'ablest judges.' " But Hays maintained that "arbitration cannot properly claim the right to be judged by the standards established by the best exemplars." Hays charged that there were grave questions about the mettle and character of the several thousand persons who were arbitrating the 20,000 cases that came to arbitration annually. At the time the NAA had only about 300 members; Hays's most disparaging comments were largely directed at non-NAA members. His harsh statements stirred sharp controversy. The NAA has continued work in promoting ethical standards and arbitrator competence. Also, designating agencies such as AAA, FMCS, and local labor relations agencies continued to enlarge their educational work for practitioners and to review standards for panel eligibility.

7. Henry Mayer, a prominent New York labor lawyer until his death in August 1983, frequently represented unions in the telephone and public utilities industries. At one time in the 1970s he represented the city of New York in an arbitration involving the Policemen's Benevolent Association's demand for pay parity with firefighters.

Chapter 3

1. Anna M. Rosenberg's career as a consultant in personnel and public relations and her activity in various educational, cultural, and philanthropic organizations spanned more than half a century, until her death in May 1983. She was one of the most influential women in the public affairs of the nation and of both New York State and New York City from the 1930s onwards, years when few women reached top leadership positions. During the Roosevelt and Truman administrations particularly, she served in many important posts, most notably in 1950–53 under Secretary of Defense George C. Marshall as assistant secretary of defense, specializing in manpower and personnel; she was then the highest ranking woman ever to serve in the national military establishment. President Truman awarded her the Medal for Merit, and President Eisenhower honored her with the Medal of Freedom. A petite woman of great charm, invariably wearing a smart hat, she was described by Bernard M. Baruch as having "the mind of a man and the soft brown eyes of a woman." (Baruch, adviser to U.S. presidents and famed for his financial acumen, chaired the War Industries Board in World War I; after World War II he was U.S. representative to the United Nations Atomic Energy Commission.)

Mayor Fiorello H. LaGuardia said Rosenberg knew "more about labor relations and human relations than any man in the country." New York mayors and governors designated her over the years to assist in settling labor-management disputes. Long prominent in the Democratic party, in 1962 she married Paul G. Hoffman, a prominent Republican who was the first administrator of the postwar Marshall Plan and later headed the UN Development Program.

2. Robert F. Wagner represented New York in the U.S. Senate from 1927 to 1949. He helped formulate pivotal labor and social laws, among which was the National Labor Relations Act (commonly called the Wagner Act).

3. Arthur S. Meyer's great skills as a labor peacemaker were first called upon

when he was 57 years old and retired from a successful career as head of Schulte Real Estate Company and Schulte Retail Stores Corporation. While taking courses at Columbia University School of Law, he attracted his professors' attention and respect. (Meyer was a remarkably brilliant individual who had to abandon college studies during his youth because of ill health.) When Prof. Karl N. Llewellyn was asked by Mayor LaGuardia in 1937 to form the City Industrial Relations Board, he took along as the other two board members his student Arthur S. Meyer and Anna M. Rosenberg. A few months later Gov. Herbert H. Lehman established the New York State Board of Mediation, superseding the city board; Meyer became a board member and then succeeded William H. Davis as chairman, remaining in that post until his retirement in 1950. He was involved in virtually every labor dispute in the state, and his talents as a mediator and dispute resolver were also enlisted by the federal government and New York City.

In 1942 the National War Labor Board named Meyer chairman of its panel in the steel industry wage dispute; the panel's award established the "Little Steel Formula," which became the pattern for World War II wage settlements. In 1946, when a transit strike was imminent in New York City, Mayor William O'Dwyer named Meyer chairman of the blue-ribbon committee that averted the strike and established collective-bargaining policy for the citywide transit system. (Other committee members were labor relations specialist Theodore W. Kheel, former New York City police commissioner Edward P. Mulrooney, Anna M. Rosenberg, and Samuel I. Rosenman, former New York State Court of Appeals justice and adviser and speechwriter for Pres. Franklin D. Roosevelt; Clara H. Friedman was the economist to the committee.) In 1947 Meyer was one of the small group of notable arbitrators who met in Chicago to establish the National Academy of Arbitrators. In 1951, when extracurricular activities in the New York City school system were shut down by teachers' protest of working conditions, Meyer was named chairman of the fact-finding committee of the Board of Education. (Other committee members were Andrew G. Clauson, Jr., Elinore M. Herrick, Vito F. Lanza, Joseph D. McGoldrick, Carl Whitmore, and Harry G. Willnus; Clara H. Friedman was the economist to the committee.) The committee's recommendations were the basis for far-reaching and seminal changes in salary compensation and grievance procedures.

Beginning in 1950, Meyer chaired the Columbia University interfaculty seminar on labor. He died in August 1955. Following his death, the *New York Times* editorialized that "he solved a thousand controversies in almost every area of labor-management relations with reasonableness, persuasion, kindness and firmness. But Mr. Meyer was more than a cold and impersonal umpire. He was a man of depth and warmth, passionately concerned with people. Perhaps that is why he was a great mediator. It is certainly why he was such a fine human being."

4. Gellhorn concluded that "the excess moneys held by the trustees should be expended in furtherance of the fund's fundamental purpose, namely, the provision of retirement income for the affected employee group." He noted that "neither past practices nor linguistic technicalities of written instruments speak so clearly as to dictate the outcome of the present controversy." He found that "first of all, the pension program was structured not to produce the possibility of a monetary refund for the *Star* but to produce the assurance of retirement pay for the *Star*'s qualified

employees." His conclusion was "reinforced by what is known of collective bargaining in general and at the *Star* in particular. . . . Especially having in mind the accelerating deterioration of the *Star*'s economic prospects during the years now involved, one cannot suppose that the *Star*'s payments into the fund were made without a quid pro quo in the form of Guild concessions concerning other matters." The pension fund payments by the *Star* were characterized as "compliance with a contractual commitment. To convert any part of them into a kind of long-term speculative investment would be to convert the actualities of the employer-employee relationship into the artificialities of a vocabulary foreign to the present situation." *Opinion of Impartial Umpire Gellhorn*, 9 December 1983, unpublished.

Chapter 4

1. "To Ida Klaus who pointed the way" is the dedication in Donald H. Wollett, Joseph R. Grodin, and June M. Weisberger, *Collective Bargaining in Public Employment*, 4th ed, American Casebook Series (St. Paul: West Publishing, 1993). The dedication cited Klaus as "the singular moving person in all the developments . . . identified as the wellsprings of public sector collective bargaining—the early attention of the Bar Association, the Federal Executive Order, and the New York City laws," and concluded that "Ida Klaus' contribution to labor relations in the public sector, beginning in the middle 1950's and continuing for well over 30 years, compelled the authors to dedicate this course book to her. Ida Klaus was not only present at the creation; she was herself a creator."

2. As NLRB solicitor, Klaus was the highest ranking female lawyer in the federal government.

3. Just as Senator Wagner's name was given to the National Labor Relations Act (popularly known as the Wagner Act), the name of his son, Mayor Robert F. Wagner, Jr., was given to the New York City law that became the blueprint for labor relations in local governments throughout the country.

4. The task force was chaired by the secretary of labor, Arthur J. Goldberg (who in October 1962 became a U.S. Supreme Court Justice), the chairman of the Civil Service Commission, the secretary of defense, the postmaster general, the director of the Bureau of the Budget, and the counsel to the president of the United States.

5. Ralph Seward's long and notable career as an arbitrator was preceded by work in areas that were training grounds for neutrals. These included service at the National Labor Relations Board in 1936 as a review attorney, at the New York State Labor Relations Board as executive secretary and then in 1939 as general counsel, at the National Defense Mediation Board as executive secretary in 1941, and at the National War Labor Board as a public member during World War II. He went on to serve as impartial umpire in numerous major contracts; among them were designations by the milk industry in the New York metropolitan area and the Teamsters Union; United States Steel and the United Steelworkers of America; General Motors and the United Automobile Workers; and Bethlehem Steel and the United Steelworkers of America.

Seward was the first president of the NAA in 1947–49; in all the years thereafter he assisted in shaping the character of the academy and the profession. In his gentle way and by his consistent example, he was a great teacher to his associates and apprentices and to new members joining the academy. It was not Seward's style to make pronouncements, but he offered some during a 1977 interview when asked if he had any advice to pass on to future generations of arbitrators. "Oh, I don't know," he said. "Never get yourself mixed up with God. Always realize the importance of having the grievant and everybody else go away from the hearing feeling that it has been a fair, thorough, and interesting process rather than a perfunctory one, and go away from the decision understanding the decision and feeling that the arbitrator has tried to be fair. You always must remember, when you go into a new hearing room, that you are opening a new book and you have to start learning all over again" ("Interview with Ralph Seward by Richard Mittenthal, April 14, 1977," *National Academy of Arbitrators Oral History Project*, Fall 1982, 84–85). Seward's advice embodied what he personally did in his arbitration work, as his colleagues well knew. Rolf Valtin observed that "Ralph was at once a brilliant and a humble person. He had a deep sense of fairness, and he was never arrogant at any of his hearings. . . . He disliked glibness. No boilerplate language was ever to be found in his opinions. Because he needed to be certain that he understood, his study of every case he ever decided was extreme. . . . The clarity and smoothness of his opinions belied the effort that went into them" (Valtin's unpublished tribute, written after Seward's death in January 1994). Alexander Porter noted some of the themes that Seward returned to again and again: "Simplify but don't oversimplify. Write in prose which speaks directly to grievant and foreman alike. Think anew as society and, within it, the industrial world evolve in new directions. . . . And always from him there was the call to be true to our trust as arbitrators and as guardians of the process he held so dear." Alexander B. Porter, "In Memoriam: Ralph Theodore Seward, 1907–1994," [National Academy of Arbitrators] *Chronicle* (April 1994).

6. Sylvester Garrett was regional chairman in Philadelphia of the National War Labor Board; earlier he had been an attorney at the National Labor Relations Board in Washington, D.C. He went on to become an arbitrator of national repute, making arbitration history by implementing comprehensive arbitration systems in industries previously marked by bitter strikes, lockouts, and deep hostility between management and labor. He left the faculty of Stanford Law School to chair the Board of Arbitration for U.S. Steel and the United Steelworkers of America at its inception in 1951, and chaired the board for 28 years. In 1963–64 he served as president of the National Academy of Arbitrators. He led the restructuring of labor relations in the U.S. Postal Service, serving as chairman in 1977 of the Joint Study Committee to establish a nationwide grievance procedure, and then as impartial chairman for arbitration of grievances between unions representing postal employees and the postal service. As a permanent umpire in other major contracts and an ad hoc arbitrator in numerous industries, Garrett's forte has been his unfailing capacity for penetrating determinations in exceedingly complex matters.

7. Saul Wallen began as a neutral in labor disputes at the National War Labor Board in 1942, and he served as chairman of the War Labor Board for the New England region. After World War II his principal work for 25 years was as an arbitrator of great skill and distinction. He was a founder of the National Academy

of Arbitrators and its president in 1954. In New York City he chaired the mayor's committee that recommended machinery for municipal collective bargaining and dispute resolution. He was a public member of the board of the Office of Collective Bargaining from its inception in 1967 until 1969. In 1968 he gave up most of his arbitration work to serve as president of the New York Urban Coalition. Although he died soon thereafter, in August 1969, during his brief tenure he launched many programs to improve the economic and social life of minority groups.

Wallen was memorialized as "a man of great wisdom and compassion, boundless energy, and contagious love of life. . . . As Bill Simkin said on a recent happier occasion, Saul was not only one of the five or six best arbitrators in the country but also an excellent mediator. The combination of these talents is rare; even more so is the sensitivity required to keep each role in its proper place. . . . Saul often broke through the rigidities of formal litigation to counsel with the parties and to bring about concurrence, or to bring about what George Taylor has called the 'consent to lose.' I have known of situations where not only did Saul bring about the consent to lose, but somehow he seemed to make the losing party feel downright good about it. He did this through no magic or trickery—for he was completely without guile— but simply by the force of his open, honest, and friendly personality. He was a person people trusted; they liked him and felt comfortable in his presence." Wallen's work at the Urban Coalition was described as "a continuing expression of his central character—active, optimistic, dedicated to the resolution of conflict, concerned that we do something about the social ills that beset us and not just bemoan our fate, insistent, in the words of the Coalition slogan, that we 'give a damn.' " James C. Hill, "For Saul Wallen," *Arbitration and the Expanding Role of Neutrals*, Proceedings of the 23d Annual Meeting, National Academy of Arbitrators (Washington, D.C.: Bureau of National Affairs, 1970), v–viii.

8. Theodore W. Kheel was in his early twenties when he became a staff attorney at the National Labor Relations Board. In later years he became a prominent mediator, arbitrator, and counselor involved in critical labor disputes, particularly in transit and newspapers. During World War II he was a public member of the War Labor Board in the New York region. In 1947 he served as labor counsel to the city of New York. His activity in labor matters continued when he became a partner in Battle Fowler & Kheel, a New York law firm. Long interested in the techniques of dispute settlement, in the late 1960s Kheel founded the Institute for Mediation and Conflict Resolution, a nonprofit public-service training organization for application of arbitration and mediation skills to the community conflicts wracking society.

9. "Checkoff" is the widespread procedure by which the employer (pursuant to authorization from the affected employees and agreement with the collective-bargaining organization) automatically deducts union dues (and perhaps other obligations, such as membership initiation fees and special assessments) from employees' wages and salaries. The employer turns over the deductions to the union. Unions commonly seek checkoffs to expedite receipt of employees' financial obligations to the union, thus aiding the union's financial stability.

10. Aaron Horvitz began arbitrating before the War Labor Board years. He was born in 1888 and educated as an attorney. At his death in September 1968, he was honored for his long life as a peacemaker: "Aaron, along with Max Copelof and a

handful of old-timers, set out the footings and laid the foundation stones of the House of Arbitration. . . . For decades, in the infancy of arbitration, he travelled by train, automobile, and plane to remote areas in the mountains, the plains, and the deserts, the large and small cities, frequently at great inconvenience, to sow the seeds of industrial peace. . . . Aaron was not a detached, aloof, or unconcerned arbitrator. His opinions were strong, pungent, forthright, and unequivocal. . . . While his procedure was frowned upon by some, it delighted and was richly appreciated by Aaron's clients. They enjoyed and valued the highly dramatic experience of being lectured to by Aaron—a procedure not recommended to arbitrators with less colorful, attractive, and forceful personalities. Aaron's strong personal views, however, did not color his decisions. Impartiality in the pursuit of his profession was, to him, like a religion" (Peter Seitz, "For Aaron Horvitz," *Arbitration and Social Change*, Proceedings of the 22d Annual Meeting, National Academy of Arbitrators [Washington, D.C.: Bureau of National Affairs, 1970], ix–x). Wayne L. Horvitz, son of Aaron Horvitz, headed the Federal Mediation and Conciliation Service in 1981.

11. Before becoming a full-time arbitrator, Peter Seitz had served as a public member of the National Wage Stabilization Board, counsel of the Federal Mediation and Conciliation Service, and director of industrial relations for the U.S. Department of Defense. As a baseball arbitrator in the early 1970s, he had major impact—and brief tenure—after awarding free-agent status to Catfish Hunter, Andy Messersmith, and Dave McNally. When he delivered his award and opinion in the Messersmith and McNally cases, he was handed a letter from the baseball team owners, dismissing him at once as grievance umpire.

Seitz "was a man of complete integrity and great courage," wrote Ralph T. Seward, in a memorial tribute. "He threw himself not only into the ordinary tasks of his profession but into its great issues and controversies; the journals and literature of arbitration have been enriched by his defense of principles and values he held dear" "In Memoriam: Peter Seitz, 1905–1983," *Arbitration 1984: Absenteeism, Recent Law, Panels and Published Decisions*, Proceedings of the 37th Annual Meeting, National Academy of Arbitrators (Washington, D.C.: Bureau of National Affairs), xi.

In arbitration circles, Seitz was esteemed and appreciated for his wit and poetry. One of his oft-quoted humorous sallies was, "Show me a new arbitrator and I'll show you someone with his hand in my pocket." Yet he was a devoted mentor to young arbitrators; for a long time he conducted, together with Eva Robins, at their own initiative, a tutorial for aspiring arbitrators that produced a number of respected arbitrators (many of them women).

12. Abram H. Stockman had been at the National War Labor Board as chief enforcement attorney in the New York region, and then as assistant general counsel and chairman of the appeals committee in Washington, D.C. Later he was executive director of the National Wage Stabilization Board and became vice chairman in the metropolitan New York region. From 1945 until his death in 1977, arbitration was his profession. He served on the Foreign Service Grievance Board and as designated arbitrator in many contracts, including Bendix Corporation and the United Automobile Workers and International Brotherhood of Teamsters, General Electric and International Union of Electrical Workers, New York City Department of Health and District Council 37-AFSCME and the Doctors Association.

Stockman was a charter member of the National Academy of Arbitrators, and a highly valued one: "To newcomers in the Academy, he was the elder statesman par excellence, giving freely of his time and wisdom. To old hands with perplexing problems, he was the patient and reliable sounding board," wrote Arthur Stark as president of the National Academy of Arbitrators in 1977, on behalf of the Board of Governors ("In Memoriam, Abram H. Stockman, 1911–1977," *Arbitration 1977*, Proceedings of the 30th Annual Meeting, National Academy of Arbitrators [Washington, D.C.: Bureau of National Affairs], vi). One of the tributes to Stockman from colleagues, quoted by Stark, was: "Abe was outstanding among arbitrators—really in a class by himself. He always wrote so carefully, wisely, and beautifully."

13. James C. Hill was a full-time arbitrator of national repute from the mid-1950s until his retirement some 20 years later. Earlier he had taught economics at Amherst College, Sarah Lawrence College, Columbia University, and Cornell University, before serving at the National War Labor Board, National Wage Stabilization Board, and New York State Board of Mediation. Hill was president of the National Academy of Arbitrators in 1969. His trademark grace and wit were saluted in a memorial tribute by Eva Robins: "To those of us who were fortunate enough to know and work with him, when we learned our craft, Jim was a great teacher. His arbitration hearings were prime examples of integrity, impartiality, and fairness. . . . No comment about Jim would be complete without recalling his wonderful, zany humor, which gave us—colleagues, friends, and parties—such joy." Eva Robins, "In Memoriam, James C. Hill, 1914–1991," *Arbitration 1991: The Changing Face of Arbitration in Theory and Practice*, Proceedings of the 44th Annual Meeting, National Academy of Arbitrators (Washington, D.C.: Bureau of National Affairs), viii–ix.

14. Louis Yagoda was a highly regarded arbitrator and mediator for almost half a century. From 1942 to 1962 he was on the staff of the New York State Board of Mediation and was assistant executive secretary when he resigned to become a full-time arbitrator. Among the critical labor situations he defused while at the New York State Board of Mediation was the impasse he mediated in the mid-1950s between tank-truck drivers and hauling companies, an impasse that threatened to cut off milk supplies to 17 million people in the New York area. In 1959 he helped settle a six-day strike of tugboat crews that had tied up New York Harbor. From 1962 until his death in 1990, he continued to serve as mediator and arbitrator in disputes throughout the United States and at U.S. government installations in the Panama Canal Zone. In 1975, when New York City was in the throes of a fiscal crisis, he and other mediators settled a five-day strike by the United Federation of Teachers that had closed down the city's schools.

Chapter 5

1. Louis Stark's labor reporting for the *New York Times* won him a Pulitzer Prize in 1942. He was widely regarded as the dean of labor reporters in the United States. From 1951 until his death in 1954, he was a member of the *New York Times* editorial board.

2. Charles H. Percy was the Republican party candidate in 1969 for the U.S. Senate seat held by Paul H. Douglas. He defeated Senator Douglas, who had been the Democratic incumbent since 1948.

3. Sidney Hillman was president for many years of the Amalgamated Clothing Workers Union of America and a founder and leader of the Congress of Industrial Organizations. He was a staunch supporter of Franklin D. Roosevelt from the beginning of the New Deal. "Clearing it with Sidney" was the bitter byword coined by Roosevelt's antilabor archcritics to suggest that Hillman was Roosevelt's éminence grise.

4. Frederick H. Bullen was a senior mediation officer at the National War Labor Board and became chairman of the Regional War Labor Board in Cleveland. In 1945 he was appointed executive secretary of the New York State Board of Mediation. Some five years later he went to the National Wage Stabilization Board as vice chairman. Subsequently, he became a partner in a major law firm in New York City. In recent years he has resumed the practice of arbitration on a full-time basis and resides in California.

5. Lewis M. Gill became a full-time arbitrator, designated throughout the country. He was president of the National Academy of Arbitrators from 1971 to 1972. Gill resides in Pennsylvania.

6. Burton B. Turkus was well known for successfully prosecuting mobsters in the 1940s when he was in the Kings County district attorney's office. *Murder, Inc.*, his best-seller account, has come into popular use as the term for organized gangsterism. In 1948 Turkus was appointed to the New York State Board of Mediation as a public member of the board. He later became a very successful full-time arbitrator. He died in November 1982.

7. Jean McKelvey's labor relations career has been as both an academic and an arbitrator. A longtime professor at Cornell University in the School of Industrial and Labor Relations, she began arbitrating during the National War Labor Board years of World War II. In 1970 McKelvey was elected president of the National Academy of Arbitrators, the first woman to hold that position. As a professor, she trained and inspired thousands of students who went on to careers in industrial relations, a goodly number as arbitrators. As an arbitrator, McKelvey was designated in major industries throughout the United States and in critical public-sector impasses. The trust she engendered is exemplified by such appointments as her longtime membership on the Public Review Board of the UAW; the Public Review Board is final arbiter of complaints by union members against their union in internal matters such as union elections and grievance handling.

8. Dorothy Copeland Stark is a sculptor whose work is found in private collections throughout the United States. Previously, she had used her professional training in economics in various labor relations positions. Among them were director of industrial relations research for the Continental Can Company, specialist in talent union contracts (chiefly television and radio) for the American Association of Advertising Agencies, and assistant executive secretary at the New York State Board of Mediation.

Chapter 6

1. Three of Ben Scheiber's anecdotes were recalled by several arbitrators interviewed for the oral histories. One was of Ben, at his ninetieth birthday celebration hosted by the New York region of the National Academy of Arbitrators, announcing that his wife had told him beforehand not to get "too sugary"; he had responded with, "A little taffy now is better than an 'epi-taph-y' later."

Another arbitrator remembered Ben's comment at an annual meeting of the National Academy of Arbitrators when the topic was the advancing age of veteran arbitrators and the paucity of younger arbitrators. A new member said, when introduced, "I am not as young as I look." James C. Hill (also a famous wit) said, when introduced as an old member, "I am not as old as I look." Whereupon Ben Scheiber, easily the oldest member present, rose to a point of personal privilege. He said he was reminded of the rabbi who was praying, shaking back and forth and saying, "Oh Lord, I am as nothing!" The cantor joined in shaking and saying, "Oh Lord, I am as nothing!" When the lowly sexton joined in, saying also, "Oh Lord, I am as nothing!" the cantor nudged the rabbi and said, "Look who's saying he is as nothing!"

Ben enjoyed talking with other arbitrators about arbitration cases. He would often interject (as the great violinist Mischa Elman reputedly did): "Enough talk about me! Now let's talk about you! How did you like my last arbitration award?" ("How did you like my last concert?" Elman would ask.)

2. Sixty years later, an article on Scheiber in a community newspaper said of him, "He's a man of many and great accomplishments—a man who, it has been said, singlehandedly brought Putnam Valley into the 20th century." *Community Current,* 30 April 1980.

A community service award presented to Scheiber on 28 August 1983 cited him as, "without dispute, the elder statesman of Putnam Valley. He is indeed 'a legend in his own time,' and his impact upon the quality of life in our community will be felt for all time. . . . Ben brought to this town extraordinary expertise as a planner, organizer and attorney. He served as our town counsel for 18 years, led the battle for centralization of the little one-room schools around Putnam Valley, and when it was won served as president of the Putnam Valley School Board for 15 years."

When the Putnam Valley School District celebrated its fiftieth anniversary in 1985, it wrote to Scheiber on 23 January: "No other individual in the history of this school district is more responsible for its birth and growth than Israel Ben Scheiber. We are all indebted to you for your magnificent contributions to the education of so many thousands of children."

3. During the two weeks preceding the scheduled taping, I met with Scheiber several times at his home, and he reminisced at great length. But on the day of the actual taping, extemporaneous conversation was too great a strain for him. The interview had to be conducted by asking leading questions based on information he had given earlier in untaped talk, to which he replied monosyllabically in the taped interview. Twice Scheiber spoke unprompted: once when he readily confided his "secret," and near the end when he asked, "Is it over?" Told that it was, he exclaimed, "Thank God!" For the chapter in this book, the taped interview has been recast in the first person, within Scheiber's characteristic style of speaking.

4. Scheiber's wife Augusta (known as Gus) was his constant companion at annual meetings of the National Academy of Arbitrators, which Ben attended faithfully until he was almost 90. They shared high ideals and great respect for arbitration's worth. Ben's "secret," his wife knew, was not a witticism; it was heartfelt. For decades Ben's humor was enjoyed by his colleagues, as was his wife's quieter and sometimes deflating wit. Ben made jokes, and Gus made music; a talented concert pianist, she was on the faculty of Mannes College of Music in New York for many years. Whenever arbitrators got together, Gus was asked to play, alone or in duets with other pianists (like Arthur Stark) or accompanying group singing. An excerpt from Gus playing Bach was used on the sound track of *Resolving Disputes without Going into Court,* a videotape series for law schools I produced in 1985 under grants from the National Institute for Dispute Resolution and Hofstra University School of Law. Gus Scheiber died in 1993.

Chapter 7

1. Friedman came to the New York State Board of Mediation after a statewide competitive civil service examination for staff mediator and arbitrator in which he ranked first.

2. This example was mentioned briefly in Friedman's article, "Problems of Cross-Examination in Labor Arbitration," *Arbitration Journal* (American Arbitration Association) 34, no. 4 (December 1979): 6–11.

Chapter 8

1. I. Robert Feinberg was a prominent lawyer and arbitrator until his death in 1975. He was assistant general counsel and chairman of the appeals committee of the National War Labor Board from 1943 to 1945, vice chairman of the War Labor Board in the New York region in 1945, and chairman of the enforcement commission of the National Wage Stabilization for New York and New Jersey in 1951–52. He was on permanent arbitration panels for Actors Equity and League of New York Theatres, New York City Board of Education and United Federation of Teachers, and panels in the aircraft and shipping industries. He was impartial chairman of the fur industry from 1968 until his death. A charter member of the National Academy of Arbitrators, he was vice president in 1956–57. Feinberg was adjunct professor of law at New York University School of Law, where he had ranked first in his graduating class.

2. Robert Moses was the chairman of major public works agencies, including the Triborough Bridge and Tunnel Authority. He transformed New York State and City with numerous new and improved highways, parks, bridges, and beaches. Moses's strong personality and imperious will were legendary.

3. Wolf's mediation tactics in the men's shirt industry were akin to mediation by Leiserson in the early 1900s in the men's clothing industry, when he headed the board of arbitration established by Hart Schaffner & Marx and the Amalgamated Clothing Workers Union. Fleming wrote of "William M. Leiserson, one of the tower-

ing figures in American labor-management history," that he "proved to be one of the great chairmen in the developmental days. Dr. Leiserson endeavored to bring about settlements by mediation. Whenever it was possible, he referred the case back to the parties for further discussion by a joint committee which he appointed. Even when mediation failed and Leiserson was forced to hand down a decision, he sought guidance from the parties. Usually he would clear his decision first with a small committee of union and management representatives in order to avoid implications which he might not see in making the award, but which might become troublesome precedents. He also discussed the contents of his decisions at union and management conferences in order to hammer out general acceptance of the principles he helped to form" (Fleming, *The Labor Arbitration Process*, 9). The appropriateness and effectiveness of Leiserson's approach at the start of the century were based on particular circumstances, history, and personalities in the arbitration system for Hart Schaffner & Marx and the Amalgamated Clothing Workers Union.

Chapter 9

1. Damon Stetson, "Candid Labor Arbitrator: Arvid Anderson," *New York Times*, 8 April 1982.

2. Anderson's decision in the salary dispute between Don Mattingly and the New York Yankees unleashed owner George M. Steinbrenner's wrath. *New York Times* sportswriter Ira Berkow wrote on 25 February 1987 that when Steinbrenner "lost the case—his figure was $1.7 million a year to Mattingly's $1.975 million— [Steinbrenner] railed that the arbitrator was a bum and 'probably never wore a jockstrap in his life.' . . . The arbitrator in the Mattingly case happened to be Arvid Anderson. . . . Arbitrators used by baseball have established reputations for impartiality, probity and sound judgment. Anderson's credentials are lofty."

3. Soon after graduating from the University of Michigan Law School in the early 1930s, Feinsinger began a lifelong career as a professor at the University of Wisconsin Law School and a mediator and arbitrator in labor disputes throughout the United States. After his death in 1983 at age 81, Fleming memorialized him as "one of the giants of the labor arbitration profession. . . . Nate became involved in the drafting, enactment, and administration of a Little Wagner Act for the State [of Wisconsin]. And when the National War Labor Board was formed at the outset of World War II he was called upon for service with that agency. It was with the NWLB that his national reputation was established, and through the 1940s he became one of the superstars of the mediation and arbitration field. If there was a major national dispute, Nate was likely to be involved. He had a sharp and incisive mind, an instinct for identifying key issues, an imagination that could repackage old issues so that they became more acceptable to the parties, a sense of humor which enabled him to hold the parties together, and a deep respect for fairness and equity." Fleming referred to the physical travail that Feinsinger did not permit to interrupt his work: "At the start of the 1950s Nate had a tragic auto accident which required a long period of recovery and impaired his physical strength the rest of his life. Though lame from the accident and often in pain, Nate refused to slow his pace and continued his national efforts

in mediation and arbitration. He also continued to teach at Wisconsin Law School. During the Korean War he took time off from Wisconsin to serve as chairman of the National Wage Stabilization Board under President Truman, and in the years thereafter was Chairman of a number of Emergency Disputes Boards and of boards privately established for the settlement of a wide variety of disputes. He was also the contract arbitrator under a number of agreements, principal among which was the General Motors–UAW contract. . . . The National Academy of Arbitrators, of which he was a founding member, will hold him in ever honored memory." Robben W. Fleming, "In Memoriam, Nathan P. Feinsinger, 1902–1983," *Arbitration 1984: Absenteeism, Recent Law, Panels, and Published Decisions,* Proceedings of the 37th Annual Meeting, National Academy of Arbitrators (Washington, D.C.: Bureau of National Affairs), vi–vii.

Fleming himself is an eminent legal scholar and arbitrator. He was president of the University of Michigan from 1968 to 1979, president of the Corporation for Public Broadcasting from 1979 to 1981, president of the Association of American Universities, and president of the National Academy of Arbitrators in 1966–67. He was the first chairman of the board of the National Institute for Dispute Resolution. Fleming's book on arbitration, *The Labor Arbitration Process* (Urbana: University of Illinois Press, 1965), continues to be a valued reference.

4. William H. Davis was the first chairman of the New York State Board of Mediation from 1937 to 1940, first chairman of the National Defense Mediation Board in 1941, first chairman of the National War Labor Board from 1942 to 1945, director of the Office of Economic Stabilization in 1945, first chairman of the Patent Advisory Panel in 1947 at the Atomic Energy Commission, and also chairman of the commission's Atomic Energy Labor Relations Panel. Davis was an outstanding patent attorney and until his death in August 1964 remained active in Davis, Hozie, Faithful & Hapgood, a law firm in New York City. His contributions to labor peace and to the Allied victory in World War II were termed "invaluable and incalculable, and at considerable sacrifice" by Supreme Court Justice Arthur J. Goldberg in his 1962 address to the New York Patent Law Association. The *New York Times* obituary of 15 August 1964 said that Davis "had a dry wit and took his philosophy from Plato: 'Creation is the product of persuasion.' [Davis] amended it by adding 'except in the case of rape.' "

5. The LaFollette family's influence on social policies began in Wisconsin and spread to the national level. The "Wisconsin Idea" was the term applied to progressive legislation enacted during Robert M. LaFollette's two terms as governor of Wisconsin from 1902 to 1906; as a U.S. senator from 1906 until 1925 he continued to champion reforms. So did his son, Robert LaFollette, Jr., who succeeded his father in the U.S. Senate and served until 1947. So also did another son, Philip LaFollette, who was governor of Wisconsin in 1931–33 and 1935–39.

6. The OCB was created in 1967 by the New York City Collective Bargaining Law, as authorized by the New York State Taylor Law. The OCB is an impartial tripartite agency with jurisdiction for labor relations over all municipal agencies and the unions representing municipal employees.

7. The two deputy chairmen serve as general counsel and overseer of dispute settlement procedures, respectively.

8. Eva Robins came to the OCB from the New York State Board of Mediation, where she had been a skilled mediator and arbitrator, the first woman to serve in that staff capacity in the agency's history. Widely respected as a dispute resolver, she was deputy OCB chairman until she resigned in February 1972 for the full-time practice of arbitration. One of the earliest women arbitrators, Robins's career has been notable. Her designations included permanent panel of the NFL and the NFL Players Association for on-the-job injuries, presidential boards in coal and railroads, and the Foreign Service Grievance Board. She wrote "A Guide for Labor Mediators," a widely used monograph published by the University of Hawaii in 1976. Robins was president of the National Academy of Arbitrators in 1980–81. In 1980 the American Arbitration Association awarded her its Distinguished Service Award for arbitration of labor-management disputes.

9. The advisory committee, established by Mayor Robert F. Wagner in 1983, included representatives of the mayor, union leaders, and impartial labor experts. The committee's work continued after John V. Lindsay became mayor. The result in 1986 was a written agreement between the unions and the city to set up the OCB as the neutral in municipal labor relations.

10. Vincent McDonnell, a labor specialist, was formerly chairman of the New York State Board of Mediation and a law partner in Shea & Gould.

Chapter 10

1. Cooper Union, the famous educational institution in New York City, was founded in 1859 by the inventor and industrialist Peter Cooper. It offers free lectures on technical, cultural, and public affairs subjects, and tuition-free college programs in art, architecture, and engineering.

2. The vice principal of DeWitt Clinton High was Angelo Patri, well known in the 1930s and 1940s as an educator and a syndicated newspaper columnist on youth problems.

Chapter 12

1. Stephen C. Vladeck was prominent as a labor and civil liberties lawyer for over three decades until his death in 1979. During World War II he was an economist with the National War Labor Board. After graduation from Columbia University School of Law, he formed a law firm in New York City, chiefly representing labor unions and dealing with labor law and social issues. He served as chairman of Group Health Inc., general counsel for the New York Civil Liberties Union, vice chairman of Mobilization for Youth Legal Services, and adjunct professor of law at New York University from 1960 to 1975.

2. "Slippery water" came into use after 1970 through the work of the New York City Rand Institute, a nonprofit research organization established at the request of Mayor John V. Lindsay; he asked the Rand Corporation, a California-based "think

tank," that was preeminent in national security studies and had also addressed some domestic policy problems, to apply its expertise to issues of concern in New York City.

New technology in firefighting was encompassed in the Rand Institute's study of urban fire problems: "In fighting a fire, the classic weapon is water from a hose. But the friction the water meets in flowing through the hose creates a classic dilemma; it dictates using a large, bulky hose to get enough water to the fire, while firemen prefer and need a small, light hose for speed and maneuverability. This dilemma has now been resolved by a technological breakthrough initiated and catalyzed by the work of Edward Blum at the Institute. This development derives from the fact that dissolving trace amounts of a special chemical (a long-chain polymer) in the water reduces the water's turbulent viscosity. We call the solution 'slippery water.' It permits the Fire Department to increase the flow through a hose at a given pressure by seventy percent or more, and to more than double the reach of the stream. With slippery water, a fireman can deliver as much water with a 1½-inch hose as he previously could only with a 2½-inch hose. With the lighter hose, fire fighters can climb stairs and reach remote locations more rapidly and with less strain, and put out fires more quickly and effectively. . . . Principally a laboratory curiosity when the project began, slippery water is now in the last stages of a joint development program aimed at bringing it into routine Fire Department use. . . . [Fire]Department officials have estimated that in the next few years . . . an increase in operational effectiveness will have been gained that otherwise would have cost many millions of dollars per year" (New York City Rand Institute, *First Annual Report* [October 1970], 1, 15–16). The institute's research projects were led by nine individuals; Clare H. Friedman headed the welfare studies.

Chapter 13

1. Dean Harry Shulman of Yale University Law School was umpire for Ford Motor Company and the UAW. He viewed the arbitrator as an integral part of the relationship between company and union, as did William Leiserson, umpire in the clothing industry, and George Taylor, umpire in the hosiery industry. "None of these parties," wrote Fleming, "viewed the umpire as a circuit-riding judge who came into the lives of the litigants simply to hear a given dispute and then depart to render a decision. [The umpire] was, on the contrary, an integral part of the company-union relationship. He was free to go anywhere and talk to anyone, and his decisions were expected to be based on much more than just the information that might be given to him in connection with the point at hand. In a substantial number of instances, the decision was, in fact, a mediated result even if it did not show this on its face." Fleming found the Ford umpire system unlike those of both General Motors and Chrysler insofar as it "swung heavily in the direction of utilizing the impartial umpire as a mediator, a wise and trusted counselor, and sometimes decision-maker. Perhaps this simply reflected the genius of Harry Shulman, who helped the parties work out the system and then became the first umpire." Fleming, *The Labor Arbitration Process*, 157, 16.

2. In June 1960 the Supreme Court decided three cases that came to be known

as the Steel Trilogy: *United Steelworkers of America v. Warrior & Gulf Nav. Co.*, 363 U.S. 574; *United Steelworkers of America v. Enterprise Wheel & Car Corp.*, 363 U.S. 593; and *United Steelworkers of America v. American Mfg. Co.*, 363 U.S. 564. Associate Justice William O. Douglas said in his opinion: "The labor arbitrator is usually chosen because of the parties' confidence in his knowledge of the common law of the shop and their trust in his personal judgment to bring to bear considerations which are not expressed in the contract as criteria for judgment. The parties expect that his judgment of a particular grievance will reflect not only what the contract says but, insofar as the collective bargaining agreement permits, such facts as the effect upon productivity of a particular result, its consequence to the morale of the shop, his judgment whether tensions will be heightened or diminished. . . . The ablest judge cannot be expected to bring the same experience and competence to bear upon the determination of a grievance, because he cannot be similarly informed." (*United Steelworkers of America v. Warrior & Gulf Nav. Co.*, 582; n. 87). This "almost ecstatic" paragraph by Douglas "caused many arbitrators to purchase new mirrors," Fleming wrote. Fleming, *The Labor Arbitration Process*, 24.

Chapter 14

1. During military service overseas in World War II, Nicolau suffered serious injuries that precluded the baseball career he had wanted.

2. The HRA is the umbrella agency that includes the Social Services Agency, which administers welfare and relief, and various other agencies for poverty-related programs such as community development and job training.

3. The burning was literal. Vandalism and rioting erupted in many cities at a time of intense racial tension.

4. The player, not identified by Nicolau, was Bernard King. His difficulties were reported in a *New York Times* column of April 1984 by sportswriter Dave Anderson, who wrote that King was cherished by his teammates as "their captain, their leader, a gentleman and a model citizen."

5. Benjamin C. Roberts was a highly regarded arbitrator who had been with the New York State Board of Mediation before he became a full-time arbitrator. He was umpire for NABET and the broadcast networks from the inception of their arbitration system until his death in 1980. He also arbitrated throughout the country in numerous industries, both in permanent capacities, as in the New York City theaters' collective-bargaining agreements, and ad hoc under other agreements. Roberts was a vice president of the National Academy of Arbitrators in 1960 and 1961.

Chapter 15

1. The American Arbitration Association was formed in 1926 at a time when the usage of commercial arbitration was popularizing arbitration in the business community. The AAA responded to the need for labor arbitration in the entertainment

industry early on when the Actors Equity Association in New York City asked AAA to handle its disputes with management because court dockets were so crowded that cases languished for years. "The liaison between the AAA and Actors' Equity proved so successful that the Association was soon performing a similar service for the Dramatists' Guild, the Authors' League, and later the Screen Actors' Guild and the American Federation of Radio Artists. In the course of establishing arbitration machinery in the amusement industry, the AAA rejected the idea that arbitration could or should be combined with conciliation efforts and strove to make it a strictly adjudicatory process." Fleming, *The Labor Arbitration Process*, 12.

In 1937 AAA responded to the widening demand for labor arbitration by establishing its Voluntary Industrial Tribunal, making a panel of labor arbitrators available to employers and unions. AAA gradually promulgated procedural rules for the conduct of arbitrations and recommended model arbitration clauses for inclusion in collective-bargaining contracts.

AAA's educational activities made it a leading advocate and resource for arbitration. "With different motives and greater success, the Association took over many tasks performed thirty years earlier by the National Civic Federation. Such tasks included publicizing the benefits of the arbitration system, providing arbitration services, refining the arbitration process, and training qualified arbitrators." Nolan and Abrams, "American Labor Arbitration," 415.

AAA's role in labor arbitration is epitomized by its being among the three groups that together formulated standards of ethical conduct in labor arbitration. "Code of Ethics and Procedural Standards for Labor-Management Arbitration" became the governing ethical guide in 1951 and was revised in 1972 as "Code of Professional Responsibility for Arbitrators of Labor-Management Disputes." The 1951 code and the 1972 revised code were drafted by the same three groups: the American Arbitration Association, the Federal Mediation and Conciliation Service, and the National Academy of Arbitrators. The codes were thereafter adopted by the three groups. The 1972 committee that drafted the revised code consisted of William E. Simkin (chairman), Frederick H. Bullen and Donald B. Straus (representing the American Arbitration Association), Lawrence B. Babcock, Jr., and L. Lawrence Schultz (representing the Federal Mediation and Conciliation Service), and Sylvester Garrett and Ralph T. Seward (representing the National Academy of Arbitrators).

Chapter 16

1. Edwin E. Witte, "Historical Survey of Labor Arbitration," Labor Relations Series (Philadelphia: University of Pennsylvania Press, 1952); R. W. Fleming, *The Labor Arbitration Process* (Urbana: University of Illinois Press, 1965), ch. 1; Ian R. Macneil, *American Arbitration Law* (New York: Oxford University Press, 1992), ch. 2.

2. John Mitchell, *Organized Labor* (Philadelphia: American Book and Bible House, 1903), chs. 40–45; Selig Perlman and Philip Taft, *History of Labor in the United States, 1896–1932* (New York: Macmillan, 1935), ch. 4; Henry F. Pringle, *Theodore Roosevelt: A Biography* (New York: Harcourt Brace, 1931), book 2, ch. 3; Theodore Roosevelt, *An Autobiography* (New York: Scribners, 1927), 464; Elting

E. Morison, *The Letters of Theodore Roosevelt* (Cambridge; Mass.: Harvard University Press, 1951), 3:329–30.

3. Jesse T. Carpenter, *Competition and Collective Bargaining in the Needle Trades, 1910–1967* (Ithaca: New York State School of Industrial and Labor Relations, Cornell University, 1972), chs. 1 and 2 (quote from p. 2); Alpheus Thomas Mason, *Brandeis: A Free Man's Life* (New York: Viking, 1946), ch. 19; Perlman and Taft, *History of Labor*, ch. 25.

4. Matthew Josephson, *Sidney Hillman: Statesman of American Labor* (New York: Doubleday, 1952), chs. 2–8; Harry A. Millis and Royal E. Montgomery, *Organized Labor* (New York: McGraw-Hill, 1945), 484, 711–12, 718; Perlman and Taft, *History of Labor*, 304–17, 436.

5. Arthur S. Link, *Woodrow Wilson and the Progressive Era, 1910–1917* (New York: Harper, 1954), chs. 2 and 3; Arthur S. Link, *Wilson: The New Freedom* (Princeton, N.J.: Princeton University Press, 1956), chs. 4, 5, 8, and 13; Millis and Montgomery, *Organized Labor*, ch. 3.

6. Irving Bernstein, *The Lean Years* (Boston: Houghton Mifflin, 1960), chs. 2, 9, and 10; Irving Bernstein, *Turbulent Years* (Boston: Houghton Mifflin, 1969); Millis and Montgomery, *Organized Labor*, 762–75; Department of Labor, Bureau of Labor Statistics, "Report on the Work of the National Defense Mediation Board, March 19, 1941–January 12, 1942, bulletin no. 714; Department of Labor, *The Termination Report, National War Labor Board*, vol. 1 (quote from p. 66).

7. The Trilogy consisted of *Steelworkers v. Enterprise Wheel*, 363 U.S. 593 (1960), *Steelworkers v. American Mfg. Co.*, 363 U.S. 564 (1960), and *Steelworkers v. Warrior & Gulf Navigation*, 363 U.S. 574 (1960); Sam Kagel, "Recent Supreme Court Decisions and the Arbitration Process," *Arbitration and Public Policy*, 14th Annual Meeting of the National Academy of Arbitrators (1961), 3–4.

8. Irving Bernstein, *Promises Kept: John F. Kennedy's New Frontier* (New York: Oxford University Press, 1991), 208–17; Benjamin Aaron, Joyce M. Najita, and James L. Stern, eds., *Public-Sector Bargaining*, 2d ed. (Washington, D.C.: Bureau of National Affairs, 1988), 5.

Appendix

1. The Columbia University Oral History Collection in New York City contains the transcript (restricted, category B) taped in 1959 of reminiscences of William H. Davis. The Columbia collection also has transcripts of 1965–67 interviews with Cyrus S. Ching, a leading figure in labor relations who died in 1967 at the age of 91. Ching was director of industrial and public relations at the U.S. Rubber Company from 1919 to 1947. Three successive U.S. presidents appointed Ching to important posts in the federal government: President Roosevelt named him in 1941 to the National Defense Mediation Board; President Truman appointed him in 1947 to head the Federal Mediation and Conciliation Service, a position he held until 1952; President Eisenhower named him in 1953 to the atomic energy labor relations panel, which he later chaired.

Index

Aaron, Benjamin, 176
ABC, 153
Abelson, Paul, 171
Abrams, Roger I., 190n1
Actors Equity, 143, 148, 150, 208n1
Administrative Conference of the United
  States, 7
Advance (labor newspaper), 56
Agency for International Development, 72
Air Line Pilots Association (ALPA), 154
Alexander, Gabriel, 176
American Arbitration Association (AAA), 6,
  11–12, 60, 76, 82, 111, 124, 149,
  158–63, 176, 177, 182, 183, 208n1
Amalgamated Clothing Workers of America,
  56, 101–3, 167
American Federation of Labor (AFL), 134,
  167, 173
American Federation of State, County and
  Municipal Employees (AFSCME), 40, 46,
  98–100, 109, 124
American Federation of Teachers, 42
Anderson, Arvid, 105–13, 145, 204n2
Anderson, Maxwell, 117
Andrews, Julie, 143
Anthracite Coal Strike Commission,
  170
Arbitration Act of 1888, 167

Baer, George F., 168, 169, 170
Bell Aircraft, 60
Bennett, Harry, 38, 39
Bernhardt, Debra, 183
Bernstein, Irving, 165–79

Bethlehem Steel, 176
Board of Arbitration, U.S. Steel and United
  Steelworkers of America, 47, 83–84, 178
Board of Inquiry, New York State, 60–61
Board of Education, New York City,
  41–43, 46, 90–91, 97, 140
Board of Mediation, New York State, 20,
  21, 59
Brandeis, Louis D., 11, 170–71, 173,
  192n1
Breed, Allan, 149
Brennan, William J., 14
Brickman, Herman, 118
Brotherhood of Railway Conductors, 61
Brown, Emily, 56
Bullen, Frederick H., 58, 59, 201n4
Bureau of Labor Statistics, U.S., 12
Bureau of National Affairs, 80, 192n2
Bush administration, 178

Carey, S. J., (Reverend Father) Philip A., 111
Carman, Harry J., 59
Carpenter, Jesse T., 170
Carter, President Jimmy, 49, 136, 178
Case, J. I., 109
Catherwood, Martin P., 61
Center for Community Justice, 149
Center for Criminal Justice, 149
Chamberlain, Joseph P., 18
Checkoff, 198n9
Chicago Board of Trade, 166
Ching, Cyrus S., 76, 210n1
Christensen, Thomas G. S., 44–45, 133–37,
  141–42

Civil Service Reform Act, 178
Clark, E. E., 170
Clark, Joseph S., Jr., 178
Cleveland, Grover, 167, 170
Code of Professional Responsibility for Arbitrators of Labor-Management Disputes, 176–77
Cogen, Charles, 44
Cohen, Julius H., 171
Cole, David L., 14, 21, 140, 141, 176, 193n5
Collective Bargaining Law, New York City, 100–101, 110, 111
Collins, Daniel G., 45, 46, 134, 139–45
Columbia University, 18; Oral History Collection, 182, 183, 210n1
Committee for Industrial Organization, 174
Commons, John R., 107
Communications Workers of America, 111, 148
Community Development Agency (CDA), New York City, 148
Congress of Industrial Organizations (CIO), 42, 56, 119, 134, 172
Cornell University: School of Industrial and Labor Relations, 63, 177, 182
Corsi, Edward, 60
Coulson, Robert, 25, 26, 157–63, 190n3
Council of National Defense, 173
Countryman, Vern, 111
Cox, Archibald, 193n6
Crane, Murray, 167
Cravath, Swaine and Moore, 45, 134, 139, 142
Crooks, Charles, 31

Danbury Hatters, 103
Darrow, Clarence S., 172
Dash, G. Allen, 176
Davis, William H., 108, 176, 205n4, 210n1
DeLury, John, 111
Denver Nuggets, 151
Department of Labor, U.S., 173; Wage and Hour Division, 55
Depression, 4, 6, 118, 174
Dewey, Thomas E., 13
Douglas, Paul H., 55, 201n2
Douglas, William O., 142, 193n6, 208n2
Drechsler and Leff, 101
Dworkin, Harry J., 190n2

Eight-Hour Act, 173
Eisenberg, Walter L., 111
English, Alex, 151
Erdman Act, 167
Ever-Ready Label Corporation, 118–19

Fair Labor Standards Act, 55
Federal Aviation Administration (FAA), 154
Federal Mediation and Conciliation Service, 48, 76, 82, 96, 159, 160, 176, 177
Federal Service Labor-Management Relations Statute, 178
Federal Services Impasse Panel, 6
Feinberg, I. Robert, 98, 203n1
Feinsinger, Nathan P., 107–8, 109, 176, 204n3
Feinstein, Barry, 111
Feldblum, Philip, 110
Filene, A. Lincoln, 170–71
Fleming, Robben W., 176, 189n1, 205n3
Ford, Henry, 38
Ford Foundation, 148–49
Ford Motor Company, 38–39, 69, 176
Foreign Service Grievance Board, 7, 72
Freund, Jules, 20
Friedman, Clara H., 183
Friedman, Milton, 46, 60, 79–93
Froessel, Charles, 140, 141
Fund for the City of New York, 148–49

Gallagher, Buell, 140, 141
Garment Workers Union, 172
Garrett, Sylvester, 38, 47, 84, 176, 197n6
Garrison, Lloyd, 42
Gellhorn, Walter, 17–34, 176, 195n4
General Electric, 176
General Motors, 55–56, 63–64, 67–69, 176
General Motors v. Ruzicka, 67
Gill, Lewis M., 58, 201n5
Goldberg, Arthur J., 30, 178, 196
Gompers, Samuel, 167, 173
Gotbaum, Victor, 98, 111
Graham, Frank P., 176
Great Depression, 4, 6, 118, 174
Great Society, 4
Greece, ancient, 10
Green, William, 54

Haber, Herbert, 99–100
Hacker, Louis M., 54
Halevy, Irving, 115–21

Hanna, Marcus (Mark), 169
Hardman, J. B. S., 56
Harriman, W. Averell, 62
Hart, Schaffner and Marx, 171–72
Hays, Paul R., 14, 193n6
Helsby, Robert, 98
Herlands, William B., 59
Herrick, Elinore M., 60
Hill, James C., 45, 176, 200n13
Hillman, Sidney, 56, 167, 172, 201n2
Horvitz, Aaron, 44, 45, 198n10
Horvitz, Wayne L., 44
Howard, Earl Dean, 172

Immigration and Naturalization Act, 143
Inland Corporation, 107
Institute for Mediation and Conflict
    Resolution, 149, 150
International Association of Machinists, 134
International Brotherhood of Teamsters, 40,
    111, 119–21
International Ladies' Garment Workers
    Union (ILGWU), 170–71, 192n1
International Longshoremen's Association,
    117
International Organization of Masters, Mates
    and Pilots, 30–32, 66–67
Iushewitz, Morris, 42

Javits, Jacob K., 62
Jersey City Policemen's Benevolent
    Association (PBA), 121
Johnson, Lyndon B., 136

Kagel, Sam, 177–78
Kennedy, John F., 4, 47, 140, 148, 178
Kharas, Ralph E., 59, 60
Kheel, Theodore W., 39, 149, 198n8
Klaus, Ida, 35–51, 140, 196n1
Kohler Corporation, 109
Korean War, 6, 11, 14, 80
Ku Klux Klan, 116

Labor (labor newspaper), 55
Labor Arbitration Reports, 80
Labor Cost Review Panel, 130
LaFollete family, 108, 205n5
LaFollette Seamen's Act, 173
Landrum-Griffin Act, 108
Larkin, John Day, 176
Lasker, Morris E., 97–98

League of Women Voters, 98
Legislative Drafting Research Fund, 18
Leiserson, William M., 54, 56, 58, 172,
    204n3
LeSauvage, George, 19
Leslie, Mabel, 59
Levin, Sam, 56
Lewis, John L., 54, 174
Lindsay, John V., 71, 111, 112, 140, 148,
    206n2
Little Steel strikes, 107
Livingston, Frederick R., 141
Long Island Lighting Company, 81
Long Island Railroad (LIRR), 13, 49

McAlpin, Baker, 57
McDonnell, Vincent, 112, 206n10
McKelvey, Jean T., 59, 63, 176, 201n7
Major Indoor Soccer League, 150
Manhattan Shirt Company, 101, 102
Manson, Julius S., 60
Marine Engineers Beneficial Association,
    31–32
Marshall, Louis, 171
Mason, Elizabeth, 183
Mattingly, Don, 204n2
Mauro, Tony, 99
Mayer, Henry, 14, 194n7
Meany, George, 19
Memorial Day Massacre, 55, 107
Metal Textile Corporation, 124
Metropolitan Transit Authority (MTA),
    New York City, 28, 49
Meyer, Arthur S., 21, 59, 76, 176, 194n3
Meyer, Carl, 172
Millis, Harry A., 55–56, 58, 63, 172
Minimum Wage Law, New York State, 19
Mitchell, James P., 61
Mitchell, John, 167, 168, 170
Morgan, J. P., 168, 169, 170
Morse, Wayne, 176
Moses, Robert, 99, 203n2
Municipal Labor Committee, New York
    City, 111
Murdock, Orrice Abram, Jr., 134
Murray, Philip, 107
My Fair Lady, 143–44

Nassau County Federation of Labor, 81
Nassau County Public Employment
    Relations Board, 82

National Academy of Arbitrators (NAA), 6, 46, 176–77, 191n5; proceedings of, 192n2

National Association of Broadcast Engineers and Technicians (NABET), 153–54

National Basketball Association, 64, 150

National Basketball Players Association, 64

National Can Company, 84

National Civic Federation, 168

National Defense Mediation Board, 174–75

National Education Association (NEA), 97–98

National Football League, 65, 151

National Guard, 109, 112

National Industrial Recovery Act (NIRA), 117, 174

National Labor Relations Act (Wagner Act), 36, 107, 117, 174, 178, 194n2, 196n3

National Labor Relations Board (NLRB), 39, 47, 48, 50, 56, 68, 134, 148, 172, 178, 184

National Maritime Union, 117, 148

National Mediation Board, 172

National Railroad Adjustment Board, 50

National Recovery Administration, 42

National War Labor Board (NWLB), 21–23, 24, 47, 62, 173–74, 175

National Youth Administration, 117

NBC, 153

Nelson, Gaylord A., 109

New Deal, 3, 36, 117, 133, 174–75

New Freedom, 173

New Jersey Laundry Association, 119–21

New Jersey State Mediation Board, 81, 82

Newspaper Guild, 24, 34, 93, 96–97

New York Central Railroad, 61

New York City, Collective Bargaining Law of, 100–101, 110, 111

New York City Bar Association, 140

New York City Board of Education, 41–43, 46, 90–91, 97, 140

New York chamber of commerce, 166

New York City Community Development Agency (CDA), 148

New York City Metropolitan Transit Authority (MTA), 28, 49

New York City Office of Municipal Labor Relations, 99

New York City Police Department, 25

New York City Rand Institute, 206n2

New York City Social Services Department, 99–100

New York City Transit Authority, 61, 62, 125

New York State Board of Mediation, 20, 21, 59, 76, 80, 81–82, 96, 124

New York State Department of Labor, 95–96

New York State Labor Relations Board (SLRB), 96, 98

New York State Minimum Wage Law, 19

New York Times, 25, 54, 93, 99

New York Stock Exchange, 12

New York University School of Law, 45, 140

New York Yankees, 204n2

NFL Players Association, 65

Nicolau, George, 64, 147–56

Nixon, Richard, 136

Nolan, Dennis R., 190n1

Odets, Clifford, 117

Office of Collective Bargaining (OCB), New York City, 25, 99, 110–12, 125, 206n6

Office of Economic Opportunity (OEO), New York State, 148

Office of Price Administration (OPA), 21

O'Neill, Eugene, 117

Orders, National War Labor Board, 22–23

Paraprofessional Grievance Panel, New York City Board of Education and United Federation of Teachers, 90–91

Percy, Charles H., 55, 200n2

Perlman, Selig, 107

Pitzele, Merlyn, 55, 59, 62

Platt, Harry H., 176

Police Department, New York City, 25

Policemen's Benevolent Association (PBA): Jersey City, 121; New York City, 25

Postal Service, 47–48, 179

Progressive Era, 167–74

Public Employment Relations Board (PERB), 32, 46, 48–49, 82, 98–100, 141, 160

Quill, Michael, J., 40

Railroad Brotherhoods, 55

Railway Labor Act, 6, 49, 61, 67, 136, 174

Rand Corporation, 206n2

Reading Company, 168
Reagan, Ronald, 136, 178
Republic Steel Corporation, 55, 107
Retail, Wholesale, and Department Store
    Workers, 119
Reynolds Metals, 84
Roberts, Benjamin C., 60, 153, 154, 208n5
Robins, Eva, 60, 110, 206n8
Rock, Eli, 46
Rockefeller, Nelson A., 13, 43, 112
Rock Island Railroad, 49
Roosevelt, Franklin D., 36, 95, 117–18,
    172, 174–75
Roosevelt, Theodore, 167, 168
Root, Elihu, 169
Rosenberg, Anna M., 42, 194n1
Rosenfarb, Joseph, 62
Rubin, Max, 42

St. Antoine, Theodore J., 143
Scanlon Plan, 119
Schaffner, Joseph, 171
Scheiber, Augusta, 203n4
Scheiber, Israel Ben, 75–77, 202n1, 202n2,
    202n3
Schiff, Jacob H., 171
Schmertz, Eric J., 45, 110, 111, 123–32,
    136, 142–43
Schofield, J. M., 169
Seitz, Peter, 45, 64, 199n11
Seitz, Reynold, 109
Senior, Clarence, 42
Service Employees Union, 128–29
Seward, Ralph T., 38, 176, 196n5
Shanker, Albert, 44
Shapiro, Irving, 60
Sharfman, I. L., 189n1
Shaw, Irwin, 117
Sherman Act, 168
Shriver, Sargent, 148
Shulman, Harry, 88, 142, 176, 193n6,
    207n1
Shultz, George, 119
Simkin, William E., 176
Simons, Jesse, 111
Singer, Linda, 149
Social Security Board, 20
Society for Professionals in Dispute
    Resolution, 6
Southern Christian Leadership Conference,
    102

Sovern, Michael I, 136
Spalding, John L., 170
Spero, Sterling, 54
Stark, Arthur, 45, 53–73
Stark, Dorothy C., 62, 201n8
Stark, Louis, 54, 200n1
State Department, 72
Steel Agreement, 47
Steel Trilogy, 13, 142, 177–78, 193n3,
    207n2
Steelworkers Organizing Committee, 55
Stein, Emanuel, 9–15, 25, 26, 176
Steinbrenner, III, George M, 204n2
Stockman, Abram H., 45, 62, 98, 99, 176,
    199n12
Stolberg, Benjamin, 54
Straus, Donald B., 158
Supreme Court, U.S., 30, 36, 39, 84,
    177–78; Steel Trilogy decisions of, 13,
    142, 177–78, 193n3, 207n2
System Board of Adjustment, U.S., 67

Taft, William Howard, 173
Taft-Hartley Act, 39, 61, 101, 108
Talmud, 10–11
Taylor, George W., 58, 63, 176, 189n1
Taylor Commission, 112
Taylor Law, 46, 82, 97, 99–100, 110
Teamsters, 40, 111, 119–21
Thompson, W. O., 172
Thucydides, 10
Topol, Julius, 98
Transport Workers Union, 61, 62
Trerotola, Joseph, 112
Triborough Bridge and Tunnel Authority,
    98–100
Truman, Harry S, 4, 134
Turkus, Burton B., 59, 201n6

Unemployment Insurance Law, New York
    State, 18
Uniformed Firefighters Association, 125,
    126–27
Uniformed Fire Officers Association, 125,
    126–27
Uniformed Sanitationmen's Association, 111
Union Pacific Railroad, 55
United Automobile Workers (UAW),
    55–56, 60, 63, 64, 67–68, 89–90, 109
United Federation of Teachers (UFT), 46,
    97–98

United Mine Workers (UMW), 167, 168, 170, 172, 173
United Office and Professional Workers, 119
U.S. Steel, 47, 83–84, 176
United Steelworkers of America, 47, 83–84
University of Chicago, 54, 55
Uviller, Harry, 62

Valtin, Rolf, 63
Van Arsdale, Harry, 112
Vladeck, Stephen C., 134, 206n1
Voice of America, 72
Voluntary Industrial Tribunal, 209n1

Wage Stabilization Board, 80
Wagner, Robert F., 39, 40, 194n2, 196n3
Wagner, Robert F., Jr., 178, 194n2, 196n3
Wagner Act. *See* National Labor Relations Act (Wagner Act)

Wallen, Saul, 38, 110, 111, 176, 197n7
Walsh, Frank P., 173
War on poverty, 4, 148
Washington Post, 24–25
Waterfront Commission, New York State, 60–61
Western Union Company, 38
Williams, John E., 172
Wilson, William B., 173
Wilson, Woodrow, 167, 173, 174
Wisconsin Employment Peace Act, 107, 108
Wisconsin Labor Relations Act, 107
Witte, Edwin E., 107, 108, 166, 189n1
Wolf, Benjamin H., 60, 95–103
World War I, 167, 173
World War II, 4, 6, 174

Yagoda, Louis, 46, 60, 200n14
Young, Edwin, 109
Youngstown Corporation, 107

The Author

Clara H. Friedman, a full-time arbitrator for over 20 years, has been involved in arbitration throughout her professional career, first as an economist at the National War Labor Board during World War II. A Ph.D. in economics from Columbia University, focusing on investment in human capital, she has headed think tank studies of complex economic and labor problems. *Resolving Disputes without Going into Court,* a videotape series of her interviews with five eminent arbitrators, is used in many law school curricula.

Photograph by Krystyna Sanderson.